THE FORENSIC PSYCHOLOGIST'S REPORT WRITING GUIDE

The Forensic Psychologist's Report Writing Guide is the first book to provide both student trainees and practitioners with best practice guidance for one of the core skills of their role.

Written and edited by an international range of experts from the UK, North America and Australasia, it provides clear advice on a range of assessments, from psychometric tests to personality functioning, and includes real-life examples to illustrate key points. Uniquely, the book also offers guidance on the range of different client groups that forensic psychologists work with across both civil and legal contexts, including juveniles, female clients, couples and those with cognitive impairments. From core principles to writing style to key issues, each chapter also includes a checklist of advice and further reading.

Comprehensive and practical, *The Forensic Psychologist's Report Writing Guide* is a user-friendly companion to this critical and often overlooked skill, and will be essential reading for both neophyte and experienced forensic psychologists alike.

Sarah Brown is a Professor in the Centre for Research in Psychology, Behaviour and Achievement at Coventry University, UK.

Erica Bowen was a Professor in the Centre for Research in Psychology, Behaviour and Achievement at Coventry University, UK and moved in 2016 to become Professor of Prevention of Violence and Abuse at the University of Worcester, UK.

David Prescott is a practising forensic practitioner in New England, USA.

THE FORENSIC PSYCHOLOGIST'S REPORT WRITING GUIDE

Edited by Sarah Brown, Erica Bowen and David Prescott

Routledge
Taylor & Francis Group

LONDON AND NEW YORK

First published 2017
by Routledge
2 Park Square, Milton Park, Abingdon, Oxon OX14 4RN

and by Routledge
711 Third Avenue, New York, NY 10017

Routledge is an imprint of the Taylor & Francis Group, an informa business

British Library Cataloguing in Publication Data
A catalogue record for this book is available from the British Library

Library of Congress Cataloging in Publication Data
Names: Brown, Sarah, 1970- editor. | Bowen, Erica, 1976- editor. | Prescott,
David S., editor.
Title: The forensic psychologists' report writing guide / edited by Sarah
Brown, Erica Bowen, and David Prescott.
Description: Abingdon, Oxon ; New York, NY : Routledge, 2017. |
Includes bibliographical references.
Identifiers: LCCN 2016043203 | ISBN 9781138841505 (hardback : alk. paper) |
ISBN 9781315732152 (eBook) | ISBN 9781138841512 (pbk : alk. paper)
Subjects: | MESH: Forensic Psychiatry—methods | Criminals—psychology |
Psychological Tests | Research Design | Research Report
Classification: LCC RA1148 | NLM W 740 | DDC 614/.15—dc23
LC record available at https://lccn.loc.gov/2016043203

ISBN: 978-1-138-84150-5 (hbk)
ISBN: 978-1-138-84151-2 (pbk)
ISBN: 978-1-315-73215-2 (ebk)

Typeset in Bembo
by diacriTech, Chennai

Printed and bound in Great Britain by
TJ International Ltd, Padstow, Cornwall

TABLE OF CONTENTS

LIST OF ILLUSTRATIONS

TABLES

FIGURES

ABOUT THE AUTHORS

Editors' Biographies

Sarah J. Brown is a professor of forensic psychology at Coventry University, where she is the deputy director of the Centre for Research in Psychology, Behaviour and Achievement. She is a registered psychologist (forensic) with the Health and Care Professions Council (HCPC) and also a chartered psychologist and associate fellow of the British Psychological Society. Sarah is vice chair of the National Organisation for the Treatment of Abusers (NOTA). She has been conducting research in relation to sexual violence since 1994 and was the editor of the *Journal of Sexual Aggression* (*JSA*) from 2008 until 2014. She is currently an associate editor of *Child Abuse and Neglect* and editorial board member of *JSA* and *Sexual Abuse: A Journal of Research and Treatment*. Brown has published on various topics including sexual aggression, intimate partner violence, offender engagement, empathy, risk assessment, evaluation and forensic testing.

Erica Bowen is a registered practitioner psychologist (forensic) with the Health and Care Professions Council (HCPC) and also a chartered psychologist and associate fellow of the British Psychological Society. Erica currently works as a professor in the psychology of violence and interpersonal aggression at Coventry University, where she is the director of the violence and interpersonal aggression (VIA) research group. Erica has conducted research into violence in intimate relationships since 2000, focusing mainly on understanding how best to rehabilitate perpetrators, culminating in the development and implementation of brief interventions for this population in the community. Her research has directly informed the development of accredited programmes for perpetrators designed and implemented by the National Offender Management Service (NOMS). Erica has practice experience of conducting violence risk assessments in prison and working as an expert witness in family court contexts.

David Prescott is the Clinical Services Development Director for the Becket Family of Services in the USA. He has produced 14 book projects and numerous articles and book chapters in the area of assessing and treating abuse and trauma. He has served on the editorial boards of *Sexual Abuse: A Journal of Research and Treatment* and the *Journal of Sexual Aggression*. Mr. Prescott is a past president of the Association for the Treatment of Sexual Abusers (ATSA) and the 2014 recipient of that organisation's Distinguished Contribution Award. Previously, he received the Bright Lights Award of the National Adolescent Perpetration Network. Mr. Prescott is a Senior Associate and Certified Trainer for the International Center for Clinical Excellence and is a member of the Motivational Interviewing Network of Trainers. He has provided lectures and workshops around the world, most recently in Australia, Japan, Iceland, Norway, Germany, Poland, Romania and Namibia. His work has been translated into Korean, Japanese, Polish, French and German.

Authors' Biographies

Dr. **Jo Bailey** is a registered practitioner psychologist (forensic) with the Health and Care Professions Council (HCPC). She has been employed since the early 1990s by the prison service and more latterly as the head of profession for psychology in the National Offender Management Service (NOMS) and the lead psychologist for Public Sector Prisons (PSP) providing leadership to the psychology community within PSP, which she has fundamentally reorganised over the last few years to improve the delivery of services for service users, and the training and development opportunities for NOMS psychology staff. Jo previously worked within a range of prisons and as the area psychologist in East Anglia, working with a number of prisoner client groups, prison officers and governors and overseeing psychology service delivery in this region. She has throughout her career held a number of positions with the Division of Forensic Psychology Committee and was a founding member of the Qualification in Forensic Psychology Board, where she held a number of roles including chief assessor and chief examiner.

Kerry Beckley is a registered practitioner psychologist (clinical and forensic) with the Health and Care Professions Council (HCPC). She is the current chair for the faculty of Forensic Clinical Psychology. She has been employed since 2009 as a consultant clinical forensic psychologist for Lincolnshire Partnership Foundation NHS Trust, working across low secure and community forensic services. She is the lead for the Personality Disorder Offender Pathway in Lincolnshire and is currently developing local services for perpetrators of domestic violence. Kerry previously worked as a clinical psychologist in the Male Personality Disorder Directorate, Rampton Hospital, Nottinghamshire Healthcare NHS Trust since 2002, where she developed the Schema Therapy service. She is an accredited Schema Therapy trainer and supervisor, and has presented her work nationally and internationally in this area. She regularly provides expert witness reports for the purposes of mental health tribunals and parole boards.

Kelley Blanchette began working at the research branch of Correctional Service of Canada (CSC) in 1993. She completed her master's and then her doctorate in forensic psychology at Carleton University in 2005. She has published research extensively in peer-reviewed and government journals and co-authored a book entitled *The Assessment and Treatment of Women Offenders*. Dr. Blanchette is an adjunct professor at Carleton University in Ottawa and at Mount Royal University in Calgary. She has held a number of management positions at CSC, including senior director, correctional research, director general in the women offender sector, director general, mental health, and most recently, Deputy Commissioner for Women.

Since Dr. **Susan Cooper** started her career in forensic psychology in 1997, she has worked with female offenders in hospital, prison and community settings. In 2005 she completed a PhD on psychopathy in adolescent offenders. As a consultant forensic psychologist she is the lead clinician in a personality disorder treatment service for women in prison. Much of her work involves the assessment of women, including risk of harm to others and trauma. She has acted as an expert witness on a regular basis since 2004, providing written and oral evidence to family and criminal courts.

Leam A. Craig, BA (Hons), MSc, PhD, FBPsS, FAcSS, CPsychol, CSci, Europsy, is a consultant forensic and clinical psychologist. He is Professor (Hon) of forensic psychology, University of Birmingham, and Visiting Professor of forensic and clinical psychology, Birmingham City University. He is a Full Member of the Academy of Experts, a Fellow of the British Psychological Society and the Academy of Social Sciences and recipient of the Senior Academic Award by the Division of Forensic Psychology. He is currently a consultant to the National Probation Service on working with offenders with personality disorders. He acts as an expert witness to civil and criminal courts in the assessment of sexual and violent offenders, and he has previously been instructed by the Catholic and Church of England dioceses, South African Police Service and the United States Air Force as an expert witness. He has over 80 publications, including 10 books, and he is a series editor to the *What Works in Offender Rehabilitation* book series for Wiley-Blackwell.

Professor **Michael Daffern** is a clinical and forensic psychologist who has worked in prisons and in general and forensic mental health services in Australia and the United Kingdom since 1992. Currently, he is professor of clinical forensic psychology with the Centre for Forensic Behavioural Science at Swinburne University of Technology. Michael's research interests focus on aggression and violence. Michael is a fellow of the Australian Psychological Society (APS) and a past chair of the APS College of Forensic Psychologists. In 2013 he was awarded the APS Distinguished

Contribution in Forensic Psychology Award. Further to his academic work Michael provides clinical consultancy for the Victorian Institute of Forensic Mental Health (Forensicare). In this role he conducts pre-sentence evaluations for the courts, assessments for the adult parole board of Victoria and treatment for a small number of incarcerated violent offenders.

Andrew Day is professor in the school of psychology at Deakin University. Before joining academia he was employed as a clinical psychologist in South Australia and the UK, having gained his doctorate in clinical psychology from the University of Birmingham and his masters in applied criminological psychology from the University of London. He is widely published in many areas of forensic psychology, with a focus on the development of effective and evidence-based approaches to offender rehabilitation.

Dr. **Lawrence Ellerby** has provided clinical services to violent and sexual offenders since 1987, working in correctional, mental health and community settings. He is in private practice in Winnipeg, Manitoba, Canada at Forensic Psychological Services: Ellerby, Kolton, Rothman and Associates. Lawrence is a consultant to the Canadian Center for Child Protection and the RCMP's crisis negotiation team. He is the chair of the sex offender management sub-group of INTERPOL'S Specialist Group on Crimes Against Children and a past president of the Association for the Treatment of Sexual Abusers. Lawrence is a lecturer for the Department of Psychiatry, University of Manitoba. He has published articles and book chapters related to clinical practice with individuals who have committed sexual and violent crimes and has given invited addresses on these topics in Canada, the United States and Europe. He is a past recipient of the Canadian Criminal Justice Association's National Crime Prevention Award.

Dr. **Mags Fenton** is a principal clinical psychologist who works in the UK in a large medium-secure unit in Greater Manchester and in a locked rehabilitation unit in Widnes in Cheshire, where she is also clinical lead for psychology. Dr. Fenton has considerable experience in the assessment, formulation and treatment of complex cases across a range of institutional and community settings, with a particular focus on personality disorder and autism spectrum disorders. She is currently undertaking research in relation to autistic spectrum disorders, personality disorder and risk.

Martin Fisher is a consultant and forensic practitioner psychologist, who has worked in the criminal justice field since 1988 with the National Offender Management Service (NOMS). He also holds appointments within NHS Secure Mental Health Services and Academia. He is currently chair of the BPS committee on test standards, a member of the BPS ethics committee and a member of the forensic faculty of clinical psychology executive committee. He maintains a high level of expertise in working with service users who have risk management needs in the areas of violent and sexual offending. He is an accredited expert witness, and certificated in the use of diagnostic tools relevant to his areas of expertise. He also undertakes consultancy work within NOMS and leads on research strategy for Public Sector Prisons Psychology. Martin also works privately with professional colleagues in publishing and editing psychological books and articles and delivering professional training to others.

Clare-Ann Fortune, PhD, PGDipClinPsyc, is a lecturer in clinical forensic psychology at the School of Psychology, Victoria University of Wellington where she teaches in the forensic psychology and clinical psychology programmes. She previously worked as a clinical psychologist in a specialist youth forensic service. Her research interests focus on risk, rehabilitation and ethical issues related to young offenders. She has published on a range of topics, including strength-based approaches to rehabilitation, risk and young people who have engaged in sexually abusive behaviours.

Gabrielle Klepfisz completed a bachelor's degree in psychology at Monash University, in addition to her fourth year honours, during which she investigated violent offender treatment change. She has continued this research as a doctoral candidate in the doctor of psychology (clinical and forensic) at Swinburne University of Technology. Ms. Klepfisz has worked as a research assistant both in Australia and in Canada. She has also gained clinical experience working with individuals presenting with various mental health concerns, including psychosis, depression and suicidality, anger, social and generalised anxiety, obsessive-compulsive disorder, hoarding disorder and past sexual/physical abuse.

Dr. **David Kolton** is a forensic and clinical psychologist in private practice in Winnipeg, Manitoba, Canada at Forensic Psychological Services: Ellerby, Kolton, Rothman and Associates. David has a doctorate from the clinical psychology programme at Simon Fraser University with specialisation in clinical forensic psychology. He has been working with offenders in a variety of clinical capacities for over 20 years. Prior to joining Forensic Psychological Services on a full-time basis in 2006, he held an academic appointment as assistant professor in the Department of Clinical Health Psychology, Faculty of Medicine, University of Manitoba. In this position he worked clinically providing assessment and treatment services at two of Manitoba's forensic hospitals. Prior to this he was employed as a psychologist with the Correctional Service of Canada (CSC) for 10 years at two federal correctional/psychiatric facilities.

Glenda Liell is a chartered and registered forensic psychologist and head of psychological services at Long Lartin High Security Prison. She has previously held the post of head of assessment and research as part of the development team of a treatment programme for psychopathic offenders rolled out in a prison personality disorder unit. Her career initially focused on the delivery of treatment to violent and sexual offenders, and currently assessments and report writing form part of her role. She has contributed to the work of the British Psychological Society (BPS) Division of Forensic Psychology (DFP), most notably as co-editor of *Forensic Update*. On the DFP committee, she has held the positions of secretary, professional conduct lead and representative to the BPS ethics committee and the expert witness advisory group. Most recently she has completed a 3-year tenure on the BPS Working Party for Standards in Forensic Testing that were published in 2016.

Caroline Logan is a consultant forensic clinical psychologist working in an NHS secure forensic mental health service. She specialises in the areas of risk assessment, formulation and management, and in personality disorder assessment and its links to offending behaviour. She has a particular interest in gender issues in offending behaviour, and in forensic clinical interviewing skills. She has published two books and a number of articles on the above subjects with several more of each in the pipeline.

Dr. **Jessica Mooney** is a clinical and forensic psychologist who currently works with adolescents in the youth justice system in Victoria, Australia involving the preparation of reports to inform the decision making of the youth parole board. Dr. Mooney's clinical background includes work in adult correctional and community forensic mental health settings. Dr. Mooney has conducted research in the area of parole decision making, including an examination of factors that impact upon parole decisions and the use of institutional behaviour in the assessment of risk for future violence.

Wendy Morgan has over 20 years' experience of working in forensic psychology settings and nearly 30 years' experience of working in clinical settings. She has been employed by or worked as a consultant to the NHS, Mencap, HM Prison Service, the parole board of England and Wales, charities, schools and the police. She also acts as an expert witness for the courts in relation to risk assessment and management. She specialises in working in a style which is both interdisciplinary and inclusive. She frequently writes and speaks about the need to avoid considering risk or treatment interventions within too narrow a focus. In addition to her UK work, Wendy has written about prevention of sexual offences within South and Latin America and has provided training for staff working in the United States of America. This chapter was prepared while Wendy was working at London Metropolitan University before her move to Glasgow Caledonian University.

Devon L.L. Polaschek, PhD, DipClinPsyc, is a clinical psychologist and when writing this chapter was professor of criminal justice psychology at Victoria University of Wellington, New Zealand. She now works at the University of Waikato, New Zealand. Her research interests include theory, intervention and intervention evaluation with serious violent and sexual offenders, psychopathy, desistance, reintegration and parole, and experimental approaches to offender assessment. She is the author of more than 90 journal articles, book chapters and books; a fellow of the Association for Psychological Science; and has had 10 years of continuous funding from the Department of Corrections in order to develop a better understanding of high-risk male prisoners, their characteristics and what works to reduce their risk of future offending.

Martin Rettenberger, MA, Dipl.-Psych., Dr. biol. hum., Priv.-Doz., is director of the Centre for Criminology (Kriminologische Zentralstelle – KrimZ) in Wiesbaden, Germany and was between 2013 and 2015 an associate professor for forensic psychology at the Department of Psychology at the Johannes Gutenberg-University Mainz (JGU), Germany. He previously worked at the Federal Evaluation Centre for Violent and Sexual Offenders (FECVSO) in the Austrian Prison System in Vienna, Austria, and at the Institute of Sex Research and Forensic Psychiatry at the University Medical Centre Hamburg-Eppendorf (UKE), Germany. Since 2016, he has served as secretary general of the International Association for the Treatment of Sexual Offenders (IATSO) and as editor of the IATSO e-journal *Sexual Offender Treatment*.

Brandie Stevenson, M.A., C.Psych.Assoc., completed her masters in applied forensic psychology and has devoted over 20 years of her career working with individuals with complex needs, such as developmental disabilities, FASD and acquired brain injury. Ms. Stevenson works with youth and adults and specialises in trauma, risk and sexual offending behaviours. She provides psychosexual risk/needs assessments, individual treatment, consultation to service agencies and staff training.

David J. Tobin, PhD, is currently the director of Clinical and Professional Services for the Commonwealth of Massachusetts Department of Developmental Services Central/West Region. He also is a psychologist at the Center for Integrative Psychological Services providing assessment services for individuals with chronic mental illness, developmental disabilities, traumatic brain injuries and other challenging co-morbid issues which also present with co-occurring problematic sexual and/or violent behaviour. His practice interests involve psychological, risk management and forensic assessments with a focus on the systemic integration of assessment into ongoing consultation and treatment efforts.

Dr. **Kylie Thomson** is a clinical and forensic psychologist. She has worked in both the United Kingdom and Australia in a variety of clinical and forensic settings for over 15 years, including prisons, forensic mental health services (maximum security, medium security and community-based) and private practice. Dr. Thomson has worked in a number of roles across these settings, including senior psychologist, manager of the Victorian Institute of Forensic Mental Health (Forensicare) Problem Behaviour Program and principal psychologist at Forensicare. Currently, Dr. Thomson has a private practice that involves court assessments, treatment of offenders, treatment of clients with significant mental health issues, provision of supervision to forensic and clinical psychologists and consultation to a variety of organisations. Dr. Thomson is also a senior lecturer at the Centre for Forensic Behavioural Science, Swinburne University of Technology.

Robin J. Wilson, PhD, ABPP, is a researcher, educator and board certified clinical psychologist who has worked with sexual and other offenders in hospital, correctional and private practice settings for more than 30 years. He presently maintains an international practice in consulting psychology based in Sarasota, Florida and is an assistant clinical professor (adjunct) of psychiatry and behavioural neurosciences at McMaster University in Hamilton, Ontario. Robin's current interests are focused on collaborative models of risk management and restoration as persons of risk are transitioned from institutional to community settings. He has published and presented internationally on the diagnosis and treatment of social and sexual psychopathology, in addition to being a member of the editorial boards of *Sexual Abuse: A Journal of Research and Treatment*, the *Journal of Sexual Aggression* and the *Howard Journal of Criminal Justice*.

INTRODUCTION

Erica Bowen

Psychological assessments involving clients within forensic settings form a core component of the roles of forensic psychologists. The written report is the 'practice-product' of forensic psychology and represents the assessment, formulation and opinions that the expert was contracted to provide (Griffith, Stankovic and Baranoski, 2010, p. 32). Forensic psychologist reports may be requested for a number of reasons: to determine risk, to inform decisions about child custody, to identify treatment need, to inform intervention sequencing, to inform decisions concerning transfer between prison or secure hospital establishments, to inform decisions about sentencing and to inform decisions concerning the likelihood of release from a secure environment. Consequently, written assessment reports are typically used to inform decisions made by other people about an individual's future, and as such these reports may be very influential.

In addition to the potential impact of reports on clients' futures, reports themselves are the most important way in which psychologists communicate with the individuals and panels that are the decision makers, and consequently, their own professional credibility rests with the quality of both the assessment conducted and the subsequent written report (White, Day, Hackett and Dalby, 2015). Indeed, recent research from a number of different countries highlights a number of high profile cases in which the quality of forensic psychological and psychiatric reports has been identified as poor (e.g. Combalbert, Andronikof, Armand, Robin and Bazex, 2014), and several authors have made recommendations for improving these reports (Duits, van der Hoorn, Wiznitzer, Wettstein and de Beurs, 2012; Giorgi-Guiameri et al., 2002; Robinson and Acklin, 2010) in order to improve the reputation of forensic psychology. It is agreed that guidelines are required for the writing of forensic psychology reports, and it has been observed that by comparison little attention is paid to training trainee psychologists in the art and science of effective report writing (White et al., 2015) relative to the emphasis upon conducting and writing empirical research reports.

The aim of this book, therefore, is to provide guidance to forensic psychologists who are tasked with writing assessment reports, in order to enhance their professional knowledge and skills in this area. Unlike previous volumes concerned with the issue of forensic psychology report writing (e.g. White et al., 2015), this book considers the requirements of writing reports in different contexts (secure and community), based on different populations (juveniles, women, individuals with learning difficulties, relationships) and with different aims (risk assessment, reporting on change, reporting on assessments of personality functioning, reporting results of psychometric tests). However, we start by considering the main overarching principles of effective assessment and report writing, drawing upon international codes of ethics and the limited scientific literature that has addressed issues of report quality. This is then followed by an outline of elements of reports that can be used within any given forensic psychological report before we provide an overview of the organisation of the book. Appendices 1 to 3 contain anonymised forensic psychology reports written by experienced practitioners, a reference the reader may find useful.

Core principles in conducting assessments

Psychologists are bound by professional codes of conduct and ethics that set out clear general principles for conducting and reporting assessments. The codes of conduct of the UK (British Psychological Society [BPS], 2009 and Health and Care Professions Council [HCPC], 2016), Australia (Australian Psychological Society [APS], 2007), New Zealand (New Zealand Psychological Society [NZPS], 2002) and North America (American Psychological Association [APA], 2002) are more or less explicit with regards to the ethical principles relevant to the conduct and reporting of assessments. In 2013, the APA also published specialist guidance for the ethical conduct and professional responsibilities of forensic psychologists. There is also specific guidance for psychologists acting as expert witnesses for the courts (e.g. BPS, 2015, 2016). Typically, the core values and responsibilities that underpin the work of psychologists concern integrity, respect, justice, beneficence and fidelity.

Integrity

This principle reflects the fact that forensic psychologists must strive for honesty, accuracy and truthfulness in their practice (APA, APS, BPS) and that they should try to resist the pressure of providing services in any manner that might be misleading, dishonest or inaccurate (APA, 2013; BPS, 2015, 2016). When writing assessment reports this means accurately and honestly reporting test results, providing an accurate synopsis of case materials, and reporting the presentation and engagement of the client in a fair and unbiased manner.

Respect

Within their practice and report writing, psychologists should respect the dignity and worth of all individuals, and the rights that individuals have to privacy, confidentiality and self-determination (BPS, APA). In cases where vulnerabilities exist that prohibit an individual from making an autonomous decision, psychologists must ensure that appropriate safeguards are in place. In addition, psychologists must be aware of and respect individual differences in relation to culture, sexuality, religion, gender, age, race, disability, language and socio-economic status. Moreover, these factors must be considered when working with members of these groups, trying to minimise the impact of any biases associated with membership of these groups on assessment and report writing practice.

Justice

Psychologists recognise that all individuals are entitled to access and benefit from psychological services, and ensure that potential biases, limitations of their knowledge and expertise and the limits of their competence do not lead to unjust practice (APA, BPS). Moreover, psychologists ensure that they do not discriminate against individuals on the basis of age, religion, sexuality, ethnicity, gender, disability or any other basis proscribed in law (APS, BPS).

Beneficence

Psychologists ensure that they do no harm through the work undertaken, and safeguard the rights and welfare of those individuals with whom they work. Moreover, psychologists should ensure that their expertise is not manipulated through personal, financial, social, organisational or political factors resulting in their influence being misused (APA).

Fidelity

Psychologists should be aware of their professional responsibilities to the communities in which they work and should therefore uphold professional standards of conduct, clarify their professional roles and obligations, accept responsibility for their own behaviour and manage conflicts of interest that could result in harm (APA, BPS). In relation to report writing, it is commonly accepted that psychologists should not conduct assessments of clients with whom they have been working therapeutically, due to the potential biases that the therapeutic role may transfer to the assessment task (White et al., 2015).

In relation to the conduct and reporting of assessments, the APA has explicit guidelines set out in section nine of the Ethical Principles document which are a useful reference. These are described below and cross-reference is made to other international codes of conduct at salient points.

Bases of assessment (APA, 9.01)

The opinion reached by a psychologist during assessment must be based on appropriate information and techniques that are sufficient to substantiate their findings (BPS). In addition, it is specified that in order to provide an opinion on an individual's functioning, a direct assessment involving the individual must be made. A clinical opinion of a client should not be based on pre-existing file information alone, unless there is no way of obtaining direct contact with the client. In these circumstances all efforts must be made to contact the client, and the reasons for lack of contact need to be explicitly stated, and the impact of the absence of this information on the reliability and validity of clinical opinion needs to be clearly reported. Moreover, if in the psychologist's opinion an assessment is not needed, then this also needs to be clearly justified in any resulting report.

Use of assessments (APA, 9.02)

There needs to be a scientific rationale for the assessments used in any individual case. Moreover, assessments that are used need to be administered, adapted, scored and interpreted as appropriate and in light of research that attests to their use (APS). Assessment tools, protocols and/or interviews need to be valid for the population and issue being assessed. It is sometimes challenging to find tests that have been validated in particular countries or on particular populations. Under these circumstances the use of non-validated assessment approaches needs to be clearly justified, and the implications of their use for the reliability and validity of the professional opinion expressed needs to be clearly stated. The strengths and weaknesses of the assessment approach need to be clearly reported. In addition, the assessment approach used needs to be conducted in the client's language of preference and competence. Where this is not possible, and should assessments proceed in an alternative language, the potential impact of this on the validity of the results and the consequent impact on the validity of your opinion and conclusions needs to be clearly stated.

Informed consent in assessments (APA, 9.03)

It is important that all assessments are conducted with the explicit consent of the client being assessed (BPS). Should this not be possible due to issues of age or intellectual capacity, or because consent is not required by law, it is imperative that consent is obtained from the person's guardian (NZPS). Moreover, it is also required that the assessment is sufficiently well planned so that only the information necessary and most relevant to the issue being assessed is collected (NZPS, APS). In addition, personal information should be retained in accordance with local data protection legislation (NZPS). The process of obtaining consent requires the psychologist to use plain language and to fully describe the purpose of the planned procedures; identify potential risks; explain how information will be collected and recorded, and how and for how long data will be stored; explain the limits of confidentiality; and describe the conditions under which the psychological service will be terminated (APS). Consent should be obtained from the client not only for their own direct participation in the assessment process but also for the collation of information from third parties where appropriate (e.g. requesting medical records) (APS). In addition, consent should be sought from the third party to provide this information.

Release of test data (APA, 9.04)

Test data refers to the raw scores and scaled scores, individual client responses to test questions or stimuli and psychologist's notes and recordings relating to a specific client (APA). Test data can only be released by psychologists to individuals named in a client/patient release (APA, APS). However, should the psychologist deem that releasing test data would lead to harm, or risk their misuse or misrepresentation, the psychologist can refrain from releasing the test data. Psychologists also need to be aware of, and work within, relevant data protection legislation that may apply to the disclosure of personal or confidential information.

Interpreting assessment data (APA, 9.06)

The interpretation of assessment data needs to be contextualised with regards to the purpose of the assessment, the reliability and validity of the approach undertaken, as well as test factors and the test-taking abilities and other relevant characteristics of the client being assessed. These characteristics may include language and linguistic abilities, cultural factors, motor/mobility limitations and personal factors. Any limitations to their interpretation of test data need to be clearly reported.

Assessment by unqualified persons (APA, 9.07)

The only circumstances under which unqualified individuals may conduct assessments is when they are engaging in training and assessments are undertaken under the supervision of someone who is appropriately qualified (BPS). When reporting the results of assessments, the qualifications of the assessor and whether the assessment was undertaken whilst under supervision should be explicitly reported.

Obsolete test and outdated test results (APA, 9.08)

Should old test data be available this should not be used to form professional opinion. Moreover, obsolete tests should not be used.

Test scoring (APA, 9.09)

When psychologists engage in the administration of psychological and/or psychometric tests, they must accurately describe the purpose, test norms, validity, reliability and application of the procedures and also any unique qualifications needed to administer the test (BPS). In addition, the decision to adopt a particular test needs to be justified on the basis of the evidence concerning its validity. Ultimately, even when tests may be computer administered and scored, or administered and scored by a third party acting on the instruction of the psychologist, the psychologist takes responsibility for their appropriate application, interpretation and use.

Explaining assessment results (APA, 9.10)

Psychologists should take all reasonable steps to ensure that the explanations of results are given to the individual or a designated representative, unless the relationship precludes this from happening as may exist within forensic evaluations. In some forensic contexts the results of assessments are not disclosed directly to the individual, but are disclosed to a third party acting on behalf of the individual. In other instances, the findings of assessments such as risk assessments may well be disclosed to the individual. This practice may vary depending on the setting and the nature of the assessment undertaken.

Core principles in writing reports

Forensic reports have intrinsic value to forensic decision makers. Poor quality assessments and poor quality reports lead to poor and/or detrimental outcomes for our clients. It is therefore imperative that we undertake good quality assessments and write good quality reports (Duits et al., 2012); but what constitutes a 'good quality' report? The process of conducting and writing up individual assessments is analogue to the process of conducting and writing up a piece of empirical psychological research, although the participant pool in assessments is typically much smaller, most often a single case, but potentially increasing to a small number of family members. However, the same principles of writing apply to both contexts. A good report will answer the questions that have been asked, be written in clear language using a coherent style and will be appropriately structured.

Answer the question(s)

Assessments are conducted by instruction; that is, a third party has a question or questions about the current or likely future functioning or behaviour of an individual. Good reports will directly address the questions that are posed by this third party. It is imperative that should there be any ambiguity about the question(s) being asked, the forensic psychologist contact the third party for clarification.

Linked to this are the ethical requirements forensic psychologists have to undertake an appropriate assessment that is tailored not only to the questions asked but to the individual client. Consensus between authors presented in this volume is that developing professional opinion, or formulating client behaviour, is the most challenging aspect of conducting forensic psychological assessments. Such opinion must be based on information gathered in a systematic, empirically informed way, and where at all possible, triangulated across informants. Opinions must be defensible based on the critical evaluation of a range of information, gathered through multiple methods.

Writing style

Report writers need to be considerate in the language used when writing reports (Griffith et al., 2010). The majority of readers of forensic reports are not forensic psychologists, but may include legal professionals (e.g. judges, lawyers), clinicians, lay representatives and the individual themselves. As noted in Chapter 2, the individual may be cognitively impaired or have low intellectual functioning, and consequently the written report must be written clearly enough to enable them to understand it. The codes of conduct and ethics referred to in the previous section are also relevant to the writing of reports. The basic ethical principle most relevant to this reflects the requirement of assessment report writers to use language that conveys respect for the dignity of others (NZ). As Fortune notes (Chapter 8), it can be easy to adopt a writing style that promotes biased thinking about a client, and professionals need to ensure that they do not use inflammatory or sensationalist language, or language that exaggerates the relevance of specific factors to the case. It is recommended that neutral language is used, but that clear logical arguments are made to illustrate the relative importance of specific factors and that these arguments are supported with reference to the evidence reviewed.

Consequently, forensic psychologists need to ensure that they adopt an appropriate writing style. This means that reports should be written in a **jargon-free** way, with key concepts clearly explained. In addition, although the legal question or instructions may require a comprehensive report to be written based on a lengthy assessment, it is important to write as **concisely** as possible. The length of the report needs to be appropriate to meet the requirements of the third party for whom it is written, and not simply reflect the amount of time the assessment took to complete.

It has been acknowledged that factors outside of the content of reports can also diminish the effectiveness of the report. In particular, grammatical errors and typographical errors have been isolated as reducing a report's effectiveness (Resnick, 2006). Moreover, Resnick guards against using words such as 'suspect', 'possibly', and 'supposedly' as they are deemed to weaken the report. Although applied to the writing of forensic psychiatry reports, Resnick's four principles of **clarity**, **simplicity**, **brevity** and **humanity** are also relevant to the writing of forensic psychology reports. Humanity refers to the fact that the use of direct verbatim quotes can make the subject of the assessment appear human and facilitates the report authors' attempts to directly address the reader (see Example Report 3 in Appendix 3).

Format and structure of reports

It is typically expected that reports are presented with a clear structure with subheadings identifying subsections, and with paragraphs that are numbered relative to each subsection (e.g. 1.0, 1.1; 2.0, 2.1, 2.1.1). There are no absolute rules for structuring forensic psychology reports, although it has been suggested by Grisso et al. (2010) that there exists consensus concerning the main sections to be included. These are broadly described as 'Introduction', 'Data', and 'Opinion'. However, authors should adopt flexibility in their approach to structuring reports to ensure that the structure best reflects the requirements of the assessment and instructions. The authors of each individual chapter within this book provide suggestions concerning the key content of reports based on the question, client group or setting for which the report is prepared. What follows therefore is an outline of the basic requirements of forensic reports, but the order in which they are presented is something that will likely vary depending on the nature of the assessment conducted and the individual practitioner. This variation is evident by examining the three sample reports reproduced in Appendices 1 to 3. Psychologists should strive, however, to produce a coherent report that has a clear logical progression of content, as it has been previously noted that not all reports achieve this and that incoherent reports are judged to be poor quality (Grisso et al., 2010).

- Title page:
  The title page will include the date, a title describing the content of the report, details of the client who was subject of the assessment, including name, date of birth and any case/client identifiers (e.g. prison number, case number).
- Contents page:
  If the written report is lengthy with many subsections, then it is useful to have a contents page that identifies these subsections in the order in which they are presented. This will help to orient the reader to the contents of the report.
- Referral information:
  A paragraph should be included which describes the reason for and origin of the referral for assessment.
- Biographical statement:
  This should include details of who was involved in conducting the assessment, his/her relevant professional qualifications and experience. This statement should serve to reassure the reader that the practitioner who undertook the assessment was working within their competence and that there were no conflicts of interest (APA, 2013). In addition, should someone assist with an assessment or part of an assessment, his/her details, qualifications and experience

also need to be reported, including a statement explicitly identifying the component of the assessment to which he/she assisted. This is likely to be relevant to individuals who are in the process of training to be fully qualified forensic psychologists, working under supervision. Individual practitioners differ in their opinion of where this statement is best to be placed. Some advocate early on in the report; others place this information in an appendix.

- Sources of information:

For complex assessments for which a number of sources of information are considered (e.g. prior psychiatric assessment reports, criminal history, medical records, previous probation pre-sentence reports, previous social work reports across the client's lifespan as well as the new assessment, which may involve interviews with more than one person, and the administration of psychometric tests), then it would be appropriate to identify the main documents and interviews that were used to inform the current opinion. Clinicians differ in opinion regarding whether this list should be at the start of the report or in an appendix, but the documents and interviews should be listed chronologically with the identified author/participant and date.

- Context:

This section should include details of the environment in which the assessment was conducted as well as the legal questions to be addressed.

- Consent process:

It is a requirement that the process of consent is described for each client. This means a paragraph describing how the client was briefed on the assessment and whether written or verbal consent was obtained. In circumstances where the client was a juvenile, or lacked capacity to give informed consent, the procedures used need to be clearly described.

- Summary of pre-existing information:

For some reports, for example reports for family court, it is expected that a summary of the existing information will be provided. This may take the form of a documented history informed by previous psychiatric or social worker assessments. Such a history will likely be broken down into early family history, education, relationship and sexual history, medical history, forensic history and summary of current events. The aim should be to document salient and relevant experiences and patterns of behaviour and to support each claim with reference to the document from which it was drawn. Specifically, reference should be made to documents examined that contained information that was material to the professional opinion you express (APA, 2013). It must be noted, however, that some practitioners will only provide one such summary, drawing upon the client's self-report, and will cross-reference issues that seem to vary between accounts documented in previous reports rather than duplicating the documented history with a summary of self-report which does not vary from the earlier accounts. This approach will undoubtedly reduce the overall length of the report.

Other reports may not need so detailed a summary, or may draw upon this information in a different way. For example, when conducting structured professional judgement risk assessments (see Chapter 5), this information will need to be summarised in relation to the specific risk factors that are being determined as present and relevant within an individual case. In this instance, it would not make sense to summarise the person's psychosexual and forensic history, and then duplicate this in relation to each of the risk factors. In contrast, actuarial risk assessments (see Chapter 2) will likely only need the identification of specific historical risk factors and will not need a lengthy narrative report. Moreover, reports of assessments of single constructs (e.g. personality) based on psychometric tests only (see Chapter 1) may need no personal history summary, but instead focus on describing current functioning as determined by the scores on the assessment used.

• Assessments used:
  Forensic psychologists have an ethical obligation to use appropriate assessment procedures and tools that have been validated on the population from which the individual client is drawn (see previous section on ethical requirements). In this section of the report the approach to assessment needs to be described and justified with reference to the scientific literature. In the case of using specific psychometrics or risk assessment tools, these need to be described along with their properties and more specifically, details of their reliability and validity when used with the client's population need to be reported. This section of the report is akin to the 'materials and procedure' section of an empirical report and should provide a well-justified defence of the methods used. Where new or emerging approaches are used, the limitations of these need to also be clearly stated (APA, 2013).
• Observations of client engagement and presentation:
  Some insight into an individual's motivation for assessment and mental state can be gleaned through observing their demeanour during the assessment process. Clients will vary in the extent to which they cooperate and comply with the requirements of the assessment process, and this may be more or less relevant to personality or current psychopathology. It can be useful to reflect on how the client is reported to have engaged with other professionals and whether there is consistency or inconsistency in their presentation, and what this might reflect that is relevant to the content of assessment. In addition, discrepancies between self-reported functioning and overt presentation may reflect underlying capacity concerns (see Chapter 2).
• Current functioning/interpretation of test scores:
  This is a key section of the report as it is where you interpret the results from the assessment methods employed and provide an account of current functioning. When psychometric tests are used, these should include accurate interpretation in relation to population norms.

- Factors influencing reliability/validity of assessment:
This section should provide details of the limitations of the assessment conducted. For example, was there evidence of faking good in the client's responses? Was a key informant missing from the assessment process? Is there evidence to suggest that the client's comprehension was not as good as expected, or that second language issues may have impacted on the validity of responses?
- Formulation:
Depending on the nature of the assessment, if it concerns risk of future violent offending, then some form of formulation will be required, unless of course only an actuarial risk assessment approach has been undertaken (see Chapter 2). In this section you need to draw together salient issues from the individual's personal history with the results of the assessments undertaken in order to develop a narrative account of how risk works for the individual client. The closer the links between evidence and formulation, the greater the coherence of the report (Guerreiro, Casoni and Santos, 2014) and the better quality reports are judged to be (Grisso et al., 2010). Chapters 4 and 5 provide further guidance on reporting formulations from two different perspectives: clinical judgement and structured professional judgement.
- Response to legal questions/opinion:
In this section, each question raised by the referring third party needs to be explicitly addressed, drawing on the evidence reviewed and assessment conducted. Authors in this volume agree that the integration of all relevant information from which to derive expert opinion is considerably challenging. Efforts should be made to make reference to the evidence that underpins the opinion formulated in response to each question. Some report authors provide a summary of their main conclusions at the start of their report before the evidence review in order to provide easy access to their opinion.
- Limits of conclusions:
It is necessary to provide the limits of the conclusions drawn. These limits may reflect factors such as relying purely on the self-report of the individual client in the absence of other informers, including previous self-report documented in historical third party reports (e.g. previous social worker, psychiatrist, probation officer reports). Threats to the validity of responding on individual measures may also have broader implications for the confidence of your overall conclusions, and these need to be described plainly.
- Next steps/intervention plans:
When writing reports that lead to recommendations for intervention, treatment or new risk management strategies, the recommendations need to link clearly to the formulation and the evidence reviewed, and also be realistic in terms of what is locally available. In addition, they should reflect interventions that the client is likely to engage with.

Outline of the book

The book is organised into three sections that try to capture: (1) the diversity of the questions asked of forensic psychologists conducting assessments and writing reports; (2) issues specific to sub-populations for which reports may be requested; and (3) issues specific to different settings in which reports may be requested.

Consequently, in **Section 1**, Chapters 1 to 7 focus on the reporting of assessments conducted to address different questions linked to client risk and responsivity (i.e. factors that might influence their ability to engage with, or benefit from, intervention; Andrews and Bonta, 1990). It is acknowledged that psychometric testing and the administration of standardised tests form the bedrock of assessment practice and can assist in understanding the risk, criminogenic needs and responsivity issues (e.g. intelligence, personality) of an individual. Chapter 1 provides a helpful consideration of the factors that need to be accounted for when reporting on this process and the results. Particular attention is paid to the relevance of reliability, validity and also the limitations of psychological tests. Chapters 2 and 6 focus on responsivity issues: Chapter 2 focuses on assessing and reporting on intellectual functioning/ cognitive capacity, and Chapter 6 focuses on reporting on assessments of personality. Both cognitive capacity and personality directly impact an individual's ability to function adaptively in general and within relationships specifically. Chapter 2 on cognitive capacity focuses on the clinical skills required to conduct effective assessments of low functioning clients and also discusses the potential pitfalls of trying to use standardised assessments with this client group. Chapter 6 provides a clear analysis of why personality is relevant to forensic assessments and how best to conduct and report standardised assessments of personality.

Chapters 3, 4 and 5 focus on reporting risk assessments: actuarial, formulation-based and structured professional judgement approaches, respectively. Although the aims of these approaches are qualitatively the same – to determine the level of risk of future offending posed by an individual – the methods employed differ in important ways. The authors of all three chapters present a clear theory that underpins each approach. In addition, the core methods of conducting these assessments are summarised, as is best practice in communicating risk relative to the approach taken. Finally, in Section 1, Chapter 7 focuses on reporting change. In this chapter, it is observed that there is limited guidance available on how best to assess and report change, despite the fact that expectations concerning change are fundamental to criminal sentencing. This chapter therefore provides a useful overview of the nature of assessing change and valid methods of doing this. In addition, clear examples of how to communicate change within reports are provided.

In **Section 2**, the focus shifts to reporting assessments of specific groups including juveniles (Chapter 8), females (Chapter 9), vulnerable clients (Chapter 10) and relationships (Chapter 11). The authors of these chapters all agree that forensic psychologists require specialist knowledge of the populations assessed in order to conduct robust assessments. The authors of Chapters 9 and 11 also draw attention to the need for practitioners to reflect on and work around stereotypical beliefs that may be held about the client group, and in both instances emphasise beliefs that women cannot be perpetrators and are only victims. The authors of Chapters 8, 9 and 10 agree that when assessing juveniles, females and vulnerable clients, attention needs to be paid to identifying and understanding their strengths as well as risk and vulnerability factors. Chapter 11 highlights the need to understand patterns of relational behaviours when assessing domestic violence specifically in order to fully understand the dynamics and motivators of these behaviours. With the focus on assessing couples, clear examples are given of how to write up key sections of reports from this perspective.

Section 3 examines the reporting requirements of secure settings (Chapter 12), parole/hearings (Chapter 13) and finally non-custodial community settings (Chapter 14). Chapter 12 provides an overview of the prison and secure hospital reporting context and identifies ethical and professional issues concerning the power that psychologists have relative to clients in these contexts and the level of coercion that exists surrounding the requirements for assessment. Chapter 13 discusses issues concerning risk assessments conducted in secure settings that are then used to inform release or recategorisation decisions by the parole board. Consequently, some of the issues and concerns raised in earlier chapters are revisited in relation to this specific context (e.g. Chapter 5). Indeed, the consideration of offence paralleling behaviours within secure environments is examined in relation to appraising risk in this context. Chapter 14 moves away from discussing the reporting of risk, to reporting around the process of treatment, including treatment intake, progress, suspension and completion. The focus, therefore, is on assessing a client's engagement and progress, motivation and areas of continuing concern or challenge. As with earlier chapters (Chapters 4 and 5), in which formulation of risk was discussed, this chapter also emphasises the need to engage in formulation in order to understand client treatment resistance and why they may engage in treatment interfering behaviors.

References

American Psychological Association. (2013). Speciality guidelines for forensic psychologists. *American Psychologist*, *63*, 7–19.

American Psychological Association. (2002). *Ethical principles of psychologists and code of conduct*. Washington, DC: APA.

Andrews, D., Bonta, J. and Hoge, R. (1990). Classification for effective rehabilitation: Rediscovering psychology. *Criminal Justice and Behavior*, *17*(1), 19–52.

Australian Psychological Society. (2007). *APS code of ethics*. Melbourne: APS.

British Psychological Society. (2016). *Psychologists as expert witnesses in the family courts in England and Wales: Standards, competencies and expectations*. Leicester, UK: BPS.

British Psychological Society. (2015). *Psychologists as expert witnesses: Guidelines and procedure*. Leicester, UK: BPS.

British Psychological Society. (2009). *Code of ethics and conduct*. Leicester, UK: BPS.

Combalbert, N., Andronikof, A., Armand, M., Robin, C. and Bazex, H. (2014). Forensic mental health assessment in France: Recommendations for quality improvement. *International Journal of Law and Psychiatry, 37*(6), 628–34.

Duits, N., van der Hoorn, S., Wiznitzer, M., Wettstein, R.M. and de Beurs, E. (2012). Quality improvement of forensic mental health evaluations and reports of youth in the Netherlands. *International Journal of Law and Psychiatry, 35*(5), 440–4.

Giorgi-Guarnieri, D., Janofsky, J., Keram, E., Lawsky, S., Merideth, P., Mossman, D., … and Zonana, H. (2002). AAPL practice guideline for forensic psychiatric evaluation of defendants raising the insanity defense. American Academy of Psychiatry and the Law. *Journal of the American Academy of Psychiatry and the Law, 30* (2 Suppl.), S3–40.

Griffith, E.E., Stankovic, A. and Baranoski, M. (2010). Conceptualizing the forensic psychiatry report as performative narrative. *Journal of the American Academy of Psychiatry and the Law Online, 38*(1), 32–42.

Grisso, T. (2010). Guidance for improving forensic reports: A review of common errors. *open Access Journal of Forensic Psychology, 2*, 102–15.

Guerreiro, J., Casoni, D. and Costa Santos, J. (2014). Relevance and coherence as measures of quality in forensic psychological reports. *Psychiatry, Psychology and Law, 21*(6), 890–902.

Health and Care Professions Council. (2016). *Standards of conduct, performance and ethics.* London: HCPC.

New Zealand Psychological Society. (2002). *Code of ethics.* Wellington, NZ: New Zealand Psychologists Board.

Resnick, P.J. (2006). Principles of psychiatric-legal report writing, *The syllabus of the forensic psychiatry review course.* Brookfield, CT: American Academy of Psychiatry and the Law.

Robinson, R. and Acklin, M.W. (2010). Fitness in paradise: Quality of forensic reports submitted to the Hawaii judiciary. *International Journal of Law and Psychiatry, 33*(3), 131–7.

White, J., Day, A., Hackett, L. and Dalby, J.T. (2015). *Writing reports for court: An international guide for psychologists who work in the criminal jurisdiction.* Brisbane, Australia: Australian Academic Press.

SECTION 1

General issues of reporting across different types of assessments

Introduction to Section 1

Forensic populations present numerous challenges for new evaluators. This receives succinct attention in Chapter 1, where the authors state:

> The majority of offenders in prison will be motivated to progress towards release, but will not necessarily engage in the assessment process in an entirely honest manner. Previous experience of testing may have resulted in them having 'learned' a strategy for completing tests. This can present itself in a particular response style that may indicate dishonesty, or perhaps an aspect of their psychopathology.

While these written words can appear straightforward in meaning, their nuanced application in conducting assessments, including the use of even seemingly simple measures, can be complicated. Far from simple test administration, forensic evaluators will wish to consider their interactions with clients and the context in which the assessment takes place. Each can influence the process of the assessment and the findings themselves.

Chapter 2 calls attention to areas that many who conduct forensic evaluations may miss. For example, approximately 10 to 15 per cent of assessment clients may experience intellectual or other cognitive limitations requiring specialised knowledge and skills. Professionals evaluating these clients can easily overlook problematic areas of functioning in cases where the client has spent his or her entire life portraying themselves as more functional than they actually are. Comprehensive assessment is a vital first step in understanding the possible influence of these limitations on the treatment and supervision of clients. These issues also become important once clients enter the legal domain, where issues of competence and fitness to stand trial may become pertinent.

Indeed, as noted in Chapter 3, unstructured clinical judgements made by professionals trying to predict future behavior are so notoriously inaccurate that they cannot properly be termed 'professional'. Humans are often very good at making social judgements (including treatment decisions), but a good measure is far more likely to be predictive of future events than a good professional. In the end, professionals are at their best using large amounts of information in the service of comprehensive assessment and treatment, but not at prediction. As this section shows, even the manner in which we convey risk assessment findings can influence those who read reports.

Fortunately, the authors in Chapter 4 and 5 provide ways forward. These ways forward include structuring information and reports in such a way that professionals can move beyond simple prediction to communicating how risk might best be formulated, managed and communicated to others. The authors emphasise the importance of structure and offer helpful suggestions for doing so.

Chapter 6 addresses the assessment of personality disorders, which are very common amongst people who repeatedly break the law. As the author notes, in addition to more common considerations, personality dysfunction is relevant to forensic practitioners in that it is often most problematic in times of crisis or despair. It is therefore an aggravating factor in the presence of conflict or frustration and can therefore be crucial in considering, formulating and managing future risks.

The final chapter in this section deals with a topic that has received scant attention in many quarters: the actual assessment of change. This can be a controversial topic at the front lines of practice. The author notes that there are two factors that can influence assessors and the public at large. These include the importance of recidivism from a policy perspective and the belief that offenders can and do fake change. These factors can combine to form a high level of cynicism among the public and even within professionals themselves.

Putting these pieces together, it can be particularly helpful for professionals to keep in mind the principles of effective correctional rehabilitation, which receive some attention in these chapters. The *risk principle* holds that the most intensive interventions should be reserved for those who pose the highest risk. To that end, professionals will wish to consider strongly their formulations and recommendations for managing risk. The *need principle* holds that effective programmes establish individualised treatment goals that are directly related to criminal recidivism processes (i.e. criminogenic needs). Finally, the *responsivity principle* holds that effective programmes tailor services to the characteristics of each client. This can include motivation, mode of intervention and even concerns related to scheduling. This last principle can apply to forensic evaluators in ways that can be difficult to predict, such as in interview processes (noted in Chapter 1).

1

REPORTING PSYCHOMETRIC TESTS

Glenda Liell and Martin Fisher

Introduction

Psychometric assessments are designed to be reliable and unbiased measures of psychological constructs that describe thinking, emotional and behavioural processes. Psychometric testing has been used in the following ways:

- To assist in diagnosis.
- To assist in the formulation of psychological and identification of areas of stress and conflict.
- To determine the nature of the deficits that are present (i.e. cognitive functioning).
- To assess severity of psychopathology and response to treatment.
- To assess general characteristics (i.e. personality).
- To assess risk in various criminal justice settings.

Knowing how a service user performs on a test is of no value unless we know how well other people from the same population are able to perform on the same test. Simply knowing the relative outcome is only one part of the process: scoring, interpretation and reporting complete the psychometric assessment process. The latter parts require particular competences and understanding (e.g. British Psychological Society Testing Committee, PTC, 2015) in order that the outcome is rendered meaningful and useful in assessment. The proper and appropriate reporting of results is often an overlooked aspect of the cycle but is vital, in that without effective communication of the psychometric testing results to the service user, and those requiring insight and understanding to inform their decision making and taking (Muir-Gray, 2001), the purpose is lost.

Psychometric tests can be judged and characterised by a series of measures concerning their relative merits. These can be summarised thus, and the test user needs to be familiar with these in order to select and assure the use of tests in their practice.

Reliability – this can be described in three particular ways.

1 Internal consistency – the extent to which items in a scale are correlated with one another; that is, the extent to which they measure the same thing. This is often measured using Cronbach's (alpha) (Kline, 2000).
2 Inter-rater reliability – agreement amongst raters – in effect the extent to which different raters score and interpret the test in the same way.
3 Test-retest reliability – a correlational measure between scores on two administrations of a test to the same subjects. A high correlation indicates high reliability.

Validity – this can be described across six measures and needs to be allied with considerations of reliability.

1 Concurrent validity – a way of determining the validity of a measure by seeing how well it correlates with some other measure the test designer believes is valid.
2 Content validity – a measure can be described as having this when its item accurately represents the thing that is being measured. It is a matter of expert judgement.
3 Construct validity – the extent to which variables accurately measure the constructs of interest. This is used to describe a scale, index or other measure of a variable that correlates with measures of other variables in ways that are predicted by, or make sense according to, a theory of how the variables are related.
4 Convergent validity – the overlap between different tests that are presumed to measure the same construct.
5 Discriminant validity – a measure of the validity of a construct that when it is high the construct *fails* to correlate with the other, theoretically distinct, constructs: a mirror of convergence.
6 Criterion-related validity – the ability of a test to make accurate predictions. Also called predictive validity.

In selecting a test to use, all of these features need to be considered to ensure that the intent and requirement of the testing process can be satisfactorily met. In the forensic context there is a need to ensure that the validation sample is relevant to the test taker's representative population. Similarly, there is a need for clarity in the relationship between the hypothesis being considered through the use of testing and the intent of the test itself in terms of the content validity: the WAIS IV does not require forensic context-specific norms, for example, because the construct ('intelligence') is common to all people, not just those being assessed in a forensic context. The aim of this chapter is to outline best practice when using and reporting the outcomes and interpretations of psychometric tests.

Best practice

How do you decide whether to use a psychometric test?

Psychometric tests are one of many methods available in the collation of information during the assessment process. The principle of using information from a range of sources applies to most settings – not just forensic ones. The process of *Triangulating Information* (see Figure 1.1) is arguably the most a crucial aspect of the assessment process. This involves collating information from a broad range of sources.

A thorough review of all the available documentation about an individual should normally be undertaken as the starting point of an assessment. In an ideal world, information that includes an individual's background and childhood is invaluable although not always available or complete if available. If someone has been in the care system or in secure hospitals for part of his/her life, this information may be held in medical records which may be accessed by a non-medical clinician only with consent. It is a clinician's responsibility to consider where else information could be held. This may involve contacting individuals who are involved in managing the case in question. Clients do not have to give consent for communication to take place between relevant and appropriate parties involved in managing their cases. However, consent may need to be sought if the information being gathered involves contacting family members. The aim of an assessment is always to gain as broad an understanding as possible of the day-to-day as well as past behaviour.

Have psychometric tests been used already?

Psychological reports are likely to be found in the files of forensic clients. Whilst the conclusion(s) drawn in these reports will be of interest, attention should also be paid to the method(s) used and the current validity of the results/interpretations. The rationale for this should be clear. Assessments of characteristics that can change will have a 'shelf-life' and the findings of 'dated' tests may no longer be relevant.

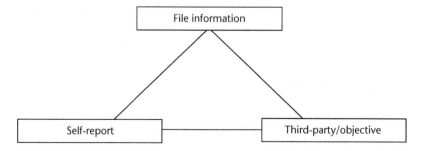

FIGURE 1.1   Triangulation of information to inform assessment

Score sheets for psychometric tests with no accompanying interpretations may be present. It is possible to refer to this test having been administered in an assessment report if it could be useful to the assessment in question. However, it will not be known whether best practice has been employed during administration and scoring and whether the reliability of the scores has been affected. A carefully thought out and justified caveat should therefore be included if the test is going to be used.

What if you disagree with the outcome of the assessment?

No clinician is infallible, and it is possible that one could come across a test that has been scored incorrectly. It may be a straightforward error in calculation, or perhaps the test taker missed an item(s). In this type of scenario, the test could be rescored, but that depends on the test.

If it is possible to rescore the test and increase its reliability, then this must be documented. The reasons why this has been done must also be documented. However, it is important to be wary of criticising the person who initially reported the inaccurate results.

Is there value in retesting using the same measure?

Repeating psychometric tests is generally not advisable – even if errors in the scoring have been uncovered. Choosing to do so carries with it a range of implications. The same psychometric test can be used over a specific period of time as part of a measure of change following treatment. If retesting is not about measuring change, what is the value of readministering the test? Is there another reason why the test outcomes could be different such that it would aid the assessment process? An example of this might be that it was clear that the client was suffering from mental health problems which may have affected how they responded.

If retesting is considered appropriate, an insufficient period of time between testing sessions can lead to test questions being answered in the same way. The questions or types of questions may be clearly remembered by the test taker. However, they could also be answered very differently for the same reason. With some tests the issue of *practice effects* has the potential to invalidate outcomes, particularly for measures of performance (i.e. the WAIS-IV) and subjects' performance on memory tests is also susceptible (i.e. McCaffrey et al., 1992). The individual may have received feedback which might also have an impact on future testing.

Choosing the right psychometric test

The first point to consider is whether the test is going to measure what you want it to; i.e. it has validity (as outlined above). Tests should have been standardised with norm groups of at least 150 people that are appropriate to the individual you are assessing. Tests with demonstrated reliability should also be used. Often tests that do not meet the recommended standards are used in forensic settings. For example, the Test of Memory Malingering (TOMM) has not been adequately validated in a forensic psychiatric setting (Orr, Woods, Conover and Feix, 2003). Indeed, proper validation studies are rare because of the sample sizes needed and the time and experience required (Toplis, Dulewicz and Fletcher, 2005). Tests can be designed on the basis of a solid theory relevant to forensic assessment which adds weight to their validity, but are in need of further development.

The psychometric test must play a part in the formulation of the case in question. That is, the ongoing development of a hypothesis about what underpins an individual's offending, and the level of risk they present to others. Tests can assist in the process of adding weight to a hypothesis or disproving it. It is often the case that clinicians choose to administer a battery of tests. There is an argument, however, that superfluous information may be being gathered that serves no purpose. Consideration should also be given to the client and the heightened levels of anxiety which testing can produce. There is no right or wrong number of tests to use; it is the rationale for using each and every test that needs to be clear and presented in the final report.

The manual accompanying a psychometric test should state whether it is suitable or has norms for use with males, females, juveniles, learning disabilities, etc. It is possible to contact the test publisher or author for further information about norms. However, where there are other issues, such as when English is not the client's first language, careful consideration should be given to whether the test can be used reliably. Attempting to explain the meaning of questions may add a layer of interpretation on the part of a test user and result in a discussion which could impact the outcome. However, it may be possible to read out the questions for those who have literacy problems. If an individual has particular cognitive deficits they may have difficulties paying attention for long periods. Certain factors such as active mental health problems may render psychometric testing unsuitable at that time.

The limitations of psychometric tests

Psychometric tests can be very useful and add a different dimension to the assessment process. However, it is important to recognise two key issues in relation to forensic settings.

1   Psychometric tests are self-report instruments.
2   Deliberate falsification of responses is easy.

Some clients will consider that it is not in their best interests to be entirely honest when participating in testing. However, this issue can also apply to other settings. It is also important to consider that factors such as fatigue, low levels of concentration or attention, and disturbed mood states may result in non-representative performances. Response style can have an impact as well as simple carelessness in how the completion of a test is approached. The same response may carry different meanings in different situations. For example, a person who describes himself as slow may be intellectually slow or just careful.

From a test design perspective, it may be very difficult to determine the true validity of measurement; i.e. there is no perfect yardstick for neuroticism against which the neuroticism rating of a test can be compared. Some test manuals will be explicit about the limitations. For example, the International Personality Disorder Inventory (IPDE [Loranger, 1999]) is essentially a self-report assessment tool which requires that individuals provide valid descriptions of aspects of their personalities. It was also not designed to assess all aspects of personality.

Screening measures

Some forensic assessments have screening measures such as the International Personality Disorder Examination (IPDE [Loranger, 1999]) and the Psychopathy Checklist-Revised (PCL-R [Hare, 2003]). These can assist with decision making around whether it is worthwhile to administer the full assessment; in most situations this is a time-saving exercise. It is not unethical to do this if, for example, there is an immovable and very tight deadline. In this case, an indication of potential problems can assist with signposting potential next steps for further assessment. A good example of this is the use of IPDE Screening Questionnaire which can assist decision making around whether to administer the full IPDE. Assuming that the test taker was truthful in the way they rated the items, it can offer an indication of what areas may be particularly problematic and will require more in-depth probing. Some psychometric tests are used as screening tools to assist with decision making around whether to use a *different*, more in-depth assessment.

Issues concerning consent and ethics

Fisher et al. (2016) discuss the issues surrounding ethics in forensic context psychometric testing at length, in terms of the potential power imbalances between test taker and test administrator, the validity of consent and how the outcomes of testing are managed and disclosed. Coaley (2014) provides a helpful and more succinct summary of the area, which in essence requires that the test administrator is satisfied that the test taker has been enabled to, and provided, valid consent to the testing process.

The test taker must also understand what is being assessed, why, using what measures and how the outcomes will be shared. In the forensic context (amongst others) there is a need to refer to valid consent as this is inclusive of the more usually referred to *informed consent*. In the forensic context the client hierarchy may be less clear, or the test taker may be detained, incarcerated or the authority requesting the testing may be a statutory body or the court. As such the test user and the test administrator need to assure that the consent for testing has meaning within the relevant code of conduct for the jurisdiction. The test taker, or his/her representative, must also have the relevant and appropriate opportunity to provide consent that is valid. Cooper and Fisher (2010) discuss various aspects of these issues in detail and in particular the need for consistency and continuity across testing situations to maintain standards of test use.

When to administer?

A fundamental part of the assessment process is to try and establish rapport with the client. For this reason, a client may not respond well to being presented with a test(s) during the first meeting. Having completed the file review, and met the client on a couple of occasions, the evidence required to form an opinion will come to light. If the intention is to use more than one test, whether to use them in one session or throughout the assessment process should be considered. The client's experience of the process should be central to this.

Client responsivity issues

The majority of offenders in prison will be motivated to progress towards release, but will not necessarily engage in the assessment process in an entirely honest manner. Previous experience of testing may have resulted in them having 'learned' a strategy for completing tests. This can present itself in a particular response style that may indicate dishonesty, or perhaps an aspect of their psychopathology.

Those using assessments such as Paulhus Deception Scales (PDS [Paulhus, 1998]) aim to identify response styles in themselves. This assessment can be used as part of a battery of self-report measures which may provide some indication of whether the desire to present in a particular way may impact on any subsequent conclusions which could be drawn. Using the test as part of a battery of assessments may also offer some indication of malingering. Any concerns regarding the reliability and validity of the tests administered need to be noted within the final report.

Scoring and interpreting test scores

There are some key principles with regards to scoring tests which should be adhered to. A methodical and meticulous approach is required for whatever type of test is being used (Coaley, 2014). The potential consequence of not doing so is invalidating the test scores. It is also the case that familiarity with a test can result in a more laid back approach to scoring it. A scoring error as a result of this can be avoided if the scoring instructions are reread every time the test is used. Another way of managing potential errors is to ask a colleague to second-score it for you. This may not be possible all the time, but planning ahead will serve to maximise best practice in this area.

Reporting test outcomes

There are three key parts to the feedback process to consider:

* The discussion between the test user and the test taker.
* The write-up of the test results which will form a standalone record that a testing session took place.
* Incorporating the outcome of the test in a report when it forms part of a broader assessment.

The person who administered the test may not be the person who will feed back the results. In which case, the test taker should have been made aware of this prior to the testing process beginning. This would have formed part of the process of seeking consent and explaining to the test taker what he/she can expect. The test taker has to be assured that the testing session and subsequent interpretation is being managed by individuals who are either trained to do so, or are being appropriately supervised.

Verbal feedback

If the test administrator will be giving verbal feedback, then this needs to be meaningful. The client should be able to choose to have another person present if they think it will be helpful for them. However, the appropriateness of this should be considered; for example, can it be another prisoner or patient? There is little point in imparting a set of raw scores with no context. It is possible to tell an individual that (s)he has good short-term memory or that his/her ability in arithmetic is higher than the average population against whom s/he was compared. The use of language is important and should be jargon-free. The person feeding back also needs to be confident that the person has understood the outcome. This can be done by asking the client to repeat back what they think are the key points of the testing outcome.

Outline of written report

The test in question and the scores (if applicable) must be appropriately filed and be accessible to relevant professionals in the future. A feedback report should include the following:

- Referral information – basic details about the client, i.e. DOB and ethnicity.
- The process of seeking consent and any concerns raised by the client.
- A brief description of the test.
- The context in which the test is being used, i.e. a report for a parole board/an assessment for the court.
- Why that particular test is the most appropriate given the context in which it is being used. What is the purpose?
- Conditions in which the test was administered. Were there any issues around the testing environment which impacted on the session? Was the testing session interrupted? This could affect reliability.
- Any concerns regarding the client, i.e. did they report feeling unwell during the session? Was it necessary to explain several questions to them? This could affect reliability.
- The report can state basic scores, and graphs can be included if appropriate. Where the testing manual contains a lot of jargon include a paragraph which clearly describes what has been found. Include any caveats in the reporting of

the scores, i.e. whether any issues arose during the testing session could affect their reliability.

- Offer an interpretation of the scores based on the manual. Use layman's terms to explain what the scores are suggesting.
- Some tests include scales relating to *response style*, i.e. exaggerating symptoms or responding randomly to questions. The impact of this will need to be commented on.
- 'Noteworthy' responses may be included which draw the test user's attention to particular areas of concern, i.e. a client is currently reporting feeling suicidal. Whether or not these have been explored further with the client should be reported.
- Consider who will be reading the report in order to decide the type of language and style to use. Do not forget that this report is also for the client.
- What can or cannot be concluded and why. Comment on the limits of the scores and any issues around reliability. Stress the dangers of using or quoting the scores in isolation and how the report should or shouldn't be used. Refer back to the reason for using the test. State where further analysis/contextual information can be found.
- Are there any 'next steps'? If so what?

It is important to bear in mind that generally people's attention will always be drawn to raw scores and cut-offs which offer only a very crude interpretation. A test such as the WAIS-IV is a good example of where people focus on the overall IQ score and consider this to be how clever someone is. In fact, the individual scale scores are often the most useful because they identify responsivity issues which can assist with the developing of strategies for how best to work with that individual. However, the overall score can be important if a referral is being made to a unit which specialises in working with those with learning disabilities.

Common difficulties/confusion

The misuse of psychometric tests

In essence, the misuse of a test is orthogonal to their appropriate use. However, some aspects of psychometric tests are more prone to misuse than others. This relates in particular to the predictive validity and the discriminant validity of tests. Understanding the application of percentiles, T scores and other derived indices requires specific competences on the part of the test user (PTC, 2015) and a failure to use tests for the purpose they were intended at design has significant adverse consequences for test takers, and where relevant, the commissioning authority. Fisher et al. (2016) discuss how the outcomes from assessment might be misconstrued by a practitioner not competent in the use of a test, or how outcomes might be used to provide support for a position which the test user prefers. Fisher et al. (Chapter 12, this volume) discuss these issues in the context of reporting bias and rule compliance (Karson and Nadkarni, 2013).

Training and CPD in the use of psychometric tests

It is the practitioner's responsibility to ensure that the rationale for using any psychometric test is clear and defensible. Correct administration and scoring is paramount, but consideration should also be given to a potential need for supervision – even if this amounts to just double-scoring. Test users should be familiar with the most up-to-date research on any test being used. Test authors may choose to revise and update their tests, and do not necessarily mind being contacted about their test. For them it can offer some valuable information about how and where the test is being used. Authors can also put clinicians in contact with others with whom they could discuss cases and share best practice.

Research may be undertaken that raises concerns about a test's use with certain individuals or in certain situations. A clinician could decide to stop using that test or introduce certain caveats when interpreting it. New tests are also published, and being aware of this is important. When in an adversarial setting in particular, clinicians should be prepared to be challenged about their use of tests and the relative value of them to the case at hand.

Protecting test information

This concerns four key issues that come under the umbrella of protecting the integrity of tests and associated materials, access to test outcomes, copyright and storage of test materials and data. The first issue around protecting integrity is related to the amount or type of information given to the test taker either prior to or after the assessment. This also concerns the sharing of the testing materials themselves. If not managed effectively, the integrity of the test may be compromised. Examples of offering a test taker too much information prior to a test session could include a personality assessment where individual scales and scoring criteria are shared. However, concerns in the area of maintaining test integrity should not be interpreted as a need to 'hide' fundamental aspect(s) of a test.

The second issue concerns how a test's integrity can be negatively affected in situations such as courts or quasi-courts (i.e. parole hearings) in terms of the amount and type of information that is shared about it. It is not generally the case that very detailed information about tests is requested for parole board hearings. A court can legally request test materials and such disclosure is permitted within the Data Protection Act (guidance to psychologists and other users of psychological tests concerning obligations when providing evidence or opinion which rests on the results of that psychometric testing, 2007). Should specific details about certain tests appear in the public domain, their usefulness can be compromised. It is the psychologist's responsibility to ensure that the potential negative impact of divulging details of standardised testing instruments is made known to the court.

Test manuals should not be given to test takers or other individuals, and test materials should not be copied. This is an infringement of copyright law and could lead to legal action by the test author or the test publisher. If a test user chances upon a photocopied test sheet in a file, (s)he should source the original from which the copy was made and destroy the unauthorised copy.

Psychologists have a significant responsibility for managing access to and the use of test data to ensure confidentially and appropriate use. However, the client has the legal right to request all records held on him/her. If records must be shared (i.e. multidisciplinary case management), then the client must know at which point any assessment or testing begins. How records are kept, and for how long, are likely to be guided by the policies of any organisation's legal and professional rules. Psychologists have a duty to follow national, local policy and legal requirements regarding the retaining or disposal of records after their work is completed.

Review task

This chapter has sought to highlight the range of issues and considerations that arise when psychometric assessment is employed in a forensic context. The use of psychometric assessment requires particular competences in the test user and the test administrator if the outcomes are to be reliable. Regular refreshing of knowledge and skills are an integral part of competent practice and familiarity with the process as well as the technical aspects of the instruments chosen is critical. Complacency can easily creep into practice with the passage of time and overconfidence in knowledge and understanding of psychometric assessment must be moderated by regular review and reference of practice. In the absence of such measures, the value and reputation of the use of psychometric testing is at risk for all, not least service users.

It can be useful over time to refer back to tests with which you feel familiar in your practice and review them in light of the guidance and discussion here. For example, reading the technical manual over again to familiarise yourself with the reliability characteristics of the test and the validation sample. Have you been administering it as per the requirement? Have you been using percentiles in the outcome description when T scores are available, and have you reflected on why the latter are more stable and preferable? The Psychological Testing Centre of the British Psychological Society provides a range of information about best practice in testing and referencing your knowledge against up-to-date best practice guidelines will assist in ensuring that your practice is as good as it can be. For example: https://ptc.bps.org.uk/sites/ptc.bps.org.uk/files/Images/The%20BPS%20Qualifications%20in%20Test%20Use%20-%20March%202015.pdf, describes all their standards and qualifications in testing, including forensic context testing.

For structured professional judgement type tests (e.g. PCL-R v2 [Hare, 2003]), maintaining your familiarity with and knowledge of the evidence base for the test will assure your competence to test takers and stakeholders alike (e.g. www.hare.org/references/new.html).

Checklist of steps/advice

1 Ensure that the test user (be that the practitioner or delegated authority) is competent in the use of testing and the particular test that has been selected.
2 Ensure that the test selected meets the requirement – that is it has an appropriate level and type of reliability and it is appropriately valid.
3 Ensure that in the administration the test taker has provided valid consent and that the administration follows the publisher's specified process.
4 Ensure that following testing appropriate and timely feedback is provided to the test taker.
5 Ensure that the outcomes of the testing are appropriately interpreted and reported as per the test publisher's intentions, and that these outcomes are integrated with other relevant information to provide a holistic assessment which provides and enhances meaning in the resulting formulation of risk assessment/management.
6 Ensure that the requirements for the handling and storage of testing material are adhered to.

Further reading

Psychometric testing is a wide field of practice and this chapter has only provided a short and practical review. The starred references below are particularly recommended for a much broader perspective to inform practice.

References

British Psychological Society. (2015). *A guide for psychologists on acting as an expert witness covering both ethical principles and practicalities.* Leicester, UK: British Psychological Society.

British Psychological Society. (2015). *Psychologists as expert witnesses: Guidelines for England, Wales and Northern Ireland.* Leicester, UK: British Psychological Society.

British Psychological Society. (2008). *Generic professional practice guidelines,* 2nd ed. Leicester, UK: British Psychological Society.

*Coaley, K. (2014). *An introduction to psychological assessment and psychometrics,* 2nd ed. London: Sage.

Cooper, S. and Fisher, M.J. (2010). Ethical considerations in the consultancy and advisory process, in Ireland, C.A. and Fisher, M.J. (eds.), *Consultancy and advising in forensic practice: Empirical and practical guidelines.* Chichester, UK: Wiley.

*Fisher, M., Brown, S.J., Barnett, G., and Wakeling, H. (2016) Forensic Context Testing. In F.T.L. Leong, D. Bartram, F. Cheung, K.F. Geisinger, and D. Iliescu (eds). *International Test Commission (ITC) Handbook of Testing and Assessment.* Oxford: Oxford University Press.

Hare, R.D. (2003). Hare Psychopathy Checklist-Revised. Technical manual. Toronto, Canada: Multi-Health Systems Inc.

Karson, M. and Nadkarni, L. (2013). *Principles of forensic report writing.* Washington, DC: APA.

Kline, P. (2000). *Handbook of psychological testing,* 2nd ed. *Oxon, UK: Routledge.*

Lichtenbrger, E.O. and Kaufman, A.S. (2012). *Essentials of WAIS-IV assessment* Hoboken, NJ: Wiley.

Loranger, A.W. (1999). *International personality disorder examination assessment*. Odessa, FL: Psychological Assessment Resources.

McCaffrey, R.J., Ortega, A., Orsillo, S.M., Nelles, W.B. and Haase, R.F. (1992). Practice effects in repeated neuropsychological assessments. *Clinical Neuropsychology*, *6*, 32–42.

Muir-Gray, J.A. (2001). Using systematic reviews for evidence-based policy making, in Egger, M., Davey-Smith, G. and Altman, D. (eds.), *Systematic reviews in health care* (pp. 410–18). London, UK: BMJ Books.

Novaco, R.W. (2003). The Novaco Anger Scale and *Provocation Inventory: Manual*. Los Angeles, CA: Western Psychological Services.

Orr, T., Woods, S. P., Conover, E. and Feix, J. (2003). A validation of the Test of Memory Malingering in a forensic psychiatric setting. *Neuropsychology, Development and Cognition*, *25*, 979–90.

Paulhus, D. L. (1998). *Paulhus Deception Scales: The balanced inventory of desirable responding-7. User manual*. New York: Multi-Health Systems.

Psychological Testing Centre (PTC). (2015). *Testing standards for forensic contexts*. Retrieved from http://ptc.bps.org.uk/how-apply-packs/bps-forensic-testing-qualifications (accessed on 4 November 2015).

*Psychological Testing Centre (PTC) and British Psychological Society. (2007). *Guidance to psychologists and other users of psychological tests concerning obligations when providing evidence or opinion which rests on the results of that psychometric testing*. Leicester, UK: BPS.

Toplis, J., Dulewicz, V. and Fletcher, C. (2005). *Psychological testing: A manager's guide*, 4th ed. London: Chartered Institute of Personnel and Development.

2

REPORTING INTELLECTUAL CAPACITY/COGNITIVE FUNCTIONING

Robin J. Wilson and David Tobin

Introduction

Writing a report about intellectual functioning or cognitive capacity is one particular area in which we are likely to see considerable use of jargon, sometimes referred to by clients and other laypersons as 'psychologese' or 'psychobabble'. Many of the difficulties experienced regarding intellectual functioning are brain-based, requiring use of complex clinical terminology and unfamiliar anatomical labels. Reporting such results necessitates a delicate balancing act in which information is professionally and precisely conveyed to expert users (other clinicians), but in a manner that is likely to be understood by those about whom the reports are written (clients, family/support persons). It is also important to remember that many of our clients will be experiencing difficulties in regard to information processing and understanding as well as difficulties with receptive and/or expressive language in the context of overall cognitive impairment. This highlights the need for assessors to choose their words carefully when composing evaluation reports in order to effectively communicate with all involved parties including the client being assessed. In this chapter, we present readers with suggestions for completing comprehensive evaluations of intellectual capacity and cognitive functioning and, most importantly, how to convey findings in a manner accessible to all who may read your reports.

Although they are not novel constructs generally, intellectual functioning and cognitive capacity are relatively new areas of focus in the world of offender assessment, treatment and risk management. As the principles of Risk, Need and Responsivity have permeated the forensic and correctional psychological fields so too has a need to make sure that the services we offer are designed to inform the process and assist the client(s) served in a manner consistent with their intellectual functioning. The focus of this chapter may be somewhat unfamiliar to some readers who work broadly with clients who offend, and the first thing we want to emphasise is the requirement for practitioners to be cognisant of their own professional limitations. That is, not all of us are specialists expert in the sorts of areas we will raise in this chapter. And there are differences to be noted between the *creators* and *users* of reports containing information about intellectual functioning and cognitive capacity – with creators needing to have a much more intimate understanding of the material at hand.

Best practice

How you proceed with your evaluation may have as much to do with the venue in which your report will be received as it has to do with specific elements of the client. When clients who have issues regarding cognitive limitations and have engaged in inappropriate conduct that brings them before the court, the presenting problem may be different than when your evaluation is being used to determine a course of intervention or risk management. It is also important to note that clinical understanding of competency may not equate fully to competency to stand trial, although certainly there are likely to be overlaps. The former may require a keen understanding of the responsivity principle, while the latter may require some process designed to restore clients to competence so that they may have their charges processed in court (see Wilson, DePass and Nelson, 2011).

Mental status evaluation and behavioral observations

In most instances you will have received a referral note from another clinician, or you will have been given some degree of problem explanation by the client or a family member or caregiver. This is the starting point leading to the opportunity to meet with and directly assess the client. After ensuring that you have appropriate consents to engage in the assessment process, which may include discussions with an alternate decision maker such as a guardian, you should then conduct a mental status examination (MSE; see Folstein, Folstein and McHugh, 1975) and begin to record your thoughts about the client's presentation and behavioral style. Mental status data can assist in making early determinations about what difficulties the client may be experiencing, the client's interactional style and what interpersonal barriers may exist. These will be working hypotheses that can be further assessed over the course of the evaluation. In some cases, especially where the client's self-report of symptoms and functioning differs significantly from the client's overt presentation, concerns may be raised about the veracity of a client's self-report which should also lead to further assessment.

The MSE and accompanying observations set the frame for the assessment results, in that those findings need to be presented within the context of the client's behavior and functioning at the time of evaluation. However, equally, if not more importantly, these data also describe the client's behavior *over the course* of the assessment, especially in regard to fluctuations in and responses to behaviors and interventions of the evaluator. This process creates a foundation for later discussion and assessment of coping and interpersonal styles that the client displays over the various demands and contexts of the assessment. For example, it will be important to document defensive coping strategies the client may demonstrate (e.g. disengagement, laughter, confabulation, aggression, agitation and/or derailment) during the assessment. A client's use of coping mechanisms – appropriate/inappropriate or effective/ineffective – provides information regarding how to interact productively with the client, as well as what might need to be addressed in the future via clinical and supervisory interventions.

As with most clients in assessment, it is important to develop rapport and trust. Keep in mind that many persons with intellectual and cognitive capacity may have been underserved or, worse still, have suffered abuse at the hands of caregivers and service providers (Hingsburger, 1995; Sobsey and Doe, 1991). These situations of abuse lead many clients to experience fear and mistrust, as well as to demonstrate a degree of acquiescence bias (a tendency to say 'yes' or to go along with instructions, regardless of the truth or possible negative outcomes). As such, it is important to ensure that the mental status interview is conducted in a calm, supportive and nonthreatening manner with particular attention to the client's perspective as well as with the provision of breaks as needed and with ample time for the client to respond to the best of their capacities.

Some simple tests exist to assist for the general screening for organic impairment masquerading as psychological symptoms (e.g. Copy-A-Figure Test, Write-A-Sentence Test and Draw-A-Clock Test [Taylor, 2007]). As their titles suggest, these tasks assist in measuring spatial conceptualisation, hand-eye coordination and memory functioning, as well as capacity for spatial relationships, ability to tell time and facility with numerical sequencing. The Draw-A-Clock task can be particularly difficult for those clients with specific brain dysfunctions. Aside from their roles in screening for organic impairment, these instruments also provide the client with an introduction to the nature of the assessment process as the evaluation switches from the conversational questioning of mental status to the increased task demands of the psychological assessment. At the same time, these introductory tasks are brief and require little to no social interaction with the evaluator as the client completes them on their own with no time constraint.

Including quick screening tests in the beginning phase of the assessment can introduce the client to the nature of evaluation and help the process be less threatening or overwhelming. For the evaluator, these brief tasks also provide an opportunity to observe how the client adapts to change and to new demands and expectations. Specifically, the evaluator can observe the client's coping, social and interactional style, including when the client resists, derails, frustrates or disengages from the tasks – the beginnings of developing strategies (e.g. cues, verbal support, encouragement, breaks) to maintain engagement while addressing frustration tolerance, focus, attention and task perseverance. There are, however, drawbacks inherent in using any assessment tool. Specifically, some individuals may experience difficulties in completing the tasks, leading to disengagement; however, it is important to recognise that this would likely have occurred with any assessment task and may not be directly related to these particular tasks. Additionally, treatment disengagement, for whatever reason and in whatever form, provides important information in and of itself about the functioning, capacities, limitations and coping styles of the client.

Intellectual capacity

Assessing intellectual capacity, along with neuropsychological inquiry (discussed in the next section), represents the most structured aspect of the assessment. In evaluating clients regarding intellectual capacity and cognitive limitations, it will be important to assess intelligence. For this process, a commonly used tool is an individually administered test known as the Wechsler Adult Intelligence Scale – 4th Edition (WAIS-IV [Wechsler, 2008]; although there are other intelligence tests that can be used, especially for those clients who are non-verbal). The WAIS-IV yields an overall score and four composite scores: Verbal Comprehension Index (VCI), Perceptual Reasoning Index (PRI), Working Memory Index (WMI) and Processing Speed Index (PSI) – all of which are helpful in establishing the client's cognitive strengths and weaknesses.

As a starting place, it is helpful to provide a general explanation of the cognitive assessment instrument utilised, in this case the Wechsler Adult Intelligence Scale – 4th Edition, prior to presentation of the assessment results. An example might include:

> *The WAIS-IV is an individually administered test of a person's intellectual ability including cognitive strengths and weaknesses. The test yields an overall score and four index scores: Verbal Comprehension Index (VCI), Perceptual Reasoning Index (PRI), Working Memory Index (WMI) and Processing Speed Index (PSI).*
>
> *In addition to an overall score summarising a person's cognitive performance, the Verbal Comprehensive Index addresses the person's ability to detect/explain similarities between objects, breadth of vocabulary and fund of general information. The Perceptual Reasoning Index addresses the person's ability to analyse and synthesise non-verbal, visual stimuli in terms of copying designs with blocks, completing matrices of visual images and analysing components of visual puzzles. The Working Memory Index assesses the person's capacity to register, hold and mentally manipulate information in short-term memory including recalling a series of digits in various order and mentally calculating mathematic problems. Lastly, the Processing Speed Index assesses the person's capacity to pair abstract symbols with numbers and search a group of symbols to detect the presence of two other symbols; both tasks are done under a time constraint.*

The results of the intelligence assessment can be depicted in a table or placed within the interpretative narrative itself. A table format displays the data in one place allowing the reader to focus on the overall pattern of results. However, the table can potentially distract from the narrative interpretation of the data by the evaluator. Table 2.1 provides an example of a results table.

TABLE 2.1 Example results table

<table>
<tr><td colspan="5" align="center">*Mr. Jones – Results table*
Wechsler Adult Intelligence Scale – 4th edition</td></tr>
<tr>
<td>*Scale*</td>
<td>*Composite score*</td>
<td>*Percentile rank*</td>
<td>*95% Confidence interval*</td>
<td>*Qualitative descriptor*</td>
</tr>
<tr>
<td>Verbal comprehension</td>
<td>70</td>
<td>2nd</td>
<td>66–77</td>
<td>Borderline</td>
</tr>
<tr>
<td>Perceptual reasoning</td>
<td>65</td>
<td>1st</td>
<td>61–73</td>
<td>Extremely low</td>
</tr>
<tr>
<td>Working memory</td>
<td>66</td>
<td>1st</td>
<td>61–75</td>
<td>Extremely low</td>
</tr>
<tr>
<td>Processing speed</td>
<td>81</td>
<td>10th</td>
<td>75–91</td>
<td>Low average</td>
</tr>
<tr>
<td>Full scale IQ score</td>
<td>65</td>
<td>1st</td>
<td>62–70</td>
<td>Extremely low</td>
</tr>
</table>

*All scores have a mean of 100 and a standard deviation of 15.

In some cases, especially when interpreting patterns and themes in the specific results, it may be beneficial to include a client's scores on the individual subtests – including the additional information in the table above. Rather than a table, the results of the cognitive assessment can also be integrated into the interpretative narrative, with the table included as an appendix. One benefit of this approach is to focus the reader on the clinical interpretation of the results rather than the numerical results in the table. For instance:

> *Mr. Jones obtained a Full Scale IQ score in an Extremely Low range (Full Scale IQ score = 65, 1st percentile, 95% confidence interval of 62 to 70), suggesting that he experiences considerable difficulties in regard to intellectual abilities.*

Interpretation of results

Generally, interpretation of intellectual abilities data should move from the most global score (i.e. the most reliable and meaningful, such as the Full Scale Score) to the more specific index scores, to the subtest scores and then, if applicable, to specific item responses. At each level of interpretation, the evaluator should assess the utility and relevance of the summary score in reflecting the person's unique capacities with the caveat that the more specific the interpretation (e.g. score on a particular subtest item), the less reliable and less generalisable the interpretation will be. In progressing from interpretation of the most global to more specific indices and subtest performances, it will be important to attend to both significant as well as unusual differences. For instance, depending on the size of the differences noted between scores, there might be indications that the full scale score may not provide an optimal summary of the client's abilities or, worse, the summary may be invalid, precluding its use. For example:

> Mr. Jones obtained a full scale IQ score in an extremely low range. His verbal-comprehensive, perceptual-reasoning and working memory abilities were similarly developed and in ranges considered borderline to extremely low. However, Mr. Jones demonstrated relative strengths with skills of processing speed performing in a range considered low average and significantly above his other capacities as assessed by the WAIS-IV. While significantly above his other capacities as assessed by the WAIS-IV (e.g. verbal comprehension, perceptual reasoning, working memory), the size of this difference was not unusually large, as compared to the respective standardisation samples. While the full scale IQ score can still be considered a valid summary of his overall cognitive functioning, it may also be useful to consider Mr. Jones' functioning in terms of his performance on the four WAIS-IV indices including his relative strength with skills of processing speed.

Integrating hypotheses derived from intellectual abilities evaluations into specific conclusions and recommendations will also be important. In the example above, Mr. Jones' overall performance in the extremely low range may be a useful summary of his cognitive functioning, but remember our recent tendency as a field to focus on strengths. In spite of his extremely low global intelligence rating, Mr. Jones' relative strengths on non-verbal tasks that rely, in part, on speed and accuracy (e.g. processing speed) suggest relatively heightened skills in visual discrimination, attention to detail and visual scanning. Integrating these strengths into recommendations for Mr. Jones will be helpful, with the following being a suggestion:

> In assessing clients who have sexually offended, focus has recently shifted from a strongly inadequacies-oriented approach to one that is primarily strength-based. Mr. Jones' test results suggest that he experiences intellectual difficulties across the board; however, inspection of subscale results suggest that he will tend to do better in tasks related to awareness of pertinent details in his world and appropriately focusing and maintaining his attention.

Indeed, this latter point is important. There may be times when the degree of variability in intellectual abilities results – either across the index or subtest scores – impacts the adequacy of the full scale or index score as a summary of a person's cognitive functioning. In one possible explanation, the full scale score may not adequately summarise the entirety of Mr. Jones' cognitive functioning. In this case, consider that across his performance on the three subtests of verbal comprehension, Mr. Jones demonstrated significantly stronger vocabulary skills as compared to considerably impaired social comprehension and verbal abstraction skills. This pattern suggests that his relatively strong vocabulary might obscure significant impairments in other areas of verbal comprehension capacities. In some clients this may be intentional – sometimes referred to as a 'cloak of competence' (see Edgerton, 1993) – the result of which being that Mr. Jones may have the capacity to communicate in a seemingly competent manner, possibly leading others to expect more from him than his actual capacities would allow. Rather than reporting and using index scores, highlighting the theme of improved vocabulary masking other verbal-comprehensive deficits would be more fruitful in understanding and working proactively with Mr. Jones.

> *In looking at trends across Mr. Jones' performance on the three subtests of Verbal Comprehension, it appears that he demonstrates what is known as a "cloak of competence", in which he appears able to discuss matters in his life with relative ease. However, it is important to note that in spite of this relative strength, Mr. Jones may not fully comprehend or appreciate how to negotiate new or challenging situations.*

Side benefits and drawbacks to intelligence testing

One salient issue associated with intelligence testing is our changing view as to what constitutes intelligence and whether or not new conceptualisations are easily slotted into the formerly popular retarded versus gifted continuum. In a field that now advocates use of strength-based approaches (see Marshall, Marshall, Serran and O'Brien, 2011), highlighting someone's limitations may not be as important as focusing on areas of strength.

Over and above the data obtained regarding intelligence, use of tools like the WAIS-IV provides an assessment of the client's capacity to problem-solve, tolerate frustration and manage impulses on highly specified and structured tasks. Situating this highly structured instrument near the beginning of the assessment – in combination with administration of tests with less or different structure – provides an opportunity for evaluators to observe client performances under varied conditions. However, as we noted above, it is important to note that many clients experience a degree of upset during evaluation, particularly in regard to their perceptions of their performance(s). Specifically, some clients may react adversely to high structure or to those tests in which difficulty levels increase over the course of the task, such as is the case in many of the scales of the WAIS-IV. Such effects are also observed in academics, in which students subjected to repeated difficulty or failure may experience progressively lower self-esteem and personal expectations. In the current context, such effects can be exacerbated by the length of time many tests take to administer (with few opportunities for breaks or rest according to standard administration). It is therefore important to consider that for some clients decreased performance may be due in part to the anxiety the instrument/process creates, rather than fully to cognitive impairment. Nonetheless, testing experiences of this sort can also provide perspective as to the client's capacity to function under conditions of duress and demand, which may ultimately have some relevance for problem-solving situations of risk in real-life community settings.

Neuropsychological screening

It is often useful to more specifically explore and describe the nature or manifestations of a client's intellectual or capacity difficulties. While causal factors for some clients will be obvious in terms of existing diagnoses (e.g. known syndromes) or developmental events (e.g. pre- or post-natal trauma), how those factors manifest may be different on a case-by-case basis. A number of neuropsychological tests exist that help to assess and describe the specific problems experienced by clients. Over and above the intellectual abilities testing noted in the preceding section, tests in this domain assist in evaluating memory, ability to organise data/concepts, perceptual tracking, attention and receptive/expressive language abilities, among other important areas of inquiry.

To assess memory, there are many commercially available tests and instruments, some of which are more involved than others. The Wechsler Memory Scale-IV is a comprehensive test battery in many ways similar to the WAIS-IV. Consistent with the theme of neuropsychological screening as well as attempting to maximise the results while decreasing stress and demands upon the client, we would suggest that administration of the WAIS-IV be paired with a selection of shorter, more to-the-point indices. For example, the Rey Auditory Verbal Learning Test (RAVLT [Meyers and Meyers, 1995]) assesses a client's memory for verbal information both immediately after presentation and after a delay. Memory for this verbal information is also assessed over time using both free-recall and recognition formats, the latter providing helpful information as to the client's ability to remember things when cued (e.g. recognition memory). As a companion to the RAVLT, the Rey Complex Figure Test (RCFT [Schmidt, 1996]) assesses a client's non-verbal organisational and memory capacity, as well as attention for detail, for a complex visual figure. The benefits of administering the RCFT are similar, but in the non-verbal domain; however, the added benefit of the RCFT is that it provides valuable information regarding hand-eye coordination leading to difficulties producing adequate, interpretable drawings.

When administering the RAVLT and RCFT or other measures with delayed memory components, it will be necessary to engage in other tasks/tests during that delay. One suggestion would be the use of the Color Trails Test (CTT [D'Elia, Satz, Uchiyama and White, 1996]), which assesses the client's perceptual tracking, sequencing and sustained attention capacities by having him/her first connect a series of colored and numbered circles in a number of ways. The CTT represents a rapid way to assess attention in a format that most clients find enjoyable or at least tolerable. It is also sufficiently different from the RAVLT and RCFT so as not to contaminate the results during the delay period.

In comparison to the relatively quick and simple tasks noted above, it may be important to engage in more comprehensive neuropsychological inquiry. The Repeatable Battery for the Assessment of Neuropsychological Status (RBANS [Randolph, 2012]) is an individually administered assessment battery testing attention, language, visuospatial/constructional and memory (immediate and delayed). Consisting of 12 subtests that comprise a total score and five index scores (e.g. immediate memory, visuospatial/constructional, language, attention and delayed memory), the RBANS is also a screening device of overall neuropsychological functioning. Of benefit, the RBANS addresses the major aspects of neuropsychological functioning in a single instrument, enabling comparison to age-appropriate normative groups as well as individualised assessment of strengths and weaknesses. However, some evaluators have expressed concerns with the language screening part of the assessment, in that clients tend to do well with the 10-item picture identification subtest (i.e. the floor is possibly too high), leading to inflated language scores that may not correspond to collateral assessment of capacities on WAIS-IV and CREVT (see next paragraph).

The Comprehensive Receptive and Expressive Vocabulary Test – 3rd Edition (CREVT-3 [Wallace and Hammill, 2013]) provides a measure of a client's understanding and expression of vocabulary. In particular, CREVT-3 quantifies oral vocabulary proficiency for both children and adults. It consists of two subtests: receptive vocabulary in which a client matches an orally stated word to a picture, and expressive vocabulary in which a client defines a series of words. A general vocabulary index is also provided, representing a combination of the Receptive and Expressive subtests. A benefit of the CREVT-3 is that while providing a comprehensive assessment of both receptive and expressive vocabulary, it is also helpful in contrasting verbal abilities with cognitive abilities, especially in situations where a client may present with good language skills (receptive, expressive or both) that may obscure underlying cognitive difficulties.

There is a wide variety of neuropsychological assessment tools available to inform a detailed expert analysis of client status in this domain. These tools highlight the difference between a neuro-screen (which we are advocating in this chapter) as a way to describe functioning with the goal of responsivity and a comprehensive neuropsychological evaluation (something we are not covering here). In writing reports including the sort of screening information advocated here, it would be helpful to add a brief statement(s) that the screen we suggest is just that, a screen, and is descriptive of particular functions such as memory and attention. One potential result of this screen, especially with disparate results (including significant differences compared to cognitive functioning) would likely necessitate consideration of a referral for more in-depth assessment with an appropriately trained and certified neuropsychological specialist.

General assessment information

In addition to the specialised information gathered in formal testing, there is also a lot to be learned in terms of the client's practical abilities – as demonstrated in a variety of life domains. Although non-disabled people generally take much of what they do for granted, many disabled persons struggle for opportunities to lead lives as 'normal' as possible given their limitations. This speaks to the need to employ the same bio–psycho–social interviewing processes that we use in most evaluation circumstances, but with something of a twist – we are looking for information that helps us to better understand both the nature and manifestations of the client's cognitive capacities. However, gathering information in these domains can sometimes require a degree of creativity, depending on the client's intellectual abilities.

In typical assessments of clients who have offended, it is important to ask questions about the client's early life and developmental experiences leading into academic experiences and early employment opportunities. Even though intellectual disabilities tend to be present from birth or very early on in clients' lives, it is also clear that the degree of stimulation and support they receive can dramatically affect development. Knowing about the client's home life, academic opportunities and extracurricular experiences will provide valuable insights regarding the client's current circumstances.

Similarly, consideration of the client's ability – or lack thereof – to effectively interact with others will also assist in both understanding the client's current functioning in interpersonal domains, as well as pinpointing areas for focus and intervention (e.g. treatment or supervision). The interplay between abilities and experiences affords clients with opportunities to grow, perhaps beyond their limitations, while providing evaluators with *in vivo* examples of strengths and weaknesses.

> *Although prognoses of Mr. Jones' likely abilities in regard to relationships and intimacy suggested that he would experience severe limitations over his lifetime, Mr. Jones' parents' determination in ensuring integrated education and social opportunities surely assisted with his better-than-expected strengths in these domains.*

In addition to client family, academic and interpersonal history data, it is also helpful to investigate what other intersections the client's life has had with professional services. For instance, information regarding health complications can help put behavior in context. Even more so, we know that many clients with intellectual disabilities have dual diagnoses, particularly in regard to mental health difficulties and problems in alcohol or substance abuse. Regarding the latter, having some knowledge as to the potential reasons for using (e.g. self-medication, soothing, problem avoidance) can be quite helpful when identifying problem areas and devising risk management plans.

Sexuality

In some assessments, e.g. when there are offences or allegations of sexual abuse, the client's experiences with respect to sexuality are important to consider. Specifically, how and when did the client learn about sex? Was it in the context of abuse, or through experimentation with peers? Whereas concerns about a dearth of effective sex education available to neurotypical youngsters is frequently a topic of discussion in the media, opportunities for meaningful sex education are even more scarce for people with disabilities. The consequence is that many people with intellectual capacity issues have poor sex knowledge, lack understanding of fundamental issues (e.g. consent) and develop attitudes reflective of their caregivers (which are, unfortunately, often repressive). Consideration of these issues is crucial in trying to understand any sexually inappropriate conduct in which the client has engaged. Using an applied behavioral analysis approach can be particularly illuminating, in which one attempts to deduce the root cause(s) of the behavior as well as the relative means available to achieve the ultimate goal. Here, we are particularly fond of this quotation from Justice Fraser in Canada (cited in Chartrand and Forbes-Chilibeck, 2003):

> *Herein lies the problem relating to the commission of sexual offences. Having a mature body beyond his intellect, he has urges for sexual gratification which leads to impulsiveness and unpremeditated behaviour without using caution and with risk taking. This is followed by non-comprehension that the behaviour was inappropriate.*

As a means to gather information about sexuality, we are fond of the Socio-Sexual Knowledge and Attitudes Tool – Revised (SSKAAT-R [Griffiths and Lunsky, 2003]). This battery addresses a variety of domains, including anatomy; men's/ women's bodies; intimacy; pregnancy, childbirth and child-rearing; birth control and STDs; and health social-sexual boundaries, using a non-threatening, largely picture-based approach. The data obtained on the SSKAAT-R are helpful in assessing the extent/absence of a client's knowledge about sexuality, as well as any values and attitudes he/she has developed that might shed light on how others might have influenced them in this domain.

Many clinics providing services to clients with intellectual and other cognitive limitations have become quite enterprising in terms of developing protocols to assess aspects of their clients' sexuality (see Wilson and Burns, 2011). However, many of these ad hoc tools are self-report in nature and their psychometric strengths and weaknesses may be unknown. As such, they are effective to the extent that the client both understands the items and is willing to respond to them. That said, a client's pattern of responding can be contrasted with available collateral information to assess the congruence or incongruence between his/her self-report and other sources of data, such as reports from caregivers. In this same vein, it may also be important to gather information about activities or daily living, particularly where the possibility exists to compare the client's perspective on his/her functional abilities with those of others.

A significant drawback to some procedures exploring sexuality in disabled clients is the sexually explicit nature of the materials or stimuli. Whereas phallometric testing (i.e. sexual arousal testing, see Freund and Blanchard, 1989) can be very helpful in establishing inappropriate sexual interests and preferences, administration of the testing requires presentation of – at least to some degree – sexually explicit materials (visual or auditory). For clients, some of the stimuli might remind them of situations of abuse they endured, while other clients may find the scenarios sexually arousing (potentially without any pre-existing education regarding the propriety of those scenarios). To get around some of these difficulties, some clinics have developed card sort protocols (e.g. Abel, Becker and Cunningham-Rathner, 1984; Hoath, Wilson, Burns, Figliola and Tough, unpublished dataset) in which clients can less imposingly answer questions informative for age-discrimination, gender preference and likes and dislikes when it comes to sexual partners and behaviors.

Concluding remarks

Although they comprise a relatively small subset of the clientele who engage in criminal behaviour, people with intellectual and other cognitive limitations can draw inordinately on already scarce resources. At times, a failure to appropriately evaluate the client's strengths and weaknesses can exacerbate existing problems while failing to account for problems to come. Ultimately, the literature shows that competent assessment, leading to effective interventions and evidence-based service provision, results in better outcomes for all. Recent history has shown a dramatic increase in the amount of effort expended in attempting to better understand sex offending clients with intellectual disabilities, but we are not quite there yet. especially in regard to ensuring that issues of responsivity are adequately considered. We hope that we have highlighted a few areas of focus for readers, and that your processes will be better informed for the experience.

Review task

Consider that you have been referred an individual who has been demonstrating great difficulties in understanding programme materials. At trial, you know that there were some issues regarding competency. Presently, the client has been expelled from programming on several occasions for being disruptive and for poor frustration tolerance (which others have deemed to be impulsivity and 'purely behavioural'). Others suggest that there may be organic processes at work. How would you go about making the distinction?

Check list of steps/advice

1   Establish the presenting problem. Why is the client being referred to you?
2   Ensure that you have comprehensive documentation of the client's past and current presentation and circumstances.
3   Ensure that you have the proper consents to conduct your evaluation, keeping in mind that many people with intellectual disabilities or other cognitive processing difficulties may have a guardian or other substitute decision maker.
4   Be comprehensive in your evaluation. Make sure you identify where the client has the greatest difficulties and be sure to explore how those difficulties will

ultimately affect functioning – both on supervision and in human service interventions (i.e. what treatment interfering factors might exist?).

5   Be judicious in your interpretation of findings – ensuring that all possible options are explored.

6   Write a report that is understandable to both professionals and receivers of service and their support persons. We understand that use of jargon can be difficult to avoid in evaluations of cognitive capacity and function.

7   Be available for a debrief, so as to ensure that the client and his/her support persons understand your findings and their implications.

Further reading

In this chapter, we have stressed the importance of adherence to the responsivity principle in the Bonta and Andrews (2016) RNR model. Readers may wish to follow up by reviewing in-depth articles or books listed in the references with an asterisk (★).

References

Abel, G.G., Becker, J.V. and Cunningham-Rathner, J. (1984). Complications, consent and cognitions in sex between children and adults. *International Journal of Law and Psychiatry*, 7, 89–103.

★Bonta, J. and Andrews, D.A. (2016). *The psychology of criminal conduct*, 6th ed. Cincinnati, OH: Anderson.

Chartrand, L.N. and Forbes-Chilibeck, E.M. (2003). The sentencing of offenders with fetal alcohol syndrome. *Health Law Journal, 11*, 35–70.

D'Elia, L.F., Satz, P., Uchiyama, C.L. and White, T. (1996). *Color Trails Test professional manual.* Lutz, FL: Psychological Assessment Resources.

★Edgerton, R.B. (1993). *The cloak of competence.* Berkeley, CA: University of California Press.

Folstein, M., Folstein, S.E., and McHugh, P.R. (1975) "Mini-Mental State" a practical method for grading the cognitive state of patients for the clinician. *Journal of Psychiatric Research, 12,* 189–98.

Freund, K. and Blanchard, R. (1989) Phallometric diagnosis of pedophilia. *Journal of Consulting and Clinical Psychology, 57,* 1–6.

Griffiths, D.M. and Lunsky, Y. (2003). *Socio-sexual knowledge and attitudes assessment tool (revised).* Wood Dale, IL: Stoelting Co.

Hingsburger, D. (1995). *Just say know! Understanding and reducing the risk of sexual victimization of people with developmental disabilities.* Angus, ON: Diverse-City Press.

Hoath, J., Wilson, R.J., Burns, M., Figliola, L. and Tough, S. (unpublished). *Sexual preference testing for intellectually-disabled persons who sexually offend: Issues, advisements, and an exploratory study.*

★Marshall, W.L., Marshall, L.E., Serran, G.A. and O'Brien, M.D. (2011). *Rehabilitating sexual offenders: A strength-based approach.* Washington, DC: American Psychological Association.

Meyers, J.E. and Meyers, K.R. (1995). *Rey Complex Figure Test and recognition trial.* Lutz, FL: Psychological Assessment Resources.

Randolph, C. (2012). *Repeatable Battery for the Assessment of Neuropsychological Status (RBANS Update).* San Antonio, TX: Pearson.

Schmidt, M. (1996). *Rey Auditory Verbal Learning Test: A handbook.* Los Angeles, CA: Western Psychological Services.

Sobsey, R. and Doe, T. (1991). Patterns of sexual abuse and assault. *Sexuality and Disability,* *9,* 243–59.

*Taylor, R.L. (2007). *Psychological masquerade: Distinguishing psychological from organic disorders,* 3rd ed. New York: Springer Publishing Company.

Wallace, G. and Hammill, D.D. (2013). *Comprehensive Receptive and Expressive Vocabulary Test,* 3rd ed. Austin, TX: Pro-Ed.

Wechsler, D. (2008). *Wechsler Adult Intelligence Scale,* 4th ed. San Antonio, TX: Pearson.

Wilson, R.J. and Burns, M. (2011). *Intellectual disability and problems in sexual behaviour: Assessment, treatment, and promotion of healthy sexuality.* Holyoke, MA: NEARI Press.

Wilson, R.J., DePass, C. and Nelson, T. (2011). Incompetent to proceed and sexual offender civil commitment: Law, policy, and clinical interventions. *Sex Offender Law Report,* *12,* 67–72.

3

REPORTING ACTUARIAL RISK

Martin Rettenberger and Leam A. Craig

Introduction

Professionals working with violent and sexual offenders are often called on to assess the risk of recidivism they present. In modern forensic psychology there are basically three different methodological approaches to risk assessment (e.g. Craig, Browne and Beech, 2008): unstructured clinical judgement (UCJ), actuarial risk assessment instruments (ARAIs) and structured professional judgement (SPJ, see Chapter 5). Intuitively made UCJs – even if done by experienced clinicians – should not be used in professional risk assessment because they cannot be regarded as a scientific procedure and, therefore, should not be named 'professional' (Hanson, 2009). The most important reason for neglecting UCJ is that – as in other areas of psychological prediction research – empirical results indicate that structured and standardised risk assessment instruments like ARAIs and SPJ instruments are more accurate in predicting recidivism than unstructured prediction methods (e.g. Bonta, Law and Hanson, 1998; Dawes, Faust and Meehl, 1989; Grove and Meehl, 1996; Grove, Zald, Lebow, Snitz and Nelson, 2000; Hanson and Morton-Bourgon, 2009). ARAIs follow an empirical approach to risk assessment usually by using quantitative statistical methods (Windelband, 1904). They represent highly structured risk assessment scales using combinations of empirically determined and thoroughly operationalised predictor variables (e.g. Craig et al. 2008; Hanson and Morton-Bourgon, 2009; Quinsey, Harris, Rice and Cormier, 2006). Based on Meehl's (1954) seminal work about the comparison between actuarial and clinical prediction methods, two core variables of ARAIs are that they use explicit methods of combining the risk factors and the total score (usually from adding up the individual item scores) is linked to an empirically derived probability figure (Dawes et al., 1989; Hanson and Morton-Bourgon, 2009).

Another kind of categorisation of risk assessment methods is based on the influential work of Andrews and Bonta (2006), which relates to all kinds of delinquent or criminal behaviour, not just sexual or violence offence. The conceptualisation of different 'generations' of risk assessment methods is based on the view that risk assessments should have the greatest possible predictive accuracy and also provide information about opportunities for risk management, i.e. about the potential risk-reducing influences of (therapeutic) interventions and sanctions (Hanson and Morton-Bourgon, 2009; Wong and Gordon, 2006). Andrews and Bonta (2006) proposed three generations of risk assessment:

- first, unstructured–intuitive clinical/professional judgement;
- second, actuarial empirically derived risk assessment methods based on predominantly or exclusively static/historical/biographical risk factors; and,
- third, actuarial risk assessment methods based on dynamic factors or crimino-genic needs (Harris and Hanson, 2010; Mann, Hanson and Thornton, 2010).

Dynamic factors can be subdivided into stable and acute factors. Stable dynamic risk factors are those that are relatively persistent but subject to change over time, such as levels of responsibility, cognitions and sexual arousal. Acute dynamic factors are rapidly changing factors such as substance misuse, isolation and negative emotional states, the presence of which is associated with sexual recidivism risk (Harris and Hanson, 2010).

The use of actuarial risk assessment instruments should be an integral part of forensic psychological practice because, first, the research has indicated that actu-arially-based instruments are the best available instruments for the prediction of recidivism risk in different offender populations (Grove and Meehl, 1996; Grove et al., 2000; Hanson and Morton-Bourgon, 2009). Second, the use of actuarial instruments can be regarded as a necessary precondition for the implementation and application of effective treatment programmes for offenders since Andrews and Bonta (2006) showed that effective interventions for offenders have to focus on three core principles: risk (i.e. the risk potential of the single offender for com-mitting new offence), need (i.e. consideration of empirically proven criminogenic needs in terms of particular treatment goals) and responsivity (i.e. the use of inter-vention techniques and treatment programmes to which the individual offender's abilities, learning style, motivation and strengths responds). The use of actuarial risk assessment could improve the risk-reducing results of treatment programmes by measuring accurately the individual level of risk with a second generation risk assessment instrument and by defining treatment targets in terms of dynamic risk factors (or criminogenic needs) with a third generation risk assessment instrument.

Nowadays, there exists a huge number of actuarial risk assessment instruments, and the first problem which has to be solved by the risk assessor is to decide which actuarial instrument (s)he should use for each individual case. The following crite-ria should be considered:

- Which kind of offences were committed and which kind of offences should be predicted (i.e. general violence, sexual violence or general criminality)?
- Should I use an actuarial risk assessment instrument for adults versus for youth (or young) offenders?

- Is it necessary to pass a special training in order to apply the actuarial instrument in clinical practice? Do I fulfil the necessary training and education preconditions?
- Are the instrument and the manual available in my language? Is there at least one cross-validation study and norms available in the jurisdiction within which I am working?

In the following sections we would like to briefly introduce the methodology of actuarial risk assessment instruments and we would like to sensitise the reader for the most relevant questions that can be raised in clinical practice when actuarial instruments are used, in order to provide a theoretical and clinical starting point to answer the above-mentioned questions. Furthermore, we will discuss additional aspects that could be relevant when actuarial instruments are used in clinical practice. Finally, we will introduce basic guidelines for interpreting and reporting the results of actuarial risk assessment instruments.

Best practice

Criminal justice professionals have increasingly endorsed actuarial measures of risk as the most reliable predictive instruments for decision making (Archer, Buffington-Vollum, Stredny and Handel, 2006; Craig and Beech, 2010). Within the field, the relative merits of the predictive accuracy of actuarial versus clinical judgment has been hotly debated, but it is now widely accepted that the former is superior in predicting recidivism compared with the latter (Grove and Meehl, 1996; Hanson and Morton-Bourgon, 2009; Quinsey et al., 2006).

There exists a plethora of validation studies for ARAIs from different countries that have consistently demonstrated a stable moderate to high predictive accuracy (e.g. Craig, Beech and Browne, 2006; Ducro and Pham, 2006; Rettenberger, Matthes, Boer and Eher, 2010). Another attraction for clinicians of using ARAIs is related to their ease of use and simplicity, as it is often a simple matter of translating risk scores into risk categories from which is it possible to extract risk tables (usually expressed in percentages) indicating future risk level. Hence, some have argued (e.g. Grove and Meehl, 1996; Quinsey et al., 2006) that failure to conduct actuarial risk assessment, or consider its results, is irrational, unscientific, unethical and unprofessional.

Actuarial risk assessment in practice

Actuarial risk assessment instruments provide several types of information that could be of value to decision makers (Hanson, Babchishin, Helmus and Thornton, 2013). First, clinicians can use so-called nominal labels for different risk scores or risk categories (including a range of risk scores), such as 'high risk category' or 'low risk category'. However, the problem with this kind of risk communication is that even experienced and trained professionals frequently disagree about what 'low', 'moderate' and 'high' risk actually represent (Hilton, Carter, Harris and Sharpe, 2008; Scurich and John, 2011; Slovic, Monahan and MacGregor, 2000). Numerical kinds of risk communication (e.g. percentiles, recidivism estimates and risk ratios), on the other hand, lead to fewer interpretation errors compared to nominal risk categories, so it is recommended that scores are directly linked to recidivism risk tables without referring to risk labels like 'low', 'moderate' or 'high' (Babchishin and Phenix, 2014; Hilton et al., 2008).

In general, the most prominent and traditional measures of risk are recidivism rate estimates that are linked to every single total score of an instrument. Relative risk measures, in contrast, provide information about a particular offender's risk relative to other offenders (i.e. to the population to which he/she belong) and can be quantified by, for example, so-called relative risk ratios or percentile ranks (Hanson, Lloyd, Helmus and Thornton, 2012). Researchers have discussed regular changes in recidivism-related norms and rates, and comprehensive empirical investigations about the stability of the relative and absolute risk estimates have been conducted (Helmus, Hanson, Thornton, Babchishin and Harris, 2012). These studies indicated that absolute recidivism rates can vary substantially across samples, whereas relative risk estimates are relatively stable over time and for different settings and jurisdictions (Hanson et al., 2013; Helmus et al., 2012). Before we review the current scientific discussions of different risk-related data sources, we would like to introduce relative and absolute risk indices and their communication form by using a concrete example. We decided in favour of the internationally most prominent actuarial risk assessment instrument for sexual offenders, the Static-99 (Hanson and Thornton, 2000), which is usually regarded as the gold standard of risk assessment for this offender subgroup.

Actuarial risk assessment for sexual offenders – the Static-99

In order to illustrate the clinical use of actuarial risk assessment instruments, we would like to introduce the Static-99 that was developed by R. Karl Hanson and David Thornton (2000). It is the most commonly used ARAI and best validated for sexual offenders (e.g. Archer et al., 2006; Hanson and Morton-Bourgon, 2009). The instrument consists of 10 predominantly static risk factors that are outlined in Table 3.1 (for further information, see Harris, Phenix, Hanson and Thornton, 2003). The total score is used to assign each individual to one of the four risk categories (low for total score 0 and 1, low-moderate for total score 2 and 3, moderate-high for total score 4 and 5 and high for total scores higher than 5), as well as to relative and absolute risk estimates (Phenix, Helmus and Hanson, 2012; for further information, see also www.static99.org).

A very intense discussion about the imperative of a revision of the Static-99 and other second generation ARAIs referred to the question about the risk-related influence of age on the recidivism risk estimates of sexual offenders

TABLE 3.1 The 10 items and their basic coding rules of the Static-99 (Hanson and Thornton, 2000), the internationally most used and best validated actuarial risk assessment instrument for sexual offenders (Harris et al., 2003; www.static99.org)

Item number	Risk factor	Basic coding rule		Item score
1	Age when exposed to risk	Aged 25 or older		0
		Aged 18–24.99		1
2	Any live-in intimate relationship for 2 or more years	Yes		0
		No		1
3	Any index offence of nonsexual violence	No		0
		Yes		1
4	Prior offences of nonsexual violence	No		0
		Yes		1
5	Prior charges or convictions for sexual offences	Charges	Convictions	
		None	None	0
		1-2	1	1
		3-5	2-3	2
		6, 6+	4, 4+	3
6	Prior sentencing dates	3 or less		0
		4 or more		1
7	Any convictions for noncontact sexual offences	No		0
		Yes		1
8	Any unrelated victims	No		0
		Yes		1
9	Any stranger victims	No		0
		Yes		1
10	And any male victims	No		0
		Yes		1
	Total score	Add up scores from individual risk factors		0–12

(Craig, 2011; Helmus, Thornton, Hanson and Babchishin, 2012; Rettenberger, Haubner-MacLean and Eher, 2013; Wollert, 2006). In order to consider the age-related influence on the Static-99-based risk assessment appropriately Helmus, Thornton et al. (2012) argued that the 'age at release' variable in the Static-99 should be weighted more heavily, which led to the development of a revised version of the Static-99, the Static-99R. In an independent cross-validation study of this newly developed revised version, Rettenberger et al. (2013) compared the predictive accuracy of the original Static-99 and the new Static-99R using a population-based sample of prison-released sexual offenders (N = 1,077). The results indicated that the original Static-99 (AUC = 0.73) performed better than the age-corrected Static-99R (AUC = 0.71). Whereas Helmus, Thornton et al. (2012) recommended using the revised age weights in applied risk assessment settings, Rettenberger et al. (2013) concluded that the original Static-99 yields better predictive accuracy than the age-corrected Static-99R for the prediction of sexual recidivism and, therefore, support the use of the original version of the instrument.

Interpreting and reporting the results of actuarial risk assessment instruments

There are three different kinds of risk communication: nominal risk labels (i.e. if the recidivism risk is 'low', 'moderate' or 'high'), absolute risk indices (i.e. the recidivism risk is XY per cent), and relative risk (i.e. XY per cent of all sexual offenders score at or above this score; alternatively, the recidivism risk is XY times the recidivism rate of the typical sexual offender). Despite the above-mentioned methodological and clinical problems associated with arbitrary nominal risk categories (Hilton et al., 2008; Slovic et al., 2000), it is well-known that forensic evaluators and decision makers usually prefer nominal categories compared to numerical risk communication strategies (Grann and Pallvik, 2002; Redding, Floyd and Hawk, 2001). Recently, researchers have tried to propose recommendations for how nominal risk categories could be linked to numerical indicators in order to improve the nominal-based risk communication by grounding nominal categories in non-arbitrary definitions, but this kind of research is still in its infancy (Babchishin and Phenix, 2014). Hanson and Phenix (2013) proposed general guidelines for reporting Static-99 results and recommended that report writers should initially introduce the instrument to juridical clients and decision makers. As an example for reporting the risk by using nominal categories, the authors suggested the following formulation:

> Mr. A received a total score of XY which places him in the Low [alternatively, Moderate-Low, Moderate-High, or High] Risk Category for being charged or convicted of another sexual offence.

Actuarial scales provide absolute recidivism risk indices in terms of probabilistic estimates that a given behaviour will occur within a given time frame. Doren (2002) pointed out that the language used when reporting actuarial data can have important implications as can be seen, for example, in the difference between saying '5 out of 10' or '50%'. Slovic et al. (2000) noted that stating results in frequency terms (i.e. 5 out of 10) leads to the perception of higher risk than describing the same statistic in percentage terms (i.e. 50 per cent). Therefore, in terms of reporting actuarial data it may be ethically prudent to use both communication formats in order to reduce this potential source of bias (Doren, 2002). Hanson and Phenix (2013) recommended the following formulation for reporting absolute recidivism risk indices for the Static-99:

> *In routine samples of sexual offenders, the average 5 year sexual recidivism rate is between 5% and 15%. This means that out of 100 sexual offenders of mixed risk levels, between 5 and 15 would be reconvicted of a new sexual offence after 5 years in the community. Conversely, between 85 and 95 would not be reconvicted of a new sexual offence during that time period.*
>
> *Mr. B's Static-99 score was YX. In routine samples with the same score, the 5 year sexual recidivism rate is between XY% and XY%. This means that out of 100 sexual offenders with the same risk score between XY and XY would be reconvicted of a new sexual offence after 5 years in the community. Conversely, between XY and XY would not be reconvicted of a new sexual offence during that time period.*

A common question under cross-examination is 'which 50 per cent group does my client fall within?' (Craig and Beech, 2010). The premise of this question is fundamentally flawed as it implies that the risk instrument is designed to predict which group a person will fall into, the recidivists or non-recidivists. But actuarial risk instruments are not tools of prediction because the term 'prediction' implies an ability to see or predict the future or a given outcome. The term 'prediction' is used colloquially and does not imply prediction in empirical terms. A response to an inviting question using the term 'prediction' under cross-examination will almost certainly result in ridicule of the forensic practitioner giving evidence. As Doren (2002) points out, if a meteorologist were to forecast that it will rain, then the prediction will either be correct or incorrect. However, the more typical meteorological statement is that there is XY per cent likelihood for rain.

Another frequently discussed concern about the validity of the Static-99 (and other ARAIs) refers to the stability or variability of the recidivism rates that are linked to every total score (Eher, Rettenberger, Schilling and Pfäfflin, 2008). Considering the fact that most data included in previous studies that have reported recidivism rates for the Static-99 is based on data sources that have their origins in the 1960s, 70s and 80s (e.g. Hanson and Thornton, 2000; Harris et al., 2003), it seems to be a relevant question for forensic practice and research whether recidivism rates have changed in the last few decades. Given the broad cultural changes during the past 40 years, Helmus, Hanson and Thornton (2009) concluded that 'it is important to consider whether the recidivism rates of sexual offenders have remained the same during that time' (p. 38). The authors further reported that crime rates peaked in the early 1990s and have in general been declining since then. In the meantime, the phenomenon of declining base rates has been extensively documented for different kinds of offences using both official crime data (Tonry, 2014) as well as victimisation surveys (Finkelhor and Jones, 2006).

The reasons for that phenomenon are still not fully understood, but Helmus et al. (2009) provided a few possible explanations: first, demographic factors (e.g. aging population, increased obesity, reliance on medications such as Prozac or other serotonin-affecting agents); second, cultural factors (e.g. changing morals regarding sexuality, increased awareness about sexual assault leading to greater vigilance and supervision of children); and, third, criminal justice system factors (e.g. offender treatment, increased supervision, deterrent and incapacitation effects of longer sentences; for further information see Finkelhor and Jones, 2006, or Tonry, 2014). Helmus et al. (2009) concluded that there are at least two research implications: on the one hand, criminologists and forensic scientists would like to know more about the causes of changing crime rates, and, on the other hand, one may know how these changes affect best practices in offender assessment, management and supervision, because – even without understanding the reasons for the change – the evidence of change may force evaluators to adjust their practice. Current empirical evidence provides further support that substantial changes in sex offender recidivism base rates have occurred, which must inevitably lead to the development of up-to-date norm tables (Rettenberger, Briken, Turner and Eher, 2015).

An alternative to reporting absolute recidivism rates (for groups of sexual offenders) as an indicator of risk is to report relative risk (Craig and Beech, 2010). Relative risk compares the risk of one person to that of another and can be expressed in percentiles or in terms of relative risk ratios. Relative risk ratios allow statements about a particular offender's recidivism rate relative to the 'typical' sexual offender. For example, the median score on Static-99 in a sample reweighted to approximate the population of adjudicated sexual offenders is 2 (Hanson et al., 2013). Using relative risk ratios, a score of 0 shows approximately half the recidivism rate of the typical sexual offender, whereas a score of 6 shows three times the recidivism rate of the typical sexual offender. Both reporting methods for relative risk indices of actuarial risk estimates may be useful when making decisions on the allocation of treatment and supervision resources (Craig and Beech, 2010). Hanson and Phenix (2013) suggested the following statement for these two risk formats:

> *For percentile ranks: Mr. C's Static-99 score was 0. In routine correctional samples, this score represents the 19th percentile, defined as a mid-point average (14% have a lower score, 76% have a higher score and 10% have the same score). In other words, out of 100 sexual offenders, 14 would have a lower score, 10 would have the same score and 76 would have a higher score.*
>
> *For relative risk ratios: Mr. D had a Static-99 score of 1. On average, offenders with this score have a sexual recidivism rate that is 3/4 the rate of offenders in the middle of the risk distribution.*

Common difficulties/confusion

Practitioners using actuarial scales must do so mindful of the boundaries of the instruments and criticism of this methodology (Craig and Beech, 2010). One criticism, for example, indicates that an underlying theory is missing in ARAIs (Boer and Hart, 2009). Furthermore, there is an absence of protective factors, a predominance of static (i.e. unchangeable) items, and the problem of generalisation across different offender subgroups and jurisdictions. The most important limitation is probably the fact that ARAIs provide no ideographic information about the risk and potential risk management strategies for the individual case, whereas most jurisdictions insist on a risk assessment approach considering the characteristics and properties of the individual case. Even if ARAIs show high predictive accuracy (Hanson and Morton-Bourgon, 2009), a clinician is always necessary in order to provide an individual explanatory model as to why this individual offender committed this individual offence. By definition, only an ideographic risk assessment approach meets these practical, ethical and legal requirements by considering the relevant facts of the single case.

Conclusions

The aim of this chapter was to summarise the strengths and weaknesses of actuarial risk data and to contribute to developing guidance on best practice when using actuarial measures in adversarial settings. Not only have we summarised the strengths and weaknesses of actuarial risk data but also offered counter-argument to some of the criticism and myths around actuarial risk data. While it is unlikely many forensic practitioners will be cross-examined on the confidence intervals of the actuarial risk instruments, it is likely they will be examined on their understanding of how these instruments were developed, the measurement and accuracy of the risk instrument, the interpretation of the actuarial data on a group and individual basis, and the factors which may impact on the application of the risk instrument (i.e. cohort base rates, age, subgroup of sexual offenders). We should point out that there are no hard and fast rules on how to present actuarial data in adversarial settings or how to respond under cross-examination. However, the recommendations made here may be interpreted as the attempt to develop a standard best practice approach to actuarial risk assessment (Craig and Beech, 2010).

Review task

What are the major advantages and what the most relevant problems of the clinical use of actuarial risk assessment instruments? Why should these instruments be an integral part of each psychologically sound risk assessment report? And why are ARAIs not able to provide an individual explanation of the reasons of the criminal behaviour of an individual offender? What are the methodological preconditions which have to be fulfilled if an assessor would like to use ARAIs in clinical practice?

Checklist of steps/advice

1   First of all, decide if the information provided by actuarial risk assessment instruments is actually helpful in the risk assessment task on which you have to work (i.e. is the information of relative and absolute risk indices really helpful or necessary?).

2   Select an appropriate actuarial risk assessment instrument for your offender population (i.e. answer the question which kind of offender you have to assess and which kind of offences you should predict).
3   Examine if you have the necessary skills to use the instrument in clinical practice (e.g. is a special training mandatory?).
4   Check if the instrument, the manual, empirical data about the psychometric properties and appropriate norm data are available in your language area and jurisdiction.
5   Use the instrument correctly, (i.e. in accordance with the manual).
6   Communicate the results of your risk assessment in a way that decision makers and colleagues understand them, even if they have no sound psychological education. Similarly, try also to communicate the main methodological strengths and weaknesses of actuarial risk assessment instruments in common in order to give decision makers and colleagues the opportunity to interpret actuarially-based results in an appropriate manner.

Further reading

Craig, L.A. and Beech, A.R. (2010). Towards a guide to best practice in conducting actuarial risk assessments with sex offenders. *Aggression and Violent Behavior, 15*, 278–93.

Grove, W.M. and Meehl, P.E. (1996). Comparative efficiency of informal (subjective, impressionistic) and formal (mechanical, algorithmic) prediction procedures: The clinical-statistical controversy. *Psychology, Public Policy, and Law, 2*, 293–323.

Hanson, R.K. (2009). The psychological assessment of risk for crime and violence. *Canadian Psychology, 50*, 172–82.

References

Andrews, D.A. and Bonta, J. (2006). *The psychology of criminal conduct*, 4th ed. Cincinnati, OH: Anderson.

Archer, R.P., Buffington-Vollum, J.K., Stredny, R.V. and Handel, R.W. (2006). A survey of psychological test use patterns among forensic psychologists. *Journal of Personality Assessment, 87*, 84–94.

Babchishin, K.M. and Phenix, A. (2014). Recommendations for non-arbitrary nominal risk labels for Static-99/R in Babchishin, K.M. (Chair), *Where are we now? Recent developments in Static-99R risk communication*. Paper presented at 33rd Annual Research and Treatment Conference of the Association for the Treatment of Sexual Abusers, November, 2014, San Diego, CA.

Boer, D.P. and Hart, S.D. (2009). Sex offender risk assessment: Research, evaluation, 'best-practice' recommendations and future directions, in Ireland, J. L., Ireland, C. A. and Birch, P. (eds.), *Violent and sexual offenders: Assessment, treatment, and management* (pp. 27–42). Cullompton, UK: Willan.

Bonta, J., Law, M. and Hanson, R.K. (1998). The prediction of criminal and violent recidivism among mentally disordered offenders: A meta-analysis. *Psychological Bulletin, 123*, 123–42.

Craig, L.A. (2011). The effect of age on sexual and violent reconviction. *International Journal of Offender Therapy and Comparative Criminology, 55*, 1, 75–97.

Craig, L.A. and Beech, A.R. (2010). Towards a guide to best practice in conducting actuarial risk assessments with sex offenders. *Aggression and Violent Behavior, 15*, 278–93.

Craig, L.A., Beech, A.R. and Browne, K.D. (2006). Cross-validation of the Risk Matrix 2000 Sexual and Violent Scales. *Journal of Interpersonal Violence, 21*, 612–33.

Craig, L.A., Browne, K.D. and Beech, A.R. (2008). *Assessing risk in sex offenders: A practitioner's guide.* Chichester, UK: Wiley.

Dawes, R.M., Faust, D. and Meehl, P.E. (1989). Clinical versus actuarial judgement. *Science, 243*, 1668–74. doi:10.1126/science.2648573

Doren, D.M. (2002). *Evaluating sex offenders: A manual for civil commitments and beyond.* Thousand Oaks, CA: Sage Publications.

Ducro, C. and Pham, T. (2006). Evaluation of the SORAG and the Static-99 on Belgian sex offenders committed to a forensic facility. *Sexual Abuse: A Journal of Research and Treatment, 18*, 15–26.

Eher, R., Rettenberger, M., Schilling, F. and Pfäfflin, F. (2008). Failure of Static-99 and SORAG to predict relevant re-offense categories in relevant sexual offender subtypes: A prospective study. *Sexual Offender Treatment, 3*, 1–14.

Finkelhor, D. and Jones, L. (2006). Why have child maltreatment and child victimization declined? *Journal of Social Issues, 62*, 685–716.

Grann, M. and Pallvik, A. (2002). An empirical investigation of written risk communication in forensic psychiatric evaluations. *Psychology, Crime and Law, 8*, 113–30.

Grove, W.M. and Meehl, P.E. (1996). Comparative efficiency of informal (subjective, impressionistic) and formal (mechanical, algorithmic) prediction procedures: The clinical-statistical controversy. *Psychology, Public Policy, and Law, 2*, 293–323.

Grove, W.M., Zald, D.H., Lebow, B.S., Snitz, B.E. and Nelson, C. (2000). Clinical versus mechanical prediction: A meta-analysis. *Psychological Assessment, 12*, 19–30.

Hanson, R.K. (2009). The psychological assessment of risk for crime and violence. *Canadian Psychology, 50*, 172–82.

Hanson, R.K. and Phenix, A. (2013). *Report writing for Static-99R and Static-2002R.* Pre-conference workshop at the 32nd Annual Research and Treatment Conference of the Association for the Treatment of Sexual Abusers, October, 2013, Chicago, IL.

Hanson, R.K., Babchishin, K.M., Helmus, L. and Thornton, D. (2013). Quantifying the relative risk of sex offenders: Risk ratios for Static-99R. *Sexual Abuse: A Journal of Research and Treatment, 24*, 482–515.

Hanson, R.K., Lloyd, C.D., Helmus, L. and Thornton, D. (2012). Developing non-arbitrary metrics for risk communication: Percentile ranks for the Static-99/R and Static-2002/R sexual offender risk tools. *International Journal of Forensic Mental Health, 11*, 9–23.

Hanson, R.K. and Morton-Bourgon, K. (2009). The accuracy of recidivism risk assessments for sexual offenders: A meta-analysis of 118 prediction studies. *Psychological Assessment, 21*, 1–21.

Hanson, R.K. and Thornton, D. (2000). Improving risk assessment for sex offenders: A comparison of three actuarial scales. *Law and Human Behavior, 24*, 119–36.

Harris, A.J.R. and Hanson, R.K. (2010). Clinical, actuarial, and dynamic risk assessment of sexual offenders: Why do things keep changing? *Journal of Sexual Aggression, 16*, 296–310.

Harris, A.J.R., Phenix, A., Hanson, R.K. and Thornton, D. (2003). *Static-99 coding rules revised – 2003.* Ottawa, Canada: Department of the Solicitor General of Canada. Retrieved from www.static99.org/pdfdocs/static-99-codingrules_e.pdf accessed 1 July 2016.

Helmus, L., Hanson, R.K. and Thornton, D. (2009). Reporting Static-99 in light of new research on recidivism norms. *The Forum, 21*, 38–45. Retrieved from http://static99.org/pdfdocs/forum_article_feb2009.pdf accessed 1 July 2016.

Helmus, L., Hanson, R.K., Thornton, D., Babchishin, K.M. and Harris, A.J.R. (2012). Absolute recidivism rates predicted by Static-99R and Static-2002R sex offender risk assessment tools vary across samples: A meta-analysis. *Criminal Justice and Behavior, 33*, 1148–71.

Helmus, L., Thornton, D., Hanson, R.K. and Babchishin, K.M. (2012). Improving the predictive accuracy of Static-99 and Static-2002 with older sex offenders: Revised age weights. *Sexual Abuse: A Journal of Research and Treatment, 24*, 64–101.

Hilton, N.Z., Carter, A.M., Harris, G.T. and Sharpe, A.J.B. (2008). Does using non-numerical terms to describe risk aid violence risk communication? Clinician agreement and decision making. *Journal of Interpersonal Violence, 23*, 171–88.

Mann, R.E., Hanson, R.K. and Thornton, D. (2010). Assessing risk for sexual recidivism: Some proposals on the nature of psychologically meaningful risk factors. *Sexual Abuse: A Journal of Research and Treatment, 22*, 191–217.

Meehl, P.E. (1954). *Clinical versus statistical prediction: A theoretical analysis and a review of the evidence.* Minneapolis, MN: University of Minnesota Press.

Phenix, A., Helmus, L. and Hanson, R.K. (2012). *Static-99R. Evaluators' workbook.* Retrieved from www.static99.org/pdfdocs/st-99rworkbookwithsamplesandsummaries.pdf accessed 1 July 2016.

Quinsey, V. L., Harris, G.T., Rice, M. E. and Cormier, C. (2006). *Violent offenders: Appraising and managing risk*, 2nd ed. Washington, DC: American Psychological Association.

Redding, R.E., Floyd, M.Y. and Hawk, G.L. (2001). What judges and lawyers think about the testimony of mental health experts: A survey of the courts and bar. *Behavioral Sciences and the Law, 19*, 583–94.

Rettenberger, M., Briken, P., Turner, D. and Eher, R. (2015). Sexual offender recidivism among a population-based prison sample. *International Journal of Offender Therapy and Comparative Criminology, 59*, 424–44.

Rettenberger, M., Haubner-MacLean, T. and Eher, R. (2013). The contribution of age to the Static-99 risk assessment in a population-based prison sample of sexual offenders. *Criminal Justice and Behavior, 40*, 1413–33.

Rettenberger, M., Matthes, A., Boer, D. P. and Eher, R. (2010). Actuarial recidivism risk assessment and sexual delinquency: A comparison of five risk assessment tools in different sexual offender subtypes. *International Journal of Offender Therapy and Comparative Criminology, 54*, 169–86.

Scurich, N. and John, R.S. (2011). The effect of framing actuarial risk probabilities on involuntary civil commitment decisions. *Law and Human Behavior, 35*, 83–91.

Slovic, P., Monahan, J. and MacGregor, D.G. (2000). Violence risk assessment and risk communication: The effects of using actual cases, providing instruction, and employing probability versus frequency formats. *Law and Human Behavior, 24*, 271–96.

Tonry, M. (2014). *Why crime rates fall, and why they don't.* Chicago: University of Chicago Press.

Windelband, W. (1904). *Theories in logic.* New York: Philosophical Library.

Wollert, R. (2006). Low base rates limit expert certainty when current actuarials are used to identify sexually violent predators: An application of Bayes's theorem. *Psychology, Public Policy, and Law, 12*, 56–85.

Wong, S.C.P. and Gordon, A.E. (2006). The validity and reliability of the Violence Risk Scale: A treatment-friendly violence risk assessment tool. *Psychology, Public Policy, and Law, 12*, 279–309.

4

REPORTING CASE FORMULATION AND OPINION

Andrew Day

Introduction

Whilst it is relatively straightforward to follow assessment protocols and administer tests, the challenges associated with integrating the results of different assessments in a way helps to develop an expert opinion are more significant. This chapter describes a particular approach to forensic assessment that involves developing a case formulation that is then used to inform an opinion about the referral questions. In many ways the opinion section is the most important part of any report as it seeks to offer an *explanation* of why a person acted as he or she did, rather than simply describing a person's level of risk or psychological functioning. This is particularly important in circumstances when decisions are being made about the future treatment of a person is, as well in making judgements about those strategies that are likely to be most effective in managing risk.

In preparing an expert opinion it is essential that the specific legal questions being considered are addressed. Often, but not always, these will relate to sentencing. For example, forensic psychologists are often asked to provide a professional opinion on the likelihood of a person reoffending, the nature and type of any further offending and the extent to which the risk of this happening can be effectively managed. As an expert, the psychologist is recognised as someone who can give an opinion in a specific area of knowledge that the court determines to lie outside the understanding of the layperson. As such, it is essential that psychological opinions are based on data that have demonstrable scientific merit and that the assessment was conducted in a manner that is regarded by the professional community as competent. There is no place in the forensic report to express personal views that cannot be substantiated.

It is often appropriate to begin an assessment by assessing risk of reoffending (see Chapters 3 and 5, this volume). However, while most risk assessment tools categorise clients in a way that can be used to determine the most appropriate level of intervention, most have little to say about the specific circumstances in which offending is likely to occur. Applying the results of a risk assessment to the individual is central to good report writing as risk will always be contingent upon situational or contextual factors. Casey, Day, Ward and Vess (2012) explain this in the following way: 'even high risk cases will not be at imminent risk at all times, but will vary in their likelihood of reoffending, depending on such factors as access to victims, current degree of alcohol or drug use, access to and compliance with treatment and supervision services, the nature of interpersonal relationships and support systems, and current mood states' (p.93). The suggestion here is that even those with similar profiles in terms of their risk assessment scores will not necessarily require the same kind of risk management plans. It is also helpful when reporting an opinion to clearly communicate the limitations of a risk assessment tool by making specific reference to data concerning the tool's predictive validity (including the likelihood of false positives), as well as providing information about the population on which this data was gathered. This allows the court to consider the validity of the assessment and its relevance to the individual who has been assessed.

The next step is to consider psychological functioning and needs, both at the time of the assessment and at the time of the offence. This can help to identify which psychological factors (e.g. the presence of a mental disorder; particular beliefs about the self, others and the world; flexibility in regulating emotion) might be relevant to the referral questions, as well as identifying additional risk factors that are not routinely assessed in structured tools, but nonetheless relevant to the person being assessed. Psychometric testing (see Chapter 1) is recommended here as it allows the assessor to place the person in relation to the 'normal' population, as well as providing a scientifically defensible basis for any opinion that uses this data. Of course, good psychometric tests are not always available to assess all of the different areas of functioning that might be considered relevant. In addition, tests are typically designed to assess current levels of functioning rather than to assess the onset and development of any problems. As such, psychometric test information should be supplemented and contextualised with information derived from interviews. Whilst interviews are often the main source of information, it is important to be aware of their limitations. For example, some people may not have insight into the causes of their behaviour. Others may have a limited capacity to self-report, due to poor attention, concentration, or memory. It is also essential that every effort is made to corroborate interview data with other sources of information given the possibility of impression management or socially desirable responding. Nonetheless, it is often the interview that identifies the clinical and legal hypotheses that become central to the forensic psychology case formulation.

Best practice in case formulation

The term 'best practice' emerged in the commercial sector to assist business and manufacturing to be more internationally competitive. The adoption of this term within the human services domain has caused some discomfort, with the concern that 'best' implies only one right way to do things, regardless of context or circumstance (Howells, Heseltine, Sarre, Davey and Day, 2004). In developing the forensic case formulation, it should be stressed that there is no single 'correct' approach. Rather, the formulation should be written in a way that is most appropriate for the audience and to the matter under consideration. Sometimes this will require a more detailed approach, depending on the type of referral question that the psychologist is seeking to answer. There are, however, a number of general comments that can be made about how to present the psychologist's interpretation of what is relevant to the particular legal questions (Grisso, 2010). This is often referred to as the case formulation and forms the basis for the opinion section of the report.

As noted above, whereas many assessment tools provide a description of the presenting problem and a person's current level of functioning, the case formulation is concerned with explaining why a person acted as he or she did. This explanation can then be used to inform an opinion about the most appropriate intervention and management. Of course, it is possible to explain as individual's behaviour in many different ways and it is here that professional judgement becomes important. The forensic psychologist should consider, for example, broader theories of why people commit crime – some of these explain offending in terms of how people respond to social and structural pressures (such as social disadvantage or gender), whereas others view offenders as personally responsible for their circumstances and behaviour. It is these latter theories that are most relevant to the psychological case formulation, as courts are typically most interested in understanding how different sanctions and incentives might influence the particular individual's attitudes and behaviour. Nonetheless, the impact of structural drivers of crime should not be overlooked as they are not only sometimes important but also can be legally relevant (see Anthony, 2010). The forensic psychologist should also use his or her experience of other cases when selecting the type of assessment information that is likely to be most relevant and helpful. As such, professional judgement should not be considered to be without basis.

There is no consensus about what should be included in a good case formulation, even among psychologists. Indeed, a wide range of different approaches to case formulation are used in practice, even within particular schools, such as cognitive-behavioural therapy (Flitcroft, James, Freeston and Wood-Mitchell, 2007). Sturmey (2010) suggests, however, that most case formulations share a number of common features. For example, they identify key aspects of a presenting problem, account for both the onset and maintenance of the problem and inform the development of a treatment plan that is tailored to meet the needs of the individual. Sturmey argues, however, that they differ in relation to which variables are considered to be important, the emphasis placed on historical antecedents to behaviour, the extent to which the formulation identifies opportunities for intervention and the role of the therapeutic relationship in the formulation process. Whilst some see these differences as relatively unimportant, 'others see them as fundamental and irreconcilable' (Sturmey, 2010, p.27). It is also perhaps worth remembering that some studies have shown low levels of inter-rater reliability when therapists formulate the same cases (Persons, Mooney and Padesky, 1995).

In the forensic setting the most widely used approach to case formulation has been derived from a method of psychological assessment known as functional analysis. Originally developed as part of the assessment process for entry into behaviour modification programmes, the aim of a functional analysis is to establish the purpose of an action or behaviour, to specify the variables that maintain the behaviour, as well as to identify other more pro-social behaviours that might satisfy a similar purpose (Daffern, Jones and Shine, 2010). This type of assessment thus focuses on the current presentation of the problem, which is then contextualised through exploration with the client of earlier formative events and experiences and how these have shaped subsequent beliefs, emotions and, importantly, behaviour (see Grant et al., 2008). Of course, in the forensic assessment the 'problem' being analysed will nearly always be the offending behaviour.

There are surprisingly few practical guides to help the forensic psychologist develop skills in functional analysis. Over 20 years ago, Meloy (1992) developed a relatively simple, but nonetheless useful, method involving a matrix where notes are made about relevant factors 'Before', 'During', and 'After' the offending. These are then cross-referenced with psychological factors labelled 'Thoughts', 'Emotions', and 'Behaviour'. Meloy's matrix is completed by asking the client to describe what the police would see as they arrive at the scene of the offence. This account is then used to explore associated feelings and thoughts. Nelson and Jackson (1989) also emphasised the need to begin with observable events described in behavioural terms, focusing on *what* happened instead of why it happened. The contribution of each event in a behavioural 'offence chain' is then evaluated to determine whether the event increased, decreased or had no effect on the probability that offending would follow. The assessor will only ask for information on how the offender interpreted events after a behavioural chain has been completed.

Casey et al. (2012) describe a variation of these approaches that they refer to as Criminogenic Needs Assessment (CNA). The initial aim of a CNA is to identify those needs that are the most directly associated with the offending behaviour for a particular individual. A major emphasis is placed on describing the events leading up to the offence in great detail, identifying patterns of thoughts, feeling and behaviour. These are then understood in relation to the earlier developmental history of the person being assessed, with the aim of arriving at an explanation of both the onset and maintenance of offending. This approach will be familiar to those who use a particular therapy developed to treat Borderline Personality Disorder, known as Dialectical Behaviour Therapy (DBT). Koerner and Linehan (1997) have described how a DBT assessment begins with a clear definition of the problem behaviour. The clinician and client then identify both *general vulnerability factors* (the context in which precipitating events have more influence on behaviour) and *specific precipitating events* that begin the chain of events that lead to the problem behaviour. The task is then to link the precipitating events to the problem behaviour to develop a detailed account of those factors that triggered the behaviour. Finally, the reactions of the client and others following the problem behaviour are considered as this provides important clues about potential reinforcers of the behaviour.

What is common to all of these approaches is the in-depth analysis of events and situations both before and after the problem behaviour, with the goal of developing an accurate and complete account of those behavioural and environmental factors that cause and maintain the behaviour. As they seek to understand offending as a process, it is important to assess every specific instance of the behaviour to see if patterns can be identified across different occurrences. The idea of documenting detailed personal offence histories is consistent with the conclusions of a number of qualitative research studies that clearly illustrate the considerable heterogeneity that exists within offender populations and the different pathways that offending can follow (see Ward, Yates and Long, 2006). This work establishes, for example, that the core issues for at least some offenders are less to do with a failure to self-regulate (e.g. the effects of stress, intoxication, low empathy or impulse control) than they are to a conscious and purposeful decision to offend in the pursuit of self-gratification. Accordingly, the pathway that each individual follows will have different developmental origins and triggers (e.g. Day and Bowen, 2015) and these can only be properly understood by assessing offending behaviour chains.

This approach, which is compatible with what is sometimes referred to as *anamnestic risk assessment*, incorporates the results of a number of other assessments (and structured risk assessment is very important), whilst paying particular attention to those factors that are specific to the individual being assessed and which might be very relevant to his or her future management (see Conroy and Murrie, 2007; Heilbrun, 2001; Otto, 2000). For example, mental disorder might be a significant risk factor for an individual who has repeatedly offended whilst experiencing psychotic reactions, even though a diagnosis of schizophrenia is not generally identified as a particularly powerful risk factor for offending. There are also cases where offending involves the participation and collaboration of an intimate partner. Whilst the existence of a long-term intimate relationship is often considered to be a protective factor against offending, it should be clearly identified as an important risk factor in such circumstances.

Presenting the case formulation

The case formulation should be presented as part of the opinion section of the forensic report and should be clearly separated from the data derived from the assessments. This is because the formulation represents a set of hypotheses about why the offending occurred and is not factual. It is important to remember that there are many different ways to explain human behaviour, many of which have validity. Thus, the formulation represents an opinion that is informed by the data (evidence), but derived from professional judgement. Indeed, it is to be expected that case formulations will change or develop as hypotheses are tested or new information comes to light – as typically happens in the course of treatment.

Given the level of interpretation required to develop a case formulation, it is unsurprising that the opinion section of the report is likely to be the most closely scrutinised. It needs to be clearly written, unambiguous and linked directly to the referral questions. Although the specific presentation will differ according to the circumstances of the case, it can be helpful to present this as a narrative that tells the story of how the offending began, developed and continued over time. Then, an opinion regarding each of the specific referral questions can be provided. Casey et al. (2012) suggest that this should be relatively brief (less than 1,000 words) and clearly identify the circumstances in which risk is likely to be highest (i.e. those future scenarios which would be of most concern), as well as the areas that might be targeted for intervention if risk is to be effectively managed.

Outline of report

In this section some extracts of forensic psychology reports are reproduced to illustrate particular aspects of how the assessment can be communicated. It is important to remember that the audience for forensic psychology reports is rarely other psychologists, but readers who cannot be expected to have detailed knowledge of the discipline. Take, for example, this paragraph on risk assessment:

> An important goal of any assessment of this type is to understand the extent to which there is ongoing risk of violence to the community. Methods of predicting who will be violent (and who will not) are commonly known as risk assessments. Risk factors are those variables that impact systematically on violence, either by increasing or decreasing its likelihood. Predicting whether someone will commit further acts of violence typically involves establishing which risk factors are relevant to the individual case.

The aim here is to provide the reader with some basic information about how the term 'risk' is used by forensic psychologists, given there is no standard definition (Risk Management Authority, 2007). This provides the context for what follows, which should involve a description of the risk assessment tool that was used in the assessment, followed by a reporting of the results in relation to those specific risk factors that were identified as present. For example, the following extract seeks to summarise the results of a widely used risk assessment tool, the HCR-20 (see Douglas and Webster, 1999):

> *Mr Brown scored highly on both the 'Clinical' and 'Risk Management' items of this protocol, resulting in an overall risk judgement of 'moderate' risk of violence. A judgement of moderate risk suggests that a risk management plan should be developed, at the very least including some mechanism for the systematic re-assessment of risk.*
>
> *Although Mr Brown is not routinely violent, it is possible to imagine a number of scenarios in which provocation will arise and lead to impulsive aggression. The main clinical risk factors identified were impulsivity, lack of insight, negative attitudes, and a lack of response to treatment. His plans to manage risk also place him at ongoing risk,*

given that they appear to lack feasibility (his main methods of risk management are either avoidance or self-medication), he continues to experience stress and de-stabilising events, and lacks personal support.

A case formulation describing a developmental history might look like this (adapted from White, Day, Hackett and Dalby, 2015).

Mr Green's early development was characterised by physical and probable emotional neglect as an infant, necessitating his removal from the care of his biological parents at 6 months of age. Such critical early experiences can contribute to an individual's attachment style, which is a particular style of relating to significant others which can remain stable across the life-course. Children with poor attachment often have difficulty trusting parental figures, and people in general, and thus can have great difficulty forming protective bonds, even when placed in stable families.

The fact that Mr Green was the recipient of severe physical punishment would, in my opinion, have exacerbated his sense of exclusion and of not truly belonging. This laid the foundation for a pervasive sense of loneliness, rejection, and probably fear, which then during his adolescence expressed itself in resentment, and anger, often at the injustice of his early life experiences.

Mr Green's 'acting out' behaviour in adolescence would seem characteristic of these early difficulties. He began, like those around him, to engage in substance abuse as a way of coping with adversity, and has maintained heavy poly-substance use for over 15 years now. Over this time he has developed entrenched anti-social attitudes, essentially the view that one must look out for oneself because no-one else will, and therefore one's own self-interest becomes superordinate to the rights and wishes of others. Mixing in peer groups and sub-cultures where such views are shared has only served to strengthen the impact of such beliefs upon Mr Green's behaviour.

This same report then provides an opinion based on a Criminogenic Needs Assessment:

In my opinion a number of historical and more recent factors combined to contribute to Mr Green's offending. Predisposing psychological features include anti-social beliefs and an adherence to stereotypical rape myths (e.g. women ask for it, women are liars, etc.), along with a sense of entitlement and long-standing pattern of asserting his own needs over the rights of others. In these offences, the impulse to act in a manner consistent with these beliefs was triggered by Mr Green witnessing his girlfriend talking to another man and being asked to leave the room. This was a situation which left Mr Green feeling angry, resentful, outraged and humiliated. Pre-existing difficulties in managing these feelings and controlling his behaviour were then further exacerbated by the disinhibiting effects of drugs and alcohol. This created a situation in which his already tenuous internal cognitive barriers to offending, such as his view that violence against women is wrong, were readily overcome.

Common difficulties with this approach

There are a number of limitations associated with the approach described in this chapter, the most obvious of which is a reliance on client self-report. In the forensic setting this can prove unreliable and it is particularly important, where possible, to corroborate self-report with other sources of information, such as from schools, employers and family members. A number of assessment tools have been developed to assess socially desirable responding or impression management and these should be used to inform an opinion on the likelihood that the person being assessed has responded in an honest and forthright manner. Notwithstanding this, problems with impression management are less likely to arise when a strong therapeutic alliance has developed. This approach requires a high degree of participation and collaboration and is often conducive to the development of an alliance. Associated with this is the danger that the type of self-disclosure required to complete the assessment will lead the assessor to conclude that the person is at higher risk than might have been determined using other methods. Accordingly, the limitations of confidentiality and all possible uses of the disclosed information must be thoroughly reviewed with all offenders before the assessment begins. However, there are also occasions when the person being assessed does not actively engage and consciously seeks to minimise (or even deny) responsibility for offending.

A related issue derives from potential conflict that arises between the assessment and the treatment role. It is generally recommended that those involved in treatment should not undertake a psychological assessment for court (see Greenberg and Shuman, 1997). The psychologist can, of course, carry out these distinct roles with separate individuals (i.e. provide treatment to some individuals and evaluate others), but the case formulation approach described in this chapter very clearly moves the assessment into territory that has been traditionally regarded as treatment. Issues of objectivity thus become paramount. It is relatively common for those being assessed to develop greater insight and motivation to change as a result of taking part in this type of assessment.

Finally, it will be apparent that this type of approach will necessarily be time and labour intensive. Each incident of offending in the individual's history must be carefully examined in an effort to establish the chain of events that resulted in an offence. In addition, the approach is obviously tailored to legal questions that concern understanding offending and managing the risk of future offending. It is obviously less suitable for use in answering other types of forensic assessment questions, such as are asked in fitness to plead or competency to stand trial cases.

Review task

After reading this chapter, try to reflect on your own approach to the forensic assessment. Consider how you understand and assess risk, the value that you place on psychometric tools and how you integrate the findings of your assessment to form an opinion that allows you to answer the relevant referral questions. Finally, think about how you present your opinion in your reports and the clarity with which you are able to explain your case formulation to a lay reader.

Checklist of steps/advice

The assessment method described in this chapter is essentially a five-step process:

1 Assess risk using a structured risk assessment tool.
2 Assess needs using validated psychological assessments and client interview.
3 Use functional analysis methods to develop a detailed offence chain for each occurrence of offending behaviour.
4 Integrate this information in a case formulation that explains why the offending occurred.
5 Present the formulation in the opinion section of the report.

Further reading

Casey, S., Day, A., Ward, T. and Vess, J. (2012). *Foundations of offender rehabilitation*. Oxford, UK: Routledge Publishing.

References

Anthony, T. (2010). *Sentencing indigenous offenders. Brief 7,* Indigenous Justice Clearinghouse. State of New South Wales through the Department of Justice and Attorney General.

Casey, S., Day, A., Ward, T. and Vess, J. (2012). *Foundations of offender rehabilitation*. Oxford, UK: Routledge Publishing.

Conroy, M.A., and Murrie, D.C. (2007). *Forensic assessment of violence risk: A guide for risk assessment and risk management*. Hoboken, NJ: Wiley.

Daffern, M., Jones, L. and Shine, J. (eds.) (2010). *Offence paralleling behaviour: A case formulation approach to offender assessment and intervention*. Chichester, UK: John Wiley and Sons.

Day, A. and Bowen, E. (2015). Offending competency and coercive control in intimate partner violence. *Aggression and Violent Behavior, 20,* 62–71.

Douglas, K.S. and Webster, C.D. (1999). The HCR-20 violence risk assessment scheme: Concurrent validity in a sample of incarcerated offenders. *Criminal Justice and Behavior, 26,* 13–9.

Flitcroft, A., James, I., Freeston, M. and Wood-Mitchell, A. (2007). Determining what is good in a good formulation. *Behavioural and Cognitive Psychotherapy, 35,* 352–64.

Grant, A., Townend, M., Mills, J. and Cocks, A. (2008). *Assessment and Case Formulation in CBT*. London, UK: Sage Publications.

Greenberg, S.A. and Shuman, D.W. (1997). Irreconcilable conflict between therapeutic and forensic roles. *Professional Psychology: Research and Practice, 28,* 50–7.

Grisso, T. (2010). Guidance for improving forensic reports: A review of common errors. *Open Access Journal of Forensic Psychology, 2,* 102–15.

Heilbrun, K. (2001). *Principles of forensic mental health assessment*. New York: Kluwer Academic/Plenum Publishers.

Howells, K., Heseltine, K., Sarre, R., Davey, L. and Day, A. (2004). *Correctional offender treatment programs: The national picture in Australia.* Report for the Criminology Research Council. Retrieved from www.aic.gov.au/crc/reports/200203-04.html (accessed 19 November 2014).

Koerner, K. and Linehan, M.M. (1997). Case formulation in dialectical behavior therapy for borderline personality disorder, in T. Eells (ed.), *Handbook of psychotherapy case formulation* (pp. 340–67). New York: Guilford Press.

Meloy, R. (1992). *Violent attachments.* Northvale, NJ: Jason Aronson.

Nelson, C. and Jackson, P. (1989). High-risk recognition: The cognitive-behavioral chain. In D.R. Laws (ed.), *Relapse prevention with sex offenders* (pp. 147–177). New York: Guilford Press.

Otto, R.K. (2000). Assessing and managing violence risk in outpatient settings. *Journal of Clinical Psychology, 56,* 1239–62.

Persons, J.B., Mooney, K. and Padesky, C. (1995). Inter-rater reliability of cognitive-behavioural case formulations. *Cognitive Therapy and Research, 19,* 21–34.

Risk Management Authority. (2007). *Risk assessment tools evaluation directory. RATED version 2.* Retrieved from www.rmascotland.gov.uk/files/5512/7306/6150/riskAssessmentTools EvaluationDirectory.pdf (accessed 19 December 2014).

Sturmey, P. (2010). Case formulation in forensic psychology, in M. Daffern, L. Jones and J. Shine (eds.), *Offence paralleling behaviour: A case formulation approach to offender assessment and intervention* (pp. 25–52). Chichester, UK: John Wiley and Sons.

Ward, T., Yates, P.M. and Long, C. (2006). *The self-regulation model of the offense and relapse process – Volume 2: Treatment.* Victoria, Canada: Trafford Publishing.

White, J., Day, A., Hackett, L. and Dalby, J.T. (2015). *Writing reports for court: An international guide for psychologists who work in the criminal jurisdiction.* Melbourne, Australia: Australian Academic Press.

5

REPORTING STRUCTURED PROFESSIONAL JUDGEMENT

Caroline Logan

Introduction

The term *structured professional judgement* (SPJ) refers to the discretionary application of evidence-based clinical guidelines for understanding complex problems in order to influence their comprehensive, positive and ongoing or continuous management (Hart and Logan, 2011). To say that a process is evidence-based is to state quite clearly that both the understanding of the problem and the action taken to attempt to remedy or manage it has been underpinned by a sound investigative method, either formal research or, where such research does not exist or is still developing, a systematic and transparent examination of the issue and theories pertaining to its origins and development (Sackett and Rosenberg, 1995; Sackett, Rosenberg, Muir Gray, Haynes, Richardson, et al., 1996). Evidence-based practice was made common in clinical medicine but it is now upheld as good practice in many areas, including understanding and managing risk by forensic practitioners. Such practice relies on the availability of information – evidence, and of sufficient range and quality – on the basis of which guidelines may be derived for the procedures necessary to understand and manage the problems that are its focus. And the availability of evidence is at the heart of the matter with respect to harmful behaviour.

What we know or think we know about the reasons why people harm themselves or one another is insufficient (Hart and Logan, 2011). Further, it is a hugely conflicted literature, with multiple and disparate theories of important challenges in the forensic field, such as violence and sexual violence. Therefore, the selection of evidence and the nature of the recommendations made in relation to problem understanding and decision making towards risk management is not straightforward and guidance of some kind is required (see Otto and Douglas, 2010).

There have developed two approaches to attempt to manage the shortfalls in the field (Hart and Logan, 2011): *discretionary* and *non-discretionary* approaches. Discretionary approaches involve the application of structured clinical guidelines as a way of anchoring practice to the available research. However, those guidelines are simply that – guidance, or a standard to which practitioners will aspire. This is because the evidence base is incomplete and flawed, which means that practitioners are required to use their judgement or discretion to bridge the gaps in their knowledge, but using those clinical guidelines (such as the *HCR-20 Version 3* or HCR-20^{V3}, Douglas, Hart, Webster and Belfrage, 2013) as their map of the terrain. In contrast, the authors of non-discretionary approaches adopt the view that practice is only truly evidence-based when there is a direct line between the empirical research and judgement, operationalised by the application of fixed and explicit rules about exactly what information is relevant to decision making about a problem, such as the prediction of future violence. Non-discretionary approaches are so prescriptive because otherwise the gaps in knowledge and understanding will invite biased thinking and decision making and therefore risk costly errors (Meehl, 1954/1996); decisions must be evidence-based or they are not valid decisions. In the risk assessment and management field, SPJ operationalises the discretionary approach while the non-discretionary approach is represented by the actuarial or statistical application of risk assessment tools (for example, the *Risk Matrix 2000* or RM2000) or instruments (see Chapter 3; Hart and Logan, 2011; Barnett, Wakeling and Howard, 2010). The contrast between these two approaches is considerable, and the debate about which is better – more accurate, justified and informative – is intense and ongoing.

This chapter focuses on SPJ, that is, on the application of discretionary clinical guidelines that support the understanding and real time management of the threat of harmful behaviour in the clients of mental health, correctional and law enforcement services. This is because SPJ, more than any other approach to evaluating risk, incorporates both empirical and professional evidence about harmful behaviour, supports transparent and professionally accountable practice and guides pragmatic risk management in the services that endeavour to work collaboratively with their users. This makes it a practically useful and flexible approach to understanding and managing risk. The chapter will begin with an account of the application of the SPJ approach, followed by a consideration of when it would and would not be regarded as best practice. The chapter will then examine how best to communicate the findings of an evaluation based on the SPJ approach in order to ensure that its author's objectives are clearly met. Some of the difficulties often encountered by evaluators using SPJ will then be considered, and a task will be outlined to help readers develop best practice in this area. The chapter will conclude with a set of recommendations for the development of expertise in SPJ.

Best practice

How do you apply the SPJ approach?

In practice, the SPJ approach is presented in the form of a manual containing guidance on navigating each step of the process of conceptualising, understanding and managing risk, where evidence of decision making at each step is recorded on a worksheet. Examples of manuals that completely operationalise the SPJ approach include the HCR-20^{V3} and the *Risk for Sexual Violence Protocol* (RSVP [Hart, Kropp, Laws, Klaver, Logan and Watt, 2003]). Manuals that support SPJ but in a less complete way (see reference below to SPJ 'lite') include the *Sexual Violence Risk-20* (SVR-20 [Boer, Hart, Kropp and Webster, 1997]), the *Structured Assessment of Violence Risk in Youth* (SAVRY [Borum, 2006]), and the *Extremism Risk Guidelines-22+* (ERG-22+ [Lloyd and Dean, 2015]). Risk of suicidal behaviour has had little attention from the SPJ movement, though one such set of guidelines is in development (Logan, 2013).

The substantial part of SPJ-informed manuals is the identification of risk factors evidenced in the research as being the most relevant to the specific risk being investigated – violence, sexual violence, youth violence and so on – and the review of evidence justifying their importance. Protective factors are included in some guidance, such as in the SAVRY, but they are excluded from most and practitioners may instead rely on a separate SPJ 'lite' evaluation using the *Structured Assessment of Protective Factors* or SAPROF (de Vogel, de Ruiter, Bouman and de Vries Robbé, 2009). Depending on the manual, guidance is then offered on evaluating overall risk and preparing for its management. Therefore, SPJ assists in the identification of the most important factors in the individual case and in understanding their meaning in terms of that person's future potential for harm. Then, based on the understanding – or formulation (see Chapter 4) – developed about his or her risk, the evaluator is 'walked' through risk management planning via a series of questions designed to prompt the evaluator to generate ideas based on what would best meet the needs of the client.

Regardless of the harmful behaviour to be managed, the complete application of the SPJ approach involves assessors working through six steps. First, on receiving and accepting the instruction to evaluate a client's risk, evaluators will gather a range of information and resources that they believe will provide them with the evidence they need about the client to comment on his or her potential. Ideally, the instruction – or referral – will communicate something of the nature of the risks posed and the problems the referrer has experienced trying to understand future potential, thus prompting their appeal to the evaluators for assistance. Risk evaluations are intended to reduce or at least characterise the uncertainty surrounding a case, and information gathering at this first step should be guided by the problem as it has been framed. As a consequence, information gathering will often be over-inclusive, focused on past similar behaviour and on the nature of current concerns about the future, and oriented around the risk and protective factors thought most important in this case. The client will be a key source of the information accessed. However, risk evaluations can and sometimes have to be carried out without the client's participation (e.g. British Psychological Society, 2009; Heilbrun, 2001) as when he or she is too paranoid to engage in the process. As this information gathering process is ongoing, practitioners will start to record the evidence they have collected on the SPJ worksheet accompanying the manual they have selected to guide them through this procedure.

Second, practitioners will turn to the manual and, using the guidance therein, make a decision as to the <u>presence</u> of each of the risk (and protective) factors listed and described within its pages. This stage provides the critical evidence base for the evaluation process – a way of ensuring that what follows is underpinned by current knowledge about the problem behaviour to be prevented. The judgement about the presence of individual factors is made on the basis of the extent to which they are present – *not at all*, *partially* or *possibly*, or *definitely present*. Already, an understanding of what has happened to the client and the nature of his or her current circumstances are shaping consideration of the case.

However, it is the third step – when evaluators determine the <u>relevance</u> of risk (and protective) factors that the idiographic nature of the evaluation becomes most apparent. In this step, evaluators decide if and how they believe a risk or protective factor that they judge to be present is relevant to future risk. For example, a client may be judged to have a history of substance use problems – for many years they have abused cocaine and other stimulants. If this client's past violence was clearly linked to intoxication, withdrawal or to the procurement of such substances, then substance use is relevant to their future potential for violence; if they abuse substances again or trade them, violence may be an outcome given the pattern noted in the past. If, however, this person's violence was related to a family feud that predates their use of stimulants, and has occurred in the recent past on occasions when the person has not been intoxicated or withdrawing from cocaine, then substance use problems while present are *not* relevant to his or her particular risk for violence. Relevance should be considered in terms of both the generation of future harm, such as to suggest it has causal relevance, and to the management of risk in the future. As with presence, relevance is determined by the evaluators in terms of *definitely*, *possibly* or *partially*, or *not at all*. The HCR-20^{V3} and the RSVP require evaluators to record both judgements – about the presence and relevance of individual risk factors – on the accompanying worksheets. Guidance that operationalises the SPJ approach only partially (SPJ 'lite') does not usually require relevance ratings, which diminishes the extent to which they can help to generate truly individualised evaluations.

Although the SPJ manual guides assessors in their review of the risk and protective factors that the evidence suggests are potentially relevant to the harmful outcome to be prevented, it is entirely possible that additional factors are important – that is, case-specific factors. This may occur because the nature of the case is unusual, such as when a person is severely hearing or sight impaired, or their first language or culture is different from that of the staff of the service in which they are being held, all of which would be very relevant to risk management. Alternatively, additional factors will need to be included in the core assessment of say, violence risk, if a client is also at risk of sexual violence or suicidal behaviour, necessitating a broader ranging evaluation.

The fourth step is critical – this is when the evaluator creates a <u>formulation</u> of the client's harm potential based on their identification of the most relevant risk and protective factors. This is the step when the evaluator attempts to *explain* the client's future harm potential based on their understanding of why the person was harmful before and the circumstances in which he or she may decide to be harmful again in the future. More detailed explanations of risk formulation are available elsewhere (e.g. Chapter 4; Logan, in press). However, important elements of the step are organising the most relevant information, such as through the application of the 4/5Ps model (Weerasekeera, 1996; Sturmey and McMurran, 2011) and scenario planning. The latter involves forecasting two or more situations in which harmful behaviour *could* happen in the future in order to anticipate the chain of events that would lead to its occurrence and highlighting the strategies that would be required to interrupt and ultimately prevent that outcome (Chermack and Lynham, 2002; van der Heijden, 1994). Narrative formulations are recommended rather than maps or diagrams in order to ensure unambiguous communication of concern, which is especially important for clients who are detained for the long term and for whom new practitioners wanting to pick up the work of their predecessors are a routine occurrence. And ideally, formulations should be simply written – therefore accessible and brief – and no more than four to six pages in length. As such, they are more likely to be read and to influence risk management.

Risk management is the fifth step in the SPJ process, the step in which the understanding described in the formulation stage is crystallised into a set of recommendations intended to minimise if not prevent the potential for future harm to occur. In the SPJ approach, risk management consists of at least three, if not four, strategies. *Treatment interventions* are the efforts made to repair or restore deficits in functioning linked to risk (Logan, 2016). They are intended to diminish the potency of the risk factors thought to be most relevant to harm potential and/or enhance the influence of protective factors to the same end. Treatment interventions should be drawn from the range of psychological (e.g. cognitive behaviour therapy), psychosocial (e.g. social skills training) and psychopharmacological approaches (e.g. antidepressants, mood stabilisers) to tackling risk factors with a direct relevance to the individual's harm potential. The selection of specific treatment strategies would depend on the emphasis placed on individual or clusters of risk factors in the formulation.

Supervision strategies target the environment or the setting in which the client is based or likely to be located in the future (Logan, 2016). Such strategies are intended to restrict the individual's access to the means by which they could be harmful again in the future (e.g. close supervision such as through a multi-agency public protection panel, or a restriction on access to substances or preferred victim type) and/or to enhance the person's access to activities or resources that will help to divert them from harmful behaviour (e.g. employment, regular financial income, stable accommodation, regular practical support with childcare). As above, the choice of supervision strategies would depend on the formulation and on the scenarios explored to create it.

In terms of risk management, *monitoring* involves the identification of early – and not so early – warning signs of deterioration in managed risk. For example, for a client whose mental ill health is highly relevant to his harm potential – because, for example, he feels compelled to respond to auditory hallucinations that 'instruct' him to hurt a close family member – a key monitoring recommendation would be to observe his compliance with prescribed medication and the quality of his inter-actions with others, especially if social withdrawal has been identified as a key way in which a deterioration in his mental state is signaled. The monitoring component of a risk management plan also involves making recommendations for what should happen – and not happen – when those early warning signs are detected. It is also important to identify when improvements have occurred, as it might be appro-priate to revise the risk management strategies. Monitoring is akin to surveillance making it much less intrusive than treatment or supervision but no less essential for cross-disciplinary and cross-service cooperation.

Finally, the management of risk of harm to others is likely to involve the prepa-ration of *victim safety plans* (such plans may have less relevance where concerns are about risk of harm to self). These plans relate to the action that is judged to be required to protect a prospective victim or victim type from harm at the hands of the client – a family member, a practitioner, an identifiable professional such as a police officer, Member of Parliament or soldier. Victim safety plans should high-light both what potential victims could be asked to do to 'harden' them as targets and what agencies should consider doing to limit the harm that might occur.

Finally, the sixth step is when recommendations are made for the level of case prioritisation – how urgent the case is in terms of the need for action – and what action needs to be taken, what other risks are indicated and the date for the next review. No risk evaluation will last forever – an individual's risk of harmful behaviour changes as their circumstances evolve – and every risk evaluation should come with a 'sell-by date', a date after which the findings should be considered due for revision.

These six steps describe the SPJ process in full. The HCR-20^{V3} and the RSVP encourage evaluators to engage in each step and to document the evidence of their activity in worksheets that are at least 10 pages in length in paper form, which is then the basis of a summary report that might itself be 5 to 10 pages in length if not more. Following this process in its entirety enables an incredible level of consideration to be given to individual clients and the concerns raised about them. It also offers a high level of transparency and accountability in thinking and decision making. SPJ 'lite' guidance, such as the SAVRY and the ERG-22+, certainly lend themselves to the full six-step process, but their worksheets are more brief and there is much less emphasis placed on relevance ratings, scenario planning and structured risk management.

When is it best practice to use the SPJ approach?

The SPJ approach described above should be regarded as best practice in clini-cal risk assessment, formulation and management. Evaluators adopting such an approach will gradually move from uncertainty towards certainty in terms of their understanding of the individual client's harm potential and its comprehen-sive and proportionate management. However, it is clearly a time-consuming process; hours if not days may be spent working through each step and preparing a report summarising the findings of the evaluation and its recommendations. Such an evaluation is suitable for only a proportion of the cases encountered by forensic practitioners on a routine basis – perhaps those they see in relation to court proceedings (e.g. to assist in sentencing decisions), or reviews such as those carried out by the parole board or mental health tribunals relating to continued detention in forensic mental health facilities, or in specialist facilities where 'deluxe' assessments are expected. Full SPJ assessments should not be seen as routine for all clients of all services as to do so is to make it a bureaucratic exercise that will lose its meaning and dilute the expertise required to carry it out well. Instead, they should be regarded as an advanced or specialist assessments. The application of SPJ 'lite' is more sustainable in terms of being repeated by evaluators over more routine cases, providing an evidential basis for a more in-depth evaluation when required. Non-discretionary actuarial approaches are more often used to screen for high-risk cases (for example, allocating a level of risk to hundreds of men and women released from prison every month in order to link them into what is thought to be the most suitable level of probation supervision). However, caution has been expressed about the use of such prediction tools to this end (Cooke and Michie, 2010).

Outline of report

For the SPJ approach to enhance a client evaluation, communication of its technique and findings made has to be of the highest quality. Communication is everything, and the best SPJ evaluation is rendered worthless by unclear purpose, ambiguous phrasing, excessive and unnecessary use of jargon, absence of detail and poor grammar. Practitioners should write sentences to be understood in one read-through and avoid making their readers have to wade through pages of dense or superfluous text that represents the author's anxious workings out, diluting the key message. Reports should be brief (a four- to six-page report is more likely to be read and acted upon than a 40- to 60-page report) and essential details reserved for the appendix so that they do not distract from the work undertaken. Evaluators should leave the reader in no doubt what they have observed and concluded. Therefore, when a forensic practitioner completes an evaluation of the risks posed by a client using the SPJ approach, it is recommended that their report include reference to the following seven points.

1   Your terms of reference. The practitioner should begin by providing a clear statement about:
    a   why the evaluation was requested (the context of the request) and from whom,
    b   the practitioner's qualifications and experience to undertake the evaluation,
    c   how the evaluation was actually carried out and what sources of information and informants were used, and
    d   the potential relevance of its findings to ongoing proceedings or care.

2   Limitations. The practitioner should state in detail both the limitations of the evaluation carried out (e.g. the client refused to cooperate) and the reason why, notwithstanding those limitations, the report's conclusions and its recommendations should still be taken seriously and acted upon by the reader.

3   Client presentation. The practitioner should describe the client's response to and engagement with the evaluation process and any relevant observations on the client's interactions with the practitioner or others during its course.

4   Key findings. Present the practioner should include key findings from the application of a specific set of SPJ guidelines, such as the HCR-20^{V3}. Focus on the clusters of the *relevant* risk and protective factors. Where specific ratings have to be reported, do put these in the appendix of the report so that they do not distract from the overall message of the document.

5   Risk formulation. Now write your risk formulation, that is, your narrative statement that is both (a) your understanding of the client's past harmful behaviour, and (b) the relevance of the past to his or her future risk.

6   Risk management plan. Describe a plan for intervention – the treatment strategies you would like to recommend, options for supervision, any monitoring points, and if relevant, a victim safety plan – all of which *must* be linked directly to the formulation and focused on moderating the influence of the most relevant risk and protective factors on future harm potential.

7   Review plan. Finally, highlight any risks in other areas, any action that is urgently required and the 'sell-by' date of the evaluation.

Common difficulties and confusions in reporting SPJ

The strengths of the SPJ approach can be tested by certain of the challenges faced by practitioners in their forensic practice. Below are listed some of the common difficulties and confusions faced by evaluators. The checklist offers suggestions as to how they may be managed in written reports.

•   The evaluation of a client's risk of harmful behaviour should be a journey towards understanding, on the basis of which relevant and proportionate interventions should follow. However, one's understanding of future risk will be severely challenged in cases where the client has carried out a single serious act of violence in the past (e.g. murder, manslaughter) in the absence of a pattern of any similar behaviour. It is difficult to extrapolate into the future from such a meagre history.

•   Relatedly, past harmful behaviour that is difficult to explain means that future potential will be hard to formulate and manage. We cannot risk manage with confidence what we do not understand (Reid and Thorne, 2007).

•   Referrers can request risk evaluations with high – sometimes too high – expectations about what practitioners can say and do (e.g. where an autism spectrum disorder is linked to risk, that the evaluator will recommend or deliver conclusive treatment when long-term and costly supervision may be the best that can be hoped for). Less experienced or confident practitioners may blame themselves for not being able to deliver on those expectations or recommend that others do so.

• While the SPJ approach is well known and widely used, there is little in the way of research that demonstrates its effectiveness. There have been lots of studies verifying that guidance like the HCR-20^{V3} contains a representative sample of risk factors (Douglas, Hart, Webster, Belfrage, Guy and Wilson, 2014), but less on the development of risk formulations or the efficacy of risk management plans in their entirety as opposed to individual interventions such as SOTP.

Review task

Select five reports, completed in the last year or so, containing an evaluation of a client's risk of harmful behaviour using the SPJ approach; or if you do not have access to such reports, review the example reports in the appendices, all of which include an SPJ assessment.

a   Do the reports contain *all seven* of the items listed in the 'Outline' section above? Rate a report with 0 if it does not contain any of the items, 1 if it covers some of the items but not others and 2 if all are mentioned in at least some detail.

b   Do the reports highlight *relevant* risk and protective factors as opposed to those that are merely present? Rate a report with 0 if it does not discuss risk factors in terms of their relevance or if protective factors are not mentioned at all, 1 if it discusses risk and protective factors in terms of presence only and 2 if *relevant* risk and protective factors are highlighted and explored.

c   Do the risk formulations state clearly *what they are risk formulations of?* (For example, 'This is a formulation of A's risk of future violence towards intimate partners'.) Rate a report with 0 if it does not contain a risk formulation at all, 1 if it has a risk formulation but the focus of the formulation is not explicit and 2 if the formulation clearly answers the 'risk of what' question.

d   Do the risk formulations *use circumspect language* or have they presented them as if they represent facts about the client? Rate a report 0 if the language used suggests that hypotheses are facts, 1 if there is a mixture of circumspect language and hypotheses expressed as facts and 2 if the language reflects the hypothetical nature of the explanation given.

e   Do the risk formulations consider the client's *future potential* as well as their past conduct? Rate a report with 0 if it does not contain a risk formulation at all, 1 if it has a risk formulation but the focus of the formulation is the client's past harmful behaviour only and 2 if the risk formulation offers hypotheses about past harmful behaviour as well as the client's future potential for harm.

f   Was scenario planning done in order to assist with preparing the formulation? Rate a report with 0 if you did not scenario plan, 1 if you considered just one scenario (e.g. the client doing again what he or she did before) and 2 if you considered two or more scenarios in preparing your risk formulation.

g   Do the risk management plans contain each of the elements of treatment interventions, supervision strategies, monitoring recommendations, and where appropriate, victim safety plans? Rate a report with 0 if the risk management section of your report does not exist; 1 if you make a mix of suggestions but are not explicit about whether they are treatment, supervision or monitoring recommendations; and 2 if you clearly set out your recommendations in each area.

Each of the reports will now have a total score out of 14. Select your highest scoring report and your lowest scoring report. Are you satisfied that the higher scoring report reflects the SPJ process more than the lower scoring report? In the future, could you make your reports higher scoring than the reports considered as part of this exercise? How useful do you think your lower scoring reports were to those who read them? Do you think you will change how you write your reports as a result of doing this exercise?

Checklist: Guidelines for the reporting of SPJ

SPJ is a demanding task for the forensic practitioner, especially if it is to be undertaken to a high standard and communicated well to those in the best position to implement the recommendations made. Here is a set of guidelines for the reporting of an evaluation based on the SPJ approach.

1   Commence work by trying to answer the 'risk of what?' question. This question is central to what you do from the moment the referral is accepted. Your referrer may be able to articulate their concerns well, or may need your assistance to progress from a statement of general unease about a client.

2   Use the six steps described in the 'Best Practice' section above as your route map for an evaluation of risk informed by the SPJ approach, whichever manual you choose.

3   Know that evaluating future risk in the absence of a pattern of past harmful behaviour will be hard for anyone to do. Acknowledge this limitation as others may expect you to be able to do this.

4   In general, when referrals are accepted, understand and manage the expectations of those making the referral and avoid over-promising what may be too hard to deliver. Note that more restrictive interventions are likely to be recommended – and justified – in cases where risk is poorly understood.

5   In reports, ensure that risk formulations make reference to future potential and do not just explain the past, and definitely ensure that risk management plans are based on the formulation and not – after all the effort it will have taken to produce it – just on one or two salient facts about the client (e.g. recommend

a sex offender treatment programme because the person committed a sexually motivated offence).

6   Ensure that formulations are written in language that is circumspect (e.g. 'It would appear that A's experience of severe abuse as a child made him feel that people around him could not be trusted . . .') and not stated as if incontrovertible fact (e.g. 'A's experience of severe abuse as a child made him distrust people . . .').

7   While SPJ supports evidence-based practice, it is still a developing field. Evaluators should be reassured by empirical evidence supporting the selection of risk factors and individual interventions but acknowledge that further research is required. They should endeavour to support that research and to monitor the literature for work relevant to their area of practice.

Further reading

Douglas, K.S., Hart, S.D., Webster, C.D. and Belfrage, H., (2013). *HCR-20: Assessing risk for violence*, 3rd ed.Vancouver, Canada: Mental Health, Law and Policy Institute, Simon Fraser University.

Otto, R.K. and Douglas, K.S. (eds.). (2010). *Handbook of violence risk assessment tools*. Milton Park, UK: Routledge.

Logan, C. and Johnstone, L. (eds.). (2013). *Managing clinical risk: A guide to effective practice*. Oxford, UK: Routledge.

Sturmey, P. and McMurran, M. (eds.). (2011). *Forensic case formulation*. Chichester, UK: Wiley-Blackwell.

References

Barnett, G.D., Waleling, H.C. and Howard, P.D. (2010). An examination of the predictive validity of the Risk Matrix 2000 in England and Wales. *Sexual Abuse, 22*, 443–70.

British Psychological Society (2009). *Code of ethics and conduct*. Leicester, UK: The British Psychological Society.

Boer, D.P., Hart, S.D., Kropp, P.R., and Webster, C.D., (1997). *Manual for the Sexual Violence Risk-20: Professional guidelines for assessing risk of sexual violence*. Vancouver, Canada: British Columbia Institute on Family Violence and the Mental Health, Law, and Policy Institute, Simon Fraser University.

Borum, R. (2006). *Manual for the structured assessment of violence risk in youth* (SAVRY). Odessa, Florida (2006). Retrieved from http://works.bepress.com/randy_borum/2/ accessed 22 July 2016.

Chermack, T.J. and Lynham, S.A. (2002). Definitions and outcome variables of resource planning. *Human Resource Development Review, 1*, 366–83.

Cooke, D.J. and Michie, C. (2010). Limitations of diagnostic precision and predictive utility in the individual case: A challenge for forensic practice. *Law and Human Behavior, 34*, 259–74.

de Vogel, V., de Ruiter, C., Bouman, Y. and de Vries Robbé, M. (2009). *Guidelines for the assessment of protective factors for violence risk*, English version. Utrecht, Netherlands: Forum Educatief.

Douglas, K.S., Hart, S.D., Webster, C.D. and Belfrage, H. (2013). *HCR-20: Assessing risk for violence*, 3rd ed. Vancouver, Canada: Mental Health, Law and Policy Institute, Simon Fraser University.

Douglas, K.S., Hart, S.D., Webster, C.D., Belfrage, H., Guy, L.S. and Wilson, C.M. (2014). Historical-clinical-risk management-20, version 3 (HCR-20^{V3}): Development and overview. *International Journal of Forensic Mental Health*, *13*, 93–108.

Hart, S.D. and Logan, C. (2011). Formulation of violence risk using evidence-based assessments: The structured professional judgement approach, in Sturmey, P. and McMurran, M. (eds.), *Forensic case formulation*. Chichester, UK: Wiley-Blackwell.

Hart, S.D., Kropp, P.K., Laws, D.R., Klaver, J., Logan, C. and Watt, K.A. (2003). *The risk for sexual violence protocol: Structured professional guidelines for assessing risk of sexual violence*. Vancouver, Canada: Mental Health, Law and Policy Institute, Simon Fraser University.

Heilbrun, K. (2001). *Risk assessment and risk management: Towards an integration*. Plenary session delivered at the International Conference, Violence Risk Assessment and Management: Bringing Science and Practice Closer Together, Sundsvall, Sweden.

Lloyd, M. and Dean, C. (2015). The development of structured guidelines for assessing risk in extremist offenders. *Journal of Threat Assessment and Management*, *2*, 40–52.

Logan, C. (2016). Structured professional judgement: Applications to sex offender risk assessment and management, in Phenix, A. and Hoberman, H. (eds.), *Sexual offenders: Predisposing antecedents, assessments and management*. New York: Springer.

Logan, C. (in press). Forensic case formulation of violence and aggression. Chapter to appear in Sturmey P. (ed.), *The Wiley handbook of violence and aggression*. Chichester, UK: John Wiley & Sons.

Meehl, P.E. (1996). *Clinical versus statistical prediction: A theoretical analysis and a review of the literature*. Northvale, NJ: Jason Aronson. (Original work published in 1954).

Otto, R.K. and Douglas, K.S. (eds.). (2010). *Handbook of violence risk assessment tools*. Milton Park, UK: Routledge.

Reid, W.H. and Thorne, S.A. (2007). Personality disorders and violence potential. *Journal of Psychiatric Practice*, *13*, 261–8.

Sackett, D.L. and Rosenberg, W.M. (1995). On the need for evidence-based medicine. *Journal of Public Health Medicine*, *17*, 330–4.

Sackett, D.L., Rosenberg, W.M., Muir Gray, J.A., Haynes, R.B. and Richardson, W.S. (1996). Evidence based medicine: What it is and what it isn't – it's about integrating individual clinical expertise and the best external evidence. *British Medical Journal*, *312*, 71–2.

Sturmey, P. and McMurran, M. (eds.). (2011). *Forensic case formulation*. Chichester, UK: Wiley Blackwell.

van der Heijden, K. (1994). Probabilistic planning and scenario planning. In G. Wright and P. Ayton (Eds.), *Subjective probability* (pp. 549–72). Chichester, UK: Wiley.

Weerasekera, P. (1996). *Multiperspective case formulation: A step toward treatment integration*. Malabar, FL: Krieger.

6

REPORTING PERSONALITY FUNCTIONING

Caroline Logan and Margaret Fenton

Introduction

Personality disorders are the most prevalent mental health condition in offender populations (e.g. Fazel and Danesh, 2002). They are identified at very high rates in men and women who break the law repeatedly (e.g. Yu, Geddes and Fazel, 2012) and are harmful towards others (ten Have, de Graaf, van Weeghel and van Dorsselaer, 2014) and themselves (Björkenstam, Björkenstam, Holm, Gerdin and Ekselius, 2015). Personality functioning is a consideration in any effort to try to understand the clinical presentation of a client (American Psychiatric Association [APA], 2013), a complete-person narrative that may be embodied in a case formulation (Sturmey and McMurran, 2011; see Day, Chapter 4). Given the importance of personality to the key tasks that forensic practitioners routinely carry out – e.g. risk assessments, optimising treatment engagement, the assessment and communication of personality relevant information – is a critical skill. However, it is infrequently the subject of formal instruction and there is little clarity about 'best practice'. Therefore, the first objective of this chapter will be to examine the ways in which the personality being assessed may be relevant to the matter in hand. This examination will provide an essential backdrop to the following brief review of options for carrying out personality assessments that are useful and of a high standard. Best practice guidelines on the clear and relevant reporting of personality functioning will be proposed.

Best practice

Why is personality functioning important to forensic practitioners?

Personality is the collection of attitudes and beliefs, thinking patterns, emotional experiences, behaviours, interpersonal styles and self-beliefs that characterise a person most of the time in most circumstances, and which are a product of both his/her genetic inheritance and his/her experiences pre- and post-birth (Livesley, 2003). Personality is regarded as disordered when the individual's characteristics are such as to impede:

- his or her ability to function in an adaptive way;
- his or her relationships due to problems with understanding and taking into consideration the feelings of others and because of challenges with the experience of and response to intimacy; and
- his or her sense of self is fragile and poorly formed and lacking in direction or control (APA, 2013).

The disordered or at least dysfunctional personality presentation is of interest to forensic practitioners because of the potential relevance of such patterns of maladaptive functioning to rule-breaking behaviour.

Personality characteristics are inferred from a combination of (a) how individuals describe themselves – what they want others to know – and (b) what they reveal indirectly through their conduct (Cooke and Hart, 2004). However, what an individual wants an evaluator to know about his or her personality and what that individual reveals may not be the same thing. This is why the assessment of personality functioning is such a skilled undertaking – because of the need to reconcile sometimes very disparate, if not contradictory, pieces of information into a coherent explanation for what is going on in a person and why. Therefore, personality assessment is an attempt to identify the most important individual characteristics through a process of both direct questioning and observation. Theoretical frameworks are often used to steer investigations and to make sense of the usually very complex array of information gathered. A structured assessment tool, such as a semi-structured clinical interview or a self-report questionnaire that operationalises the theoretical framework, aids the identification of commonly occurring characteristics and the measurement of strengths and interactions with other variables, co-occurring conditions (e.g. substance misuse, post-traumatic stress disorder) and circumstances (e.g. unemployment, family break-up).

In general, the outcome of a personality assessment will be a narrative statement of several paragraphs or pages in length (see 'Outline of Report' section below). This statement will convert the findings of structured assessments into a communication about the *essence* of the person, that is, the mechanism of his or her characterological functioning as a human being and its relevance to the specific question or questions that initiated the enquiry.

People with personality disorder are generally held to be legally responsible for their actions (Hart, 2001). This is in contrast to the responsibility of those with severe mental illness, which may be regarded as diminished or even non-existent. Therefore, there is a requirement to explain their complex and often damaging behaviour and to assume in so doing that the choices they made were deliberate and their conduct wholly within their control. In the absence of mental illness, personality will be a key source of information towards such an explanation. This is because the assessment of personality is an evaluation of the underlying drivers for the behaviours requiring explanation – for example, 'his violence towards his partner was motivated by his excessive self-centredness'. However, such an endeavour requires attention to the interplay and possible co-existence of mental health and personality problems and the attribution of causality. Therefore, the assessment of personality requires a good understanding of *both* personality and the interplay between personality and mental disorders, especially those that may produce some of the same behavioural outcomes.

An additional reason for the relevance of personality to forensic practitioners is that personality dysfunction is often most obvious in times of crisis or despair; it can be an aggravating factor in the presence of conflict or frustration (Hart, 2001) and highly relevant to any consideration of future risk (Douglas, Hart, Webster and Belfrage, 2013). Therefore, people with personality difficulties may be vulnerable to do again what they have done before, especially in the absence of interventions that may be able to support them to think and behave in alternative ways. Thus, having a clear understanding of both the nature and the potential role of personality in the commission of past and future harmful acts and the means by which its influence may be modified are further reasons why practitioners must be competent in the assessment and communication of personality dysfunction.

The Big 5 personality dimensions of neuroticism, extroversion, openness, agreeableness and conscientiousness are frequently used to understand and explore personality (Gore and Widiger, 2013), and are increasingly relevant to our thinking about personality disorder (APA, 2013; Lynam, 2011). Two of the most important dimensions are agreeableness and conscientiousness, in particular the ends of the dimensions identifying antagonistic (low agreeableness) and disinhibited (low conscientiousness) characteristics respectively. A person with antagonistic traits can demonstrate a tendency towards arrogance and single-mindedness, which, if pronounced, can lead to conflict with others, especially similarly-minded others. A person who has traits of disinhibition can demonstrate a marked tendency towards spontaneous, even impulsive conduct and a lifestyle that is somewhat disorganised and lacking in focus or direction. Antagonism and disinhibition are key elemental parts of both antisocial and borderline personality disorders (Lynam, 2011). Therefore, understanding the way these traits can function to create for the individual circumstances in which conflict and despair may arise is a critical part of the assessment and reporting task. As the task of explaining the functional link between personality disorder and violence is so under-researched (Duggan and Howard, 2009), it remains a largely speculative task.

The expression of personality traits is 'coloured' by the environments in which they are demonstrated, the choice of which is in turn influenced by personality. For example, a hostile environment (e.g. prison) may make a person with antagonistic traits more likely to demonstrate those traits as a way of preserving his or her sense of self and as a form of physical self-preservation. However, these characteristics encouraged rule-breaking choices that have put him or her into such an environment. Similarly, unstable environments such as a residence occupied by a loosely cohering group of unemployed drug and alcohol abusers will support if not exaggerate the lack of constraint of someone with disinhibition (and tendencies towards substance misuse).

One further way in which the assessment of personality is 'coloured' is by the circumstances in which the assessment is undertaken. Most forensic assessments take place in the context of some level of coercion (Meloy, 2005). This has the potential to affect significantly the veracity of the information offered face-to-face. This is not a crippling situation, but its existence requires the assessor to implement a degree of creativity in his/her assessments – such as through the triangulation of assessment methods in order to avoid reliance on self-report (see next section) and through the exercise of a high level of interview craft (e.g. Cooke and Logan, 2016).

These and other considerations make the challenge of explaining personality functioning all the more demanding. However, it can be a far less daunting task if the evaluation process is structured by the use of formal assessment methods, which is the subject to which we will now turn.

How can I assess personality functioning in a coherent and systematic way?

A key recommendation is that assessments of personality functioning be triangulated whenever possible. This means that personality is assessed using more than one measure or method of evaluation. Ideally, assessors would endeavour to utilise three or more methods of personality assessment. However, this is a tall order in busy correctional and forensic mental health settings. Two assessment methods should be regarded as a minimum requirement.

In general, assessments of personality may be (a) unstructured and therefore a loose kind of educated guess, (b) broadly structured but undetailed, as would be the case in the application of a screening assessment or a classification system such as the *Diagnostic and Statistical Manual,* 5th Edition (DSM-5 [APA, 2013]) or the *International Classification of Diseases,* 10th Edition (ICD-10 [World Health Organisation, 1992]), or (c) very structured in the form of a detailed examination of traits and characteristics and, to varying degrees depending on the instrument, their association with resultant behaviours.

Unstructured assessments – educated guesses – are to be avoided. They lack validity and reliability and are much more likely to be influenced by salient traits and those most recently observed, or most prominent, in the environment in which the assessment takes place. Co-morbid or co-occurring mental health problems are more likely to obscure personality traits and distract the unstructured assessor from the important task of differentiating personality dysfunction from dysfunction generated by other causes.

In terms of broadly structured assessments, there are a small number of screening assessments available; for example, the *Structured Assessment of Personality: Abbreviated Scale* (SAPAS [Moran, Leese, Lee, Walters, Thornicroft and Mann, 2003]), or the screening questionnaires that accompany the *International Personality Disorder Examination* (IPDE [Loranger, 1999]), or the *Structured Clinical Interview for DSM-5 Disorders* (SCID-5-CV [First, Williams, Karg and Spitzer, 2015]). They are all fairly crude and not true screens in the sense in which the term is used in, for example, the medical field. However, what they offer is a brief or abbreviated assessment of the subject of interest, the results of which can be used to decide whether a more comprehensive assessment should follow.

Diagnostic systems – the DSM-5 and ICD-10, soon to be ICD-11 – may also be used as a framework for loosely arranging information towards a diagnosis of personality disorder. That is, a practitioner may ask questions based on his/her understanding of the diagnostic criteria – more like an impressionistic comparison of client and description. Whilst this is probably how many formal diagnoses are derived, it is only a little better than unstructured assessment and subject to the same sources of bias and distortion. Trained diagnosticians are likely to argue otherwise. However, in the complex field of personality disorder, more rigorous forms of evaluation and inquiry are recommended – and equate far more closely to 'best practice'.

Fully structured assessments of personality are on the whole more reliable and valid than any of the alternatives and are therefore recommended. They are available in five main forms.

1 Self-report questionnaires, of which the most commonly used in forensic settings include the *Millon Clinical Multi-axial Inventory,* 3rd Edition (MCMI-III [Millon and Davis, 1997]), the *Personality Assessment Inventory* (PAI [Morey, 1991]), the *Minnesota Multiphasic Personality Inventory,* 2nd Edition (MMPI-2 [Butcher, Dahlstrom, Graham, Tellegen and Kaemmer, 1989]), and the more recent *Dimensional Assessment of Personality Pathology* (DAPP [Livesley and Jackson, 2007]). Key requirements for use with offender populations are that they

    a take account of literacy levels given that literacy is generally poor in offender populations, and

    b contain sub-scales that measure response styles and, therefore, allow the assessor a means of validating the responses given and thus determining the client's approach to the evaluation.

    Therefore, while the MMPI-2 has several excellent response style indices and is written in plain text, it has 567 items and takes around an hour to complete in one sitting, so is not for those challenged by problems with concentration. However, self-report questionnaires benefit from being quick to administer and reliable. Validity is an issue though because of the potential for respondents to respond falsely, and they are therefore unsuitable for use to diagnose personality disorder (British Psychological Society, 2006).

2 Personality disorder should only be diagnosed on the basis of a combination of (a) interview-generated information – that is, the observations of a trained observer structured via the use of a theoretically underpinned assessment tool – and

(b) evidence from collateral sources. Such assessments are possible through the use of semi-structured clinical interview assessments, e.g. the SCID–5–CV and the IPDE. (The latter remains valid for the assessment of DSM-5 given that the section II disorders remain the same as those in DSM-IV [APA, 2000]). The ICD-10 interview module in the IPDE, the only interview available to assess current ICD-10 personality disorder criteria, is acceptable until the publication of ICD-11, which is expected to be in 2018. Semi-structured clinical interviews work by supporting trained and appropriately experienced evaluators to make expert observer ratings of personality disorder symptoms during the course of an engagement with a client. During this engagement, an evaluator asks questions of the client in order to elicit information directly (e.g. their declared attitudes towards others) and indirectly (e.g. how they describe others in the course of reviewing their work history, how they respond to the evaluator). Through the course of discussion and bearing in mind a range of collateral information, he/she comes to a decision about the exact form of each trait that is subject to scrutiny. The detailed questioning and rating options mean that the outcome of an interview-based assessment is both a diagnosis of personality disorder *and* an evaluation of the traits of disorder as dimensions. Problems can arise if the client refuses to engage with the assessment or he or she withdraws partway through. However, there are options for completing a personality assessment despite non-cooperation.

3   The *Psychopathy Checklist Revised* (PCL-R [Hare, 2003]) is almost a semi-structured interview. This widely known and used measure of a severe disorder of personality – psychopathy – involves an interview of the client (if the client will agree) and a review of file information and then the rating of 20 items thought to be related to the psychopathy construct. If the client cannot be encouraged to engage in the interview, the assessment could be completed on the basis of file information only. However, this option is strongly discouraged. The consequences of identifying psychopathic traits in a client are potentially very negative and lastingly so, and it is definitely best practice to engage a client in such an assessment and to report the results as they relate to the underlying facets of personality, rather than using the diagnosis of 'psychopath'. As with the IPDE and SCID-5-CV, specialist training is essential before the PCL-R can be used.

4   There are two further methods of assessing personality that can be exceptionally useful adjuncts to self-report and/or interview assessments. Personality could be assessed through the application of structured observation tools. There are not many examples of such tools, but a small number do exist. Someone other than the client or the interviewer undertakes the observations – often his or her primary nurse in a forensic mental health setting or his or her personal officer in a correctional setting. This allows a further perspective on the client from an expert observer not directly involved with the ongoing assessment. A good example of a structured observation tool used in forensic or correctional settings is the *Chart of Interpersonal Relations in Closed Living Environments*

(CIRCLE [Blackburn and Renwick, 1996; Glasgow and Blackburn, 2006]). This assessment, completed by two practitioners (nurses or prison officers, depending on the location of the client), evaluates the interpersonal style characteristics featuring on the interpersonal circumplex. Other examples include the *Comprehensive Assessment of Psychopathic Personality – Informant Rating Form* (CAPP-IRF [Cooke and Logan, in press; Cooke, Hart, Logan and Michie, 2012]), and the *Interpersonal Measure of Psychopathy* (IMP [Kosson, Steuerwald, Forth and Kirkhart, 1997]).

5 Also, personality could be assessed in a structured way through the use of projective tests such as the *Rorschach Ink Blots* and the *Thematic Apperception Test*. Their use in forensic settings, however, is very patchy – something of a 'dark art', they are used extensively in North America and Scandinavia and Finland but in a much more limited way in Europe because of concerns about their subjectivity.

Therefore, three broadly different ways exist of assessing personality and its dysfunctional presentations. Interview-based, structured assessments are the most credible way of making diagnoses of personality disorder – approaching a 'gold standard' – especially if used in combination with self-report measures. However, interviews such as the SCID-5-CV and the IPDE are only as good as the skills of the interviewer administering the instrument, which is the reason why interview craft is such a key skill in the assessment of personality disorder (e.g. Cooke and Logan, in press).

Outline of report

When a forensic practitioner has completed the personality assessment of his or her client, the following six aspects should be reported in turn.

1 The practitioner should begin by providing a clear statement about
   a why a personality assessment was requested and from whom,
   b how the assessment was actually carried out and what sources of information and informants were used, and
   c the potential relevance of its findings to ongoing proceedings.
2 The practitioner should state in detail both the limitations of the assessment carried out and the reason why, notwithstanding those limitations, the report's conclusions and recommendations should still be taken seriously and acted upon by the reader.
3 The practitioner should describe the client's response to and engagement with the evaluation process and any relevant observations on the client's interactions with the practitioner or with others during its course.
4 The findings from the application of specific assessment instruments should then be summarised. Be sure to summarise here if there is a need for a more detailed description of the evidence for and against ratings given to the client or a breakdown of item ratings, such as might be the case with a PCL-R

assessment. Try to put these in the appendix of the report so that such details do not distract from the overall findings.

5   Now write your formulation, that is, your narrative statement that is both (a) your understanding of the client's personality presentation, and (b) the relevance of his or her personality presentation to the reason why the evaluation was carried out (see Chapter 4, this volume; and Logan, 2016).

6   Finally, describe a plan for intervention – treatments, supervision strategies, any monitoring recommendations, and if relevant, a victim safety plan – that will be linked directly to the personality formulation and will endeavour to moderate the influence of personality on problem experiences or behaviours.

Client involvement in formulation and intervention planning is strongly recommended (Logan, 2016), especially if the client is likely to disagree with the practitioner's findings. This is because there is the potential for valuable information to be gleaned about insight and motivation to engage from such a collaborative process.

Common difficulties/confusion

There are a number of common difficulties and confusions in the practice of reporting personality dysfunction that are best anticipated and avoided (see also Grisso, 2010). Practitioners should avoid using their favourite personality assessment instrument for every personality assessment they do. Instead, they should use the most appropriate instrument for the task in hand. Choice should be influenced, therefore, by

a   evidence suggesting the validity and reliability of the instrument in the population from which the client is drawn, making it suitable for use with the client,

b   evidence demonstrating the use of the instrument in similar clients, allowing the assessor to draw comparisons between the client and others,

c   the time available to undertake the assessment (interviews take longer to administer than self-report questionnaires but self-report questionnaires produce less information about offending clients than interviews, unless supplemented by other assessment techniques, such as structured observations), and

d   the capacity of the client to engage in an assessment of personality pathology, which might affect the volume of information that can be collected from the client directly as opposed to others.

An evaluation of personality functioning should be independent – of the clinician's own personal viewpoint and that of the service in which they work – and must endeavour to make sense of all observations, including those that oppose the consensus view (Grisso, 2010). Personality assessments are inevitably founded on information – from the client and from collateral sources – that is contradictory at least to some degree. There are likely to be a number of plausible explanations for any given behaviour, and there may be many differing views as to whether the person can be best explained by one diagnosis or another, one formulation or any other. Therefore, although it may be tempting to present only the information that supports the outcome of the assessment, this can lead to confusion if non-reported (opposing) information later comes to light (Griffith, Stankovic and Baranoski, 2010). Instead, all relevant information should be acknowledged and reported with a clear rationale as to why it has been interpreted, scored or weighted as it has.

Finally, if practitioners want to undertake quality assessments of personality, they need to understand

a   personality and its relationship to the disordered form, and
b   the complexity of its assessment both in terms of the application of instruments and interview craft.

They also need to write clear, comprehensible and useful reports. Failure to acquire skills in each of these areas will render assessments and reports of personality functioning little more than useless.

Review task

Think about the assessments that you have carried out or witnessed to date. These could be assessments of any kind – intellectual functioning, risk and so on – not necessarily of personality. Consider the following questions in relation to those assessments:

- How were the assessments introduced to the client and how did the client respond? Was he or she willing to go along with the assessment or not? How was the client encouraged to engage and to stay engaged?
- When you left the room, how did you *feel* – and what kind of adjectives did you use to describe the client to yourself or to your colleagues? Get used to putting into words – formulating – the personality style of your clients, whether these are the direct focus of your attention or not. They will be relevant.
- Think about the interview and assessment methods.
- List what you think was good or positive about the interview and assessment method, and what was less good. What would you have done differently, and why?

Checklist of steps/advice

1   *The assessment of personality functioning is a specialised undertaking.* Practitioners assessing personality functioning should know about the conditions they are trying to detect and understand. In the absence of such knowledge, assessment reports will be at best incomplete and at worst, incorrect. Given the relevance of personality disorder to offending behaviour and to risk assessment

and risk management, incomplete and ill-informed assessment reports should be avoided at all costs.

2   *Select the assessment tools that best suit your needs.* Assessment tools may be differentiated in terms of their perspective (self-report, interview) and focus (personality traits, personality disorder symptoms and diagnosis). Tools validated with one population (e.g. outpatient psychiatric population) may be less informative when used with a different population (e.g. offenders) due to problems such as poor insight and motivation to deceive or misrepresent. In addition, some tools (e.g. self-report questionnaires) are less useful with clients who have co-morbid conditions that produce symptoms similar to those of personality pathology. In order to provide positively useful reports, select assessment tools that have been validated for use in the population of interest, and understand the strengths and weaknesses of the tools selected with that population. Avoid using tools just because they are familiar and favoured.

3   *Honour the hierarchy of assessment.* No characteristic of the client should be identified as a symptom of personality disorder if it can be better accounted for by another mental health problem. In turn, such mental health problems should not be diagnosed if the client's presentation can be better accounted for by organic conditions. Thus, personality disorder assessments should take place only after organic conditions and mental health problems have been assessed and their role in determining behaviour and inner experience understood. In the event that the personality assessor is not able to undertake these evaluations him or herself, they should be requested from others (e.g. a psychiatrist in the case of a possible psychotic disorder), or the personality assessment regarded as provisional until such assessments are completed and their findings examined in relation to the findings of the personality evaluation. Further, in order to attribute behaviours to personality, rather than, for example, an autism spectrum disorder, the practitioner must be aware of the full range of differential diagnoses and have the ability to assess (or have access to appropriate consultation) on whether any warrant further consideration before being discarded. The rationale for undertaking – or not undertaking – further assessment or consultation should also be recorded in reports.

4   *Use multiple personality assessment methods.* Ideally, practitioners should triangulate their personality assessments by including interview and self-report and/ or structured observation evaluations. This deluxe three-way approach is not always possible where, for example, time is limited. However, assessors should endeavour to include more than one assessment format, and in assessments of personality dysfunction, they should not rely on self-report methods alone. The rationale for selecting assessment tools should be a part of any report on personality functioning.

5   *The clinical interviewing skills required to undertake and complete an assessment of personality dysfunction should be regarded as specialist.* Interviews with clients with suspected – or known – personality dysfunction should be planned and

undertaken with consideration by practitioners who understand that they and not their questionnaires or interview schedules are the means by which personality characteristics can be exposed and evaluated. Practitioners who attend to their interview craft give themselves the best opportunity to write helpful and informative reports.

6   *Always take into consideration the client's context.* The developmental origins of any personality pathology detected should be explained in reports, as should be the influence of the person's current circumstances. Thus, a person with a learning disability who has an excessive dependency on others should not be diagnosed with dependent personality disorder unless his/her presentation is extreme and not explicable by his/her disability. And a person in prison who is very paranoid should not be diagnosed with paranoid personality disorder when it is functional for him/her in prison to be suspicious about the intentions of others, unless the paranoia is extreme even for those around him/her.

7   *Tooled personality assessment is a means to an end; the point is to understand the role of personality pathology in problem behaviour.* Assessors should always explain in their reports what their findings mean in relation to the reason for their assessments. That is, if their personality assessments are intended to contribute towards the evaluation of their clients' risks of harming others, then the role of personality pathology should be clearly accounted for. It is not sufficient to offer simply a diagnosis of personality disorder or a description of personality pathology – the underlying mechanism connecting personality to risk needs to be accounted for too.

Further reading

Griffith, E.E., Stankovic, A. and Baranoski, M. (2010). Conceptualising the forensic psychiatry report as performative narrative. *Journal of the American Academy of Psychiatry and the Law Online, 38,* 32–42.

Grisso, T. (2010). Guidance for improving forensic reports: A review of common errors. *Psychiatry Publications and Presentations,* paper 282. Available from http://escholarship .umassmed.edu/psych_pp/282

Meloy, J.R. (2005). The forensic interview. In R.J. Craig (ed.), *Clinical and diagnostic interviewing* (pp. 422–43). Lanham, ML: Jason Aronson Inc.

References

American Psychiatric Association. (2000). *Diagnostic and statistical manual,* 4th ed. text revision. Washington, DC: American Psychiatric Association.

American Psychiatric Association. (2013). *Diagnostic and statistical manual,* 5th ed. Washington, DC: American Psychiatric Association.

Björkenstam, E., Björkenstam, C., Holm, H., Gerdin, B. and Ekselius, L. (2015). Excess cause-specific mortality in inpatient-treated individuals with personality disorder: 25-year nationwide population-based study. *British Journal of Psychiatry, 207,* 1–7.

Blackburn, R. and Glasgow, D. (2006). *Manual for the chart of interpersonal reactions in closed living environments (CIRCLE)*. Unpublished manuscript, University of Liverpool, England.

Blackburn, R. and Renwick, S.J. (1996). Rating scales for measuring the interpersonal circle in forensic psychiatric patients. *Psychological Assessment, 8*, 76–84.

British Psychological Society. (2006). *Understanding personality disorder: A report by the British Psychological Society*. Leicester, UK: British Psychological Society.

Butcher, J.N., Dahlstrom, W.G., Graham, J.R., Tellegen, A. and Kaemmer, B. (1989). *Manual for the restandardized Minnesota multiphasic personality inventory: MMPI-2; An administrative and interpretative guide*. Minneapolis, MN: University of Minnesota Press.

Cooke, D.J. and Hart, S.D. (2004). Personality disorders. In E.C. Johnstone (ed.), *Companion to Psychiatric Studies* (pp. 502–26). Churchill Livingstone.

Cooke, D.J., Hart, S.D., Logan, C. and Michie, C. (2012). Explicating the construct of psychopathy: Development and validation of a conceptual model, the Comprehensive Assessment of Psychopathic Personality (CAPP). *International Journal of Forensic Mental Health, 11*, 242–52.

Cooke, D.J. and Logan, C. (in press). Capturing psychopathic personality: Penetrating the mask of sanity through clinical interview. In C.J. Patrick (ed.), *Handbook of psychopathy*, 2nd ed. New York: Guilford Press.

Douglas, K.S., Hart, S.D., Webster, C.D. and Belfrage, H. (2013). *HCR-20: Assessing risk for violence*, 3rd ed. Vancouver: Mental Health, Law and Policy Institute, Simon Fraser University.

Duggan, C. and Howard, R. (2009). The 'functional link' between personality disorder and violence: A critical appraisal. In P. Sturmey and M. McMurran (eds.), *Personality, personality disorder and violence* (pp. 19–37). Chichester, UK: Wiley Blackwell.

Fazel, S. and Danesh, J. (2002). Serious mental disorder in 23,000 prisoners: A systematic review of 62 surveys. *The Lancet, 359*, 545–50.

First, M.B., Williams, J.B., Karg, R.S. and Spitzer, R.L. (2015). *Structured clinical interview for DSM-5 Disorders (SCID-5-CV), clinician version*. New York: Biometrics Research, New York State Psychiatric Institute.

Gore, W.L. and Widiger, T.A. (2013). The DSM-5 dimensional trait model and five-factor models of general personality. *Journal of Abnormal Psychology, 122*, 816-21.

Hare, R.D. (2003). *The psychopathy checklist-revised*, 2nd ed. Toronto, Canada: MultiHealth Systems.

Hart, S.D. (2001). Forensic issues, in Livesley, W.J. (ed.), *Handbook of personality disorders: Theory, research, and treatment* (pp. 555-69). New York: Guilford Press.

Kosson, D., Steuerwald, B.L., Forth, A.E. and Kirkhart, K. (1997). A new method for assessing the interpersonal behaviour of psychopathic individuals: Preliminary validation studies. *Psychological Assessment, 9*, 89-101.

Livesley, W.J. (2003). *Practical management of personality disorder*. New York: Guilford Press.

Livesley, W.J. and Jackson, D.N. (2007). *Manual for the dimensional assessment of personality problems-basic questionnaire (DAPP-BQ)*. Port Huron, MI: Sigma Assessment Systems.

Logan, C. (2016). Risk formulation: The new frontier in risk assessment and management. In D.R. Laws and W.T. O'Donohue (eds.), *Treatment of sex offenders: Strengths and weaknesses in assessment and intervention*. Cham, Switzerland: Springer.

Loranger, A.W. (1999). *IPDE: International personality disorder examination: DSM-IV and ICD-10 interviews*. Lutz, FL: Psychological Assessment Resources.

Lynam, D.R. (2011). Psychopathy and narcissism. In W.K. Campbell and J.D. Miller (eds.), *The handbook of narcissism and narcissistic personality disorder: Theoretical approaches, empirical findings, and treatments* (272-82). Hoboken, NJ: John Wiley and Sons.

Millon, T. and Davis, R.D. (1997). *Manual for the Millon Clinical Multiaxial Inventory-III (MCMI-III)*. Minneapolis, MN: National Computer Systems.

Moran, P., Leese, M., Lee, T., Walters, P., Thornicroft, G. and Mann, A. (2003). Standardised Assessment of Personality–Abbreviated Scale (SAPAS): Preliminary validation of a brief screen for personality disorder. *British Journal of Psychiatry, 183*, 228-32.

Morey, L.C. (1991). Personality assessment inventory (PAI). Tampa, FL. Psychological Assessment Resources.

Sturmey, P. and McMurran, M. (eds.). (2011). *Forensic case formulation*. Chichester, UK: Wiley Blackwell.

Ten Have, M., De Graaf, R., Van Weeghel, J. and Van Dorsselaer, S. (2014). The association between common mental disorders and violence: To what extent is it influenced by prior victimization, negative life events and low levels of social support. *Psychological Medicine, 14*, 1485-98.

World Health Organisation. (1992). *International classification of diseases,* 10th revision. Geneva, Switzerland: World Health Organisation.

Yu, R., Geddes, J.R. and Fazel, S. (2012). Personality disorders, violence and antisocial behavior: A systematic review and meta-regression analysis. *Journal of Personality Disorders, 26*, 775-92.

7

REPORTING CHANGE

Devon Polaschek

Introduction

Expectations about offender change are part of the backbone of criminal sentencing. Many sentences are given with the hope that they will reform the offender. Yet the measurement and reporting of change has received scant attention. Instead change is assumed from the passing of time, or the completion of interventions. So it should be no surprise that there is no current best practice for reporting change. Change reporting depends on several other key tasks, starting with the competent assessment of change. Good baseline assessments are essential precursors to assessing change, requiring an understanding of the factors that need to change for that person. Most typically the relevant factors are those that underpin the person's *current* level of criminal risk: this is the focus taken here.

Change assessments are usually undertaken for two main purposes: (a) to evaluate the effects of a specific intervention, and (b) to determine whether an offender's current level of risk has reduced or remains above a specific legal threshold. Sometimes these two purposes co-occur: for instance, when a prisoner is appearing to a parole board following a period of prison-based treatment. However, change may also occur during periods when people are not in treatment. Life experiences that lead an offender to deliberately change direction, or simply the course of human development and learning, can lead to both improvements and deterioration on indices related to criminal risk.

People on long sentences or repeatedly appearing before the court for new offences may have one or more previous assessments that can serve as a reference point for determining whether change has occurred. Such determinations are often important for those making major decisions about the offender's life (e.g. parole, type of new sentence). Change reporting often goes hand in hand with recommendations for the next steps in the process of reducing and/or managing risk. However, change assessments also may be useful for determining whether treatment is complete.

This chapter considers change in people in prison, on community sentences or in mental health facilities because of repeated criminal or violent behaviour, where assessment of change is pertinent because of its relationship to criminal risk and thus is most often based on dynamic risk factors. However, other less direct possibilities exist, for example, progress on a clinical condition or mental disorder that has been determined during assessment to partially underpin the behaviour concerned. Sometimes change reports focus on the important area of responsivity (e.g. ability to engage in the change process), or, to put it another way, changes that may be preconditions for risk-related change. Positive changes can often be described in terms of the development of protective factors, and this language should be used if it fits.

Several challenging theoretical issues affect current understanding of change. The most notable is our limited understanding of what dynamic risk factors actually *are* and how they interact with each other (Ward, in press). Similarly problematic is the lack of agreement on what constitutes a good model of change (Day, Bryan, Davey and Casey, 2006). Change measurement does not directly require a clinical formulation (Evans, 2013; see Chapter 4), but we do need to understand *how* dynamic risk factors change in order to produce a meaningful and defensible professional opinion.

There also are challenging practical issues in conducting professionally defensible and scientifically valid risk-related change assessments. In most cases we do not know what a particular amount of change means for future behaviour. The accuracy of change assessments is inevitably evaluated against distal and indirect outcomes (e.g. reconviction). This is a problematic test. It assumes that whatever change has occurred, it will be (a) sufficient to support the non-occurrence of an offence over a long period, and (b) maintained at the current level, or continue to develop in a consistent direction over time. Very few of us achieve these standards with our own attempts at personal change: think of those New Year's resolutions!

Two factors – the importance of recidivism from a policy perspective, and the belief that offenders fake change – contribute to a degree of anxiety or cynicism about whether observed change is 'real' or 'genuine'. This concern is amplified when change assessments do not translate into greater long-term desistance in those who have changed the most. Much of the literature is informed by these concerns and fails to adequately consider that common processes that threaten predictive validity in assessments for non-offenders may be more parsimonious explanations for weak predictive relationships between change and long-term recidivism outcomes (e.g. measurement error, regression to the mean, benign influences on self-reporting of change, backsliding).

Best practice in assessing change

Reporting change requires consideration of the following questions:

- Compared to what?
- Change on what?
- How much?
- Is the change meaningful (i.e. is it a significant reduction or increase; is it likely to translate into changes in criminal behaviour)?

For the first question, it may not be possible to conduct and report a change assessment in a professionally defensible way if the previous assessment was inadequate for this purpose. The current assessor then must decide whether to repeat previous methods or, instead, choose new or additional ones with no baseline data. The quality of historic file information may enable the assessor to make retrospectively an assessment of the change status on the relevant risk factors at the time of the previous assessment, and then document change with reference to current behaviour.

Exactly which of the remaining questions is relevant to a particular reassessment will depend on the referral question. Decision makers commonly make referrals for (re)assessment when they need to know such things as how much progress a long-sentenced offender has made toward release – perhaps a recommended intervention has now been undertaken – or whether a person's current level of risk has reduced from a level that was above a particular legal threshold.

Sources of information on change

Most studies of change have explored treatment or rehabilitation effects, recognising that 'completion or not' for programmes with fixed curricula is an insensitive method of determining change. The most common sources of information about change are offender self-report questionnaires and psychometric tests (see Chapter 1), which require offenders to report on a variety of their own qualities, including beliefs, skills and behaviour. When the chosen assessments map onto validated dynamic risk factor domains (e.g. antisocial personality pattern, antisocial beliefs, anger) changes can be predictive of recidivism, but often they are not (Serin, Lloyd, Helmus, Derkzen and Luong, 2013). Even when they are, there is no simple way to assess the relationship of a particular volume of score change to changes in recidivism likelihood.

Other major sources of information are gathered in structured risk-change tools. Typically, trained assessors or therapists complete these instruments by gathering together information from as wide a range of sources as possible. In custodial environments, residential staff can provide valuable observational data, and family members or close friends, if available, may be useful informants. It is worth bearing in mind that although questionnaires/psychometric tests may intuitively seem like the best way to measure beliefs and other cognitive and emotional variables, externally observable behaviours can provide good indicators of cognitive change or its absence (e.g. how people respond to events around them) and of improvements in emotional regulation.

Offender interviews are important sources of information. For example, an instrument such as the Violence Risk Scale (VRS [Wong and Gordon, 2000]) assumes that apparent changes in behaviour are at least partly due to the conscious efforts of the offender. Investigating whether offenders are aware of the improvements in their behaviour noted by other informants can establish whether that change is under the control of the offender or is more likely due to some change in the environment, an important consideration for generalisation. Similarly, exploring possible examples of 'near misses' or lapses into previous criminogenic behaviour with an offender can lead to a more complete picture of progress.

Clinically significant change

The clinically significant change (CSC) approach is based on the premise that a measure – usually an offender self-report questionnaire – is collecting information on a clinically relevant problem that is linked to offending, and that change is only significant when the person's pre-change score was in a range indicative of clinical-level dysfunction. Its strength is that it determines the statistical significance of change after accounting for measurement error—a substantial problem, especially when often only two measurement points are used. For change to be 'clinically significant', a person's score must move from the 'dysfunctional' range to the range that is indistinguishable from a non-disordered population. However, many tools have not been fully developed and validated psychometrically, nor are there any meaningful 'normal' comparison scores.

Applying this approach to individual self-report psychometric tests can lead to a pattern of inconsistent results that is difficult to interpret (Klepfisz, O'Brien and Daffern, 2014). Furthermore, dynamic risk factors work together in complex ways, meaning that the interactions between them may be as important as individual scores (Monahan et al., 2001). The risk factors that such tools assess often have weak relationships to recidivism, and therefore their predictive power lies in combining them. In addition, self-report is unlikely to be the best way to assess changes in *behaviour*, just as it is of limited benefit in assessing skills (e.g. empathy or intelligence). Its usefulness may be as an adjunct method for accessing information about covert experiences such as thinking and emotional events. The acid test for reducing recidivism is behaviour change, which is probably best measured through observation.

The CSC approach can be used with other forms of measurement, such as dynamic risk assessment instruments (e.g. Olver, Christofferson and Wong, 2015). Olver et al. confirmed the need to control for pre-treatment overall *risk* levels in interpreting treatment change, which the CSC approach does not do. Their results raise significant concerns about whether the CSC approach should be used in clinical settings to report change to decision makers, because differences in subsequent recidivism by offenders in different change categories were largely accounted for by pre-treatment differences in risk levels, rather than the amount of change. Clearly these results require replication, not least because the method used to establish the 'normal' reference scores could be contentious. However, they do suggest that when data are available using tools that are not self-report-based and cover multiple risk domains, other approaches to reporting change represent better practice.

Change on dynamic risk assessment tools

Several scales developed over the last decade contain changeable risk factors, making them suitable for tracking change, including treatment change. They include the LS:CMI (Andrews, Bonta and Wormith, 2004), the Stable-2000 (Hanson, Harris, Scott and Helmus, 2007), the HCR-20^{V3} (Douglas, Hart, Webster and Belfrage, 2013), the SAPROF (de Vogel, de Ruiter, Bouman and de Vries Robbé, 2012), the VRS (Wong and Gordon, 2000) and the DRAOR (Serin, 2015). Some of these scales also contain dynamic 'protective factors', although to date most of these appear to function as reverse-scored risk factors. Many are useful in custodial settings, and most measure change by scoring the instrument in full at each time-point. Some of these scales also include acute items and are designed to monitor change in, for example, offenders on community supervision (e.g. the DRAOR).

The VRS is uniquely designed to measure change in custodial treatment settings. At the first point of measurement, the 6 static and 20 dynamic items are all rated, along with a current stage of change for all dynamic items scored above 1 out of 3, based on Prochaska, DiClemente and Norcross's (1992) stage of change model (see Day et al., 2006). At reassessment, only the current stage of change on those same items is scored. The difference between the two is the amount of overall change in risk. The authors have produced regression lines that enable estimation of the likelihood of general and violent recidivism, given particular scores (Wong and Gordon, 2006).

Other method of assessing change

The other main method is the measurement of treatment response. Here, scales may be used to evaluate whether the client has achieved particular milestones deemed to be important in treatment-related success (e.g. developing victim empathy, understanding of offence cycle, formulation of risk management plan). There is typically no pre-treatment measurement, the measures may not be well-developed psychometrically and often have shown no relationship to recidivism. Consequently, at present this method is not recommended for assessing change that is to be reported to decision makers (see Beggs, 2010).

Analogue behaviour

Change measurement is often done in settings (e.g. custodial environments and residential treatment) that differ importantly from how the offender usually lives. The challenge then is to factor in the contribution of these settings to altered behaviour. For example, for a child-sex offender such environments *may* lack some of the characteristics involved in building up to an offence. Similarly, behaviour that is topographically similar (e.g. prison violence) may not be an analogue to community violence. Offenders themselves are often confident of change without adequately allowing for the influence of absent environmental cues. If a prisoner has not had a sip of alcohol for 10 years while in prison, will it be easy for him to abstain in the community?

A method of assessing change (or lack of it) taking these issues into account is based on the concept of offence-paralleling behaviour (Daffern, Jones and Shine, 2010). It requires the use of information to identify individualised historic sequences of antecedent environmental or social stimuli, cognitions, emotions and problematic behaviour. Knowledge of such sequences can be used to determine whether functionally similar – but potentially topographically different – sequences are still occurring, which may indicate limited progress.

A simpler pair of concepts – Offence Analogue Behaviours ([OABs] idiosyncratic patterns of behaviour indicative of dynamic risk factors) and Offence Reduction Behaviours ([ORBs] behaviours that indicate reducing risk in a controlled environment) – can be useful in indicating whether change related to dynamic risk factors has occurred. Gordon and Wong (2009) developed a VRS companion rating guide to inform the identification of risk-change relevant behaviour within the constraints of custodial settings, and it can readily be used to identify relevant evidence for change (increased ORBs; e.g. use of prosocial skills to negotiate conflict) or lack of it. The use of these approaches helps promote a search for observations both of positive and negative evidence.

Resilience of change and generalisation

Perhaps the biggest challenge for assessors of change is in considering how durable or resilient change will be. With so few studies having evaluated change over more than two time-points, little is known about this issue. When assessing people on indeterminate orders over multiple time-points, systematic evaluation of the environmental context will be needed to understand any apparent improvements or deteriorations.

A recent study using the VRS showed that when prisoners were assessed before and after treatment and then 6 to 12 months later while still in custody, the pattern of change in treatment was not indicative of the pattern of change in the follow-up period. For example, medium-high risk offenders either maintained the change they made in treatment or continued to gain, while the highest risk offenders showed some 'backsliding' after treatment was finished (Yesberg and Polaschek, 2014). One possibility for this divergence is that, on average, these prisoners leave treatment in the 'preparation' stage of change (on the VRS), meaning that new prosocial behaviour is not yet fully consolidated (Polaschek, Yesberg, Bell, Casey and Dickson, 2016).

Best practice in reporting change

The final decision about how to assess and report change must be made on the basis of what the reassessor believes represents the best possible practice under the circumstances. A good general approach is to start with a summary of the results of the previous assessment, against which the reader can then judge subsequent changes. If those assessment data are detailed in a report that is also available to the decision maker, then the new summary may be brief. A good initial assessment will have detailed the areas of dynamic risk that were considered significant enough to warrant remediation, along with recommendations for future intervention or management of the offender.

Regardless of the method of change measurement used, it is important to note the level of assessed risk (and of what) posed by the offender at the time of the previous assessment. If this has not been done in the previous assessment, a static scale could be used retrospectively to establish this information. This practice is important because not only do higher and lower risk offenders often make different amounts of change (Olver et al., 2015), the amount of change may have different implications for a high-risk than for a low-risk offender. Reductions in factors where such changes are linked to lower recidivism will probably have more potential to reduce recidivism likelihood in a high-risk offender, but they may also be less enduring for higher-risk individuals.

There will also be a section detailing important events that have occurred since the last assessment. These may be reviewed against the recommendations for future treatment/management made in the previous report. Has the intended treatment or programme been undertaken? What information is available on how the offender progressed in that intervention? If something did not occur that was recommended, why not? Such events may be important for explaining any changes.

Next comes the report of actual change as you have reassessed it. This section is often preceded by a description of the sources of information, if they were not listed earlier, and the methods and specific tools that were used to conduct the reassessment, along with a justification for why these methods were chosen (e.g. to replicate the previous assessment; to address a specific referral issue). There may be additional pre- and post-measures available since the last assessment (e.g. if the offender has completed a treatment programme).

Methods for reporting change are in part influenced by developing practices in risk communication itself. The preferable approach – not referred to here as the 'best practice approach' because at present more often than not it cannot be done—is to use a well-validated scale and to report progress in terms of non-arbitrary metrics. In recent times, significant progress on reporting sex offender risk has been made with the promotion of several non-arbitrary metrics; these make communication clearer and less prone to misinterpretation than simply describing offenders' risk levels as 'low', 'medium' and 'high' (Hanson, Babchishin and Thornton, 2012; Hanson, Lloyd, Helmus and Thornton, 2012; see Chapter 3, this volume).

Evaluations of how 'risky' a person is, or still is, after treatment requires that the scores on the instrument are benchmarked against recidivism base rates for the relevant local population of offenders. This sort of benchmarking has been reported for some dynamic tools (e.g. VRS [Wong and Gordon, 2006]). Such figures could be used to estimate changes in the likelihood of reconviction before and after treatment. Olver, Christofferson, Grace and Wong (2014) have gone one step farther and calculated estimated recidivism rates for combinations of pre-treatment and change scores. These estimates were compared with actual rates of recidivism and the results suggest that this approach may offer a more accurate and informative way of reporting the effects of change on recidivism, if it is adopted more widely.

However, this approach is not yet generally available (a demonstration of the current rudimentary nature of our science when it comes to the reporting of change). So what to do when it is not? All we can do is report what we can, transparently, and communicate what it means as informatively as possible. Regardless of whether benchmarking data are available, we can still report those issues identified previously as underpinning dynamic risk and the progress, if any, that has been made. It is much more useful to address actual changes in behaviour than to report simply on attendance or engagement in different treatment tasks that were intended to make such changes. We can then identify our best guess about what remains still to be addressed, how further progress might be achieved, indicators to watch out for in order to ascertain that progress has been made and possible challenges to generalisation of change, if these have been detected. This practice leaves it to the decision maker to decide how to use what we have reported.

The opinion section of the report is the most challenging. It is the task of the reassessor to form an opinion about the overall picture of change – including progress on areas targeted for change, along with any changes that occurred apparently spontaneously – and how that picture contributes to the referral question. It is also important to consider sources of change. A change assessment can be invalid when there appears to have been a change for better or worse, but in fact all that has happened is that better information is available about an earlier period. The clinical interpretation or professional opinion of the overall change picture – ideally accompanied by some recommendations for ways to maintain or continue to enhance change – is usually separated clearly from the basis for that opinion. It should be possible for the reader to distinguish the information from the interpretation.

Outline of report

Included here are some sample report sections that illustrate distinct elements in the communication of change-related information. Depending on the audience – which is rarely other forensic psychologists—it will be helpful to include some explanation of the context of the information provided to aid in its interpretation in a manner that will be more valid for decision making. This approach is important for a number of reasons. For example, offenders and decision makers can have unrealistic expectations about what the effects of change may be in both low- and high-risk offenders. Substantial change in a low-risk offender may not appreciably change the anticipated recidivism outcome, which was low in the first place.

More concerningly, a high-risk offender who has made excellent progress may still remain at high risk of recidivism.

Example 1: Reporting results of previous assessment

Mr. A's first parole board assessment was 12 months ago. At that time, he was in the high-medium security area of S prison. The assessing psychologist noted that he was at high risk of future violent offences, and at very high risk of further non-violent offences, based on his scores on the ABCDE tool, which has been well validated with this population. Although superficially cooperative with the assessment process, he indicated that he is unable to undertake any programming, education or work because of his security status. Records showed that status to be a function largely of ongoing drug use infractions; otherwise his behaviour had improved noticeably over the previous 2 years. The psychological assessment suggested he had the following intervention needs which, if addressed, could reduce his current risk levels further: antisocial cognitions, drug and alcohol use, association with criminal peers, emotional regulation and problem-solving deficits. It was recommended that he complete individual drug and alcohol treatment in order to improve his security level. Following completion of this individual treatment, a more intensive cognitive-behavioural group programme was considered necessary, with work parole if progress was sufficient.

Example 2: Reporting change using an actuarial tool and non-arbitrary metrics

For his previous appearance to the board, Mr. C was fully assessed by Dr. R, using the Violence Risk Scale (VRS), along with two static risk assessment tools: the ABCDE and the LMNOP. Scores on the static scale of the VRS and the other two tools agreed that Mr. C was at high risk of further offending of any type, and at medium-high risk of further violent offending and of offending leading to imprisonment. The VRS completed using interview information from Mr. C, file information, and the results of an interview with his older brother, HC, indicated that Mr. C's dynamic risk for violence has reduced in the last 2 years, as evidenced by several significant changes noted by both family members and custodial staff. Most notably, Mr. C's risk factor of criminal peers has significantly reduced since he renounced his gang membership and became more selective in the associations he forms in the prison. He has also been treated for alcohol and drug misuse and has had continually clean alcohol and drug tests for the last 18 months.

The assessment noted several additional areas that if reduced in severity would further reduce his risk for violence. They were safety planning and skills for identifying and managing high-risk situations, and work ethic. Since this assessment, Mr. C, who prior to prison had no significant work history, has worked diligently for over 6 months as the unit cleaner and has reliably attended literacy class where the teacher has noted his efforts to improve both his reading, and especially his writing skills.

Mr. C has also attended six individual sessions with a rehabilitation worker where, despite his literacy issues, he has developed a clearer understanding of the triggers for his offending and is beginning to use these skills in other situations around the unit. Custodial staff consider him to be more reliable, less demanding and more even-tempered than previously and suggest he seems much more mature. Factoring these gains into the previous VRS assessment and comparing Mr. C with norms created using information from previous prisoners with similar characteristics suggests that Mr. C's risk of violence over the next 3 years has reduced from the previous estimate of 45 percent to about 42 percent. Similarly, his estimated likelihood of any reoffending over the next 3 years is reduced from 78 percent to 72 percent. Several changes are recent and additional steps are necessary (e.g. additional work experience, release planning) in order to ascertain that these changes are durable and generalise into more testing situations.

Common difficulties/confusion

A number of difficulties with assessing and reporting change have been noted throughout this chapter. Assessing change is a complex and underdeveloped area of practice that can require a good deal of high-level clinical reasoning. One remaining area of difficulty is the handling of contradictory results. Risk assessments in general often use more than one tool in order to triangulate the overall assessment of the level posed for different types of acts. Change assessments seldom make use of enough tools to run into this sort of difficulty, but when change is calibrated against risk levels, a widening gap can open up between static and dynamic estimates; especially in older offenders who may be past the peak of their offending career, so that the historically-based static tool still remains high while the dynamically-based score may be reducing. Resolving such differences requires an understanding of the most likely source of the discrepancies and an evaluation of the level of confidence placed in the dynamically-based assessment. A good rule in this situation is to always rely more on assessments based on observed behavioural change than on an offender's reports of change, or on apparent changes in insight or other cognitive factors.

Review task

After reading this chapter, think about the sources of information you have available to you when evaluating change in a client. Are there observations from others you could draw on? Are there tools you could use that you need more experience with? How do you think about what to look for when assessing change on dynamic risk factors? How do you decide whether behaviour in the assessment setting will generalise? Do you remember to look for both positive and negative evidence? How do you present your opinion? And do the people who are the main consumers of your reports need more general information or training about the context of your psychological change assessments?

Checklist of steps/advice

To conclude, best practice in evaluating change is to:

1   Make a combined assessment of as many potentially relevant dynamic risk factors as possible;
2   use a wide range of information sources, including offender interview, staff observations and significant others; never rely solely on offender self-report;
3   take into account pre-existing risk levels; a high-risk offender who makes a lot of change is likely still to be higher risk than a lower-risk offender who made no change;
4   not rely on a previous assessment as a benchmark if you judge that it did not meet adequate professional standards; instead make your own best assessment of the actual benchmarks at that time, or refuse to provide a change assessment on the grounds that you cannot adequately determine what to compare current behaviour against;
5   ideally make change measurements across more than two time-points;
6   look both for examples of positive change – often manifested in the development of protective factors – *and* evidence that change has not occurred, or that deterioration is evident; and
7   consider educating consumers of reports/decision makers in the approach taken, to enable them to better interpret report information in context.

Further reading

Evans, I.M. (2013). *How and why people change: Foundations of psychological therapy.* New York: OUP.

Olver, M.E., Christofferson, S.M.B. and Wong, S.C.P. (2015). Evaluation and applications of the clinically significant change method with the Violence Risk Scale-Sexual Offender Version: Implications for risk-change communication. *Behavioral Sciences and the Law, 33,* 92–110.

Serin, R.C., Lloyd, C.D., Helmus, L., Derkzen, D.M. and Luong, D. (2013). Does intra-individual change predict offender recidivism? Searching for the Holy Grail in assessing offender change. *Aggression and Violent Behavior, 18,* 32–53.

References

Andrews, D.A., Bonta, J. and Wormith, J.S. (2004). *The level of service/case management inventory (LS/CMI).* Toronto, Canada: Multi-Health Systems.

Beggs, S. (2010). Within-treatment outcome among sexual offenders: A review. *Aggression and Violent Behavior, 15,* 369–79.

Daffern, M., Jones, L. and Shine, J. (eds.). (2010). *Offence paralleling behaviour: A case formulation approach to offender assessment and intervention.* Chichester, UK: Wiley.

Day, A., Bryan, J., Davey, L. and Casey, S. (2006). The process of change in offender rehabilitation programmes. *Psychology, Crime and Law, 12,* 473–87.

Douglas, K.S., Hart, S.D., Webster, C.D. and Belfrage, H. (2013). *HCR-20^{V3}: Assessing risk for violence – user guide.* Burnaby, Canada: Mental Health, Law, and Policy Institute, Simon Fraser University.

Evans, I.M. (2013). *How and why people change: Foundations of psychological therapy.* New York: OUP.

Gordon, A. and Wong, S.C.P. (2009). *The offence analogue and offence reduction behaviour rating guide.* Unpublished user manual.

Hanson, R.K., Babchishin, K.M. and Thornton, D. (2012). Quantifying the relative risk of sex offenders: Risk ratios for the Static-99R. *Sexual Abuse: A Journal of Research and Treatment, 25*, 482–515.

Hanson, R.K., Harris, A.J.R., Scott, T.L. and Helmus, L. (2007). *Assessing the risk of sexual offenders on community supervision: The dynamic supervision project,* Ottawa, Ontario. Retrieved from www.ps-sp.gc.ca/res/cor/rep.

Hanson, R.K., Lloyd, C.D., Helmus, L. and Thornton, D. (2012). Developing non-arbitrary metrics for risk communication: Percentile ranks for the Static-99/R and Static-2002/R sexual offender risk tools. *International Journal of Forensic Mental Health, 11*, 9–23.

Klepfisz, G., O'Brien, K. and Daffern, M. (2014). Violent offenders' within-treatment change in anger, criminal attitudes, and violence risk: Associations with violent recidivism. *International Journal of Forensic Mental Health, 13*, 348–62.

Monahan, J., Steadman, H.J., Silver, E., Appelbaum, P.S., Robbin, P.C., Mulvey, E.P., Mulvey, E., Roth, L., Grisso, T., and Banks, S. (2001). *Rethinking risk assessment: The MacArthur study of mental disorder and violence.* Oxford, UK: Oxford University Press.

Olver, M.E., Christofferson, S.M.B., Grace, R.C. and Wong, S.C.P. (2014). Incorporating change information into sexual offender risk assessments using the Violence Risk Scale-Sexual Offender Version. *Sexual Abuse: A Journal of Research and Treatment, 26*, 472–99.

Olver, M.E., Christofferson, S.M.B. and Wong, S.C.P. (2015). Evaluation and applications of the clinically significant change method with the Violence Risk Scale-Sexual Offender Version: Implications for risk-change communication. *Behavioral Sciences and the Law, 33*, 92–110.

Polaschek, D.L.L., Yesberg, J.A., Bell, R.K., Casey, A.R. and Dickson, S.R. (2016). Intensive psychological treatment of high-risk violent offenders: Outcomes and pre-release mechanisms. *Psychology, Crime, and Law, 22*, 344–65.

Prochaska, J.O., DiClemente, C.C. and Norcross, J.C. (1992). In search of how people change: Applications to addictive behaviors. *American Psychologist, 47*, 1102–14.

Serin, R.C. (2015). *The dynamic risk assessment for offender re-entry (DRAOR): Pilot implementation Manual.* Ontario, Canada: Carleton University. Unpublished user manual.

Serin, R.C., Lloyd, C.D., Helmus, L., Derkzen, D.M. and Luong, D. (2013). Does intra-individual change predict offender recidivism? Searching for the Holy Grail in assessing offender change. *Aggression and Violent Behavior, 18*, 32–53.

Ward, T. (2016). Dynamic risk factors: Scientific kinds or predictive constructs. *Psychology, Crime and Law, 22*, 2–16.

Wong, S. and Gordon, A. (2000). *Violence Risk Scale.* University of Saskatchewan, Canada.

Wong, S. and Gordon, A. (2006). The validity and reliability of the Violence Risk Scale: A treatment-friendly violence risk assessment tool. *Psychology, Public Policy, and Law, 12*, 279–309.

Yesberg, J.A. and Polaschek, D. L. L. (2014). Using information from the Violence Risk Scale to understand different patterns of treatment response: Implications for the management of intensively treated life-sentenced prisoners. *Journal of Interpersonal Violence, 29*, 2991-3013.

Considerations when reporting on specific client groups

Introduction to Section 2

This section focuses on special populations for whom assessment considerations are not often clear. As discussed throughout, the qualifications for general forensic practice do not necessarily mean expertise with juvenile, female or otherwise vulnerable clients, or clients who abuse within the context of a relationship. Competence in these areas can take years to acquire, and so the chapters in this section are intended as both a starting point and ongoing resource for professionals.

Chapter 8 notes the importance of four principles of forensic assessments with juveniles that are worthy of emphasis:

1   ensure fairness and the protection of the legal rights of the young person.
2   protect the public from youth crime.
3   pay attention to the special needs of youth who have offended, and
4   provide guidance and correction to help youths become responsible members of the community.

Sadly, as the author notes, many legal professionals (e.g. judges and lawyers) are not trained in differentiating between good and poor quality reports, and so it is particularly important that professionals adhere to the rigorous standards laid out throughout this volume.

The author further notes the importance of understanding the youth in terms of their development and positive attributes. Of course, adolescence can be a time of emotional upheaval and so it is vital that assessments consider other areas that might be outside the usual focus of referral questions, such as suicide risk and substance abuse.

Chapter 9 focuses on assessments with females and stresses the importance of risk of harm to others, risk of self-injury and suicide, suitability to be transferred to less secure settings and progress in therapy. The chapter describes three gendered pathways to women's incarceration:

1   childhood victimisation as a precursor to mental illness and substance abuse;
2   women's dysfunctional intimate relationships enabled adult victimisation, reduced self-efficacy and current mental illness and substance abuse; and
3   women's needs in the areas of education, family support and self-efficacy, as well as relationship dysfunction, contributed to employment/financial difficulties and, ultimately, imprisonment.

The chapter next emphasises the importance of key areas to best practices in forensic reports on females. These include considering the pathways to offending in report writing, the importance of gender-sensitive models and theories of offending behaviour and the use of gender-sensitive tools. The chapter also discusses the contribution of approaches such as the Good Lives Model (Yates, Prescott, and Ward, 2010) as well as the importance of engagement issues, especially given the propensity of female clients to experience shame. The replication of earlier life experiences within interactions with professionals can be a serious obstacle to assessment as well as therapy.

Chapter 10 focuses on vulnerable clients and observes that as many as 20 per cent of clients who engage in offending behaviours have intellectual, cognitive or mental health difficulties that would render them 'special needs' in regard to assessment, treatment and risk management. Indeed, programmes often have difficulty in offering services that fully take into consideration the individualised aspects of the clients they serve. This is rarely more apparent than in treating people who are intellectually disabled, severely mentally ill, cognitively limited (due to head injury, age-related cognitive decline or other brain-based difficulties), elderly and other less common presentations that would render clients both vulnerable and hard to serve. The chapter then offers helpful suggestions in conducting assessments and treatment plans in accordance with the principles of risk, need and responsivity.

Chapter 11 focuses on intimate partner violence and abuse. This can be a particularly challenging endeavor for professionals. The author observes that the focus of these assessments should not be solely on physical violence. Other forms of abuse (such as psychological abuse) are important to understanding, formulating and managing risk. Effective risk assessment in the area of intimate partner violence and abuse requires an understanding of a range of risk factors, offence patterns, potential victims (including children/other family members) and relationship dynamics. The hypothesis-testing approach to assessment described in this chapter helps the professional detect and control for biases, such as those caused by a failure to incorporate all information or an uncritical acceptance of previous assessments.

In discussing best practice, the author illustrates how intimate partner violence includes a range of different behaviours, including psychological, sexual, financial or physical abuse. Likewise, it is vital to understand and detect patterns in these behaviours, even as intimate partner violence and abuse can take many forms. The psychological aspects of this abuse can be significant, and professionals should remember that men can be victimised within relationships as well as women. Not surprisingly, there can be many reasons why people who are victimised under these conditions choose not to report their experiences to authorities.

Finally, the chapter concludes with considerations that can be uncomfortable to think about, such as each professional's position on whether violence by men against their female partners is more prevalent, dangerous and frequent than violence by women against men.

Reference

Yates, P.M., Prescott, D.S., and Ward, T. (2010) *Applying the Good Lives and Self-Regulation Models to sex offender treatment: a practical guide for clinicians*. Brandon, VT: Safer Society.

8

REPORTING ON JUVENILE CLIENTS

Clare-Ann Fortune

Introduction

Most Western countries have traditionally had justice systems that are interested in things other than pure punishment in order to divert young people away from criminal life trajectories. This is reflected in youth justice systems that take a child/youth-focused approach (Romaine, Sevin Goldstein, Hunt and DeMatteo, 2011) and are adapted to meet the unique developmental needs of young people. Psychologists have a long-standing involvement in youth justice systems, providing both assessment and intervention services (Hecker and Steinberg, 2002). Reports prepared in relation to youth offer professionals a unique opportunity to broaden their scope beyond topics traditionally covered in reports in order to make a meaningful contribution to both legal and client-oriented outcomes.

There are numerous reasons why a psychologist may prepare a report in relation to a youth, including general information for the court, issues of competence to stand trial or responsibility for their actions, dispositional issues, treatment amenability and recommendations (e.g. see Cruise, 2006; Romaine et al., 2011; Ryba, Cooper and Zapf, 2003). Whatever the issue, it is important to answer the legal question as well as outline the basis for the decision (Christy, Douglas, Otto and Petrila, 2004). Hence, it is important to know the legislation and relevant guidelines and address any legal question in the report, which will vary between jurisdictions. This chapter will cover the general elements of youth-oriented reports as it is well beyond the scope of the current chapter to cover specific jurisdictions.

In general, the purpose of forensic reports is to provide information on 'possible psychopathology, needs, risk of reoffending and possibilities of treatment', as these play an important role in the courts' decisions (Duits, van der Hoorn, Wiznitzer, Wettstein and de Beurs, 2012, p. 440). Poor quality assessments and reports can have implications for youth, their families, victim(s) and the wider community; therefore, it is vital that psychologists undertake high quality assessments and produce high quality reports (Duits et al., 2012).

Young people in youth justice systems present with a wide range of issues; the most frequently identified include: behaviour and/or learning problems at school, alcohol and drug abuse, mental health problems, family dysfunction and violence or physical acting out (Thompson and Webster, 2003). Psychologists in the youth justice domain should therefore consider the broader needs of young people, beyond criminogenic needs, and do so within a developmental and broader systems context (e.g. family, school/work, peers and community; Thomson and Webster, 2003).

In order to achieve their goals, psychologists working with youths should be trained in this area. Adolescence is a period of a range of developmentally normative changes, such as those in the social, cognitive and physical domains that can be impacted by a range of psychosocial influences, including those in the peer, school, family and community domains (Cruise, 2006). Psychologists have an ethical obligation to ensure that we possess the relevant expertise to undertake these assessments, not only in terms of knowledge relevant to legal competencies, if pertinent, but it is also essential psychologists 'have a thorough background in and understanding of normative changes that occur during the adolescent developmental period' (Cruise, 2006, p. 181). Cruise (2006) stated that '[h]aving broad training in general psychiatry and psychology, and speciality training in conducting adult forensic evaluations, does not make one competent to conduct juvenile forensic evaluations' (p. 184). Although there are similarities and consistencies between youth and adults, there are also developmental differences that should be taken into account – e.g. during risk assessment (Borum, 2000). Hecker and Steinberg (2002) noted, therefore, that preparing youth justice reports requires psychologists to have 'specialized knowledge and skill not typically required in more generalist clinical training programs' (p. 305). Psychologists must possess adequate knowledge about adolescent development as well as specific familiarity with theory and research on youth aggression and delinquency, as well as skills in the area of child and adolescent mental health assessment and diagnosis of psychopathology (Cruise, 2006). Such knowledge is essential, otherwise aspects of the youth's functioning that are relevant to the referral question and adequate understanding of the youth's presentation may be overlooked (Hecker and Steinberg, 2002).

Alongside specialist knowledge and the skills necessary to assess the relevant domains (Griffith, Stankovi and Baranoski, 2010), psychologists must report the assessment information in a manner that is accessible to their audiences (Hecker and Steinberg, 2002). Our primary audiences are those outside the profession who do not have the same 'education, language, or professional mission' (Griffith et al., 2010, p. 33). It is not only about recording facts following an assessment but writing reports that allow for the accurate transfer of ideas. Written communication is therefore a core skill for psychologists working in the youth justice arena (Roose et al., 2009), as reports must clearly communicate the youths' circumstances (Hecker and Steinberg, 2002). We should work from a position that is guided by the principles of respect for the person and 'truth-telling' and avoid biased language and ambiguity (Griffith et al., 2010).

Four key principles have been identified to guide professionals working in the youth justice area:

1   Ensure fairness and the protection of the legal rights of the young person,
2   protect the public from youth crime,
3   pay attention to the special needs of youth who have offended, and
4   provide guidance and correction to help youths become responsible members of the community (Thomson and Webster, 2003).

To adhere to these key principles, psychologists must ensure their reports address the individual needs and circumstances of the young person, their risk of further offending and amenability to engaging in treatment that will address their needs and risk factors (Thomson and Webster, 2003). In order to achieve this, the following best practice guidelines are recommended, while recognising report structure and content may vary in response to factors including local jurisdiction, the purpose of the assessment and report and individual clients.

Best practice

It has been claimed that there is 'no empirically validated gold standard [that] yet exists' (Hecker and Steinberg, 2002, p. 306) for those writing youth reports. Thus we must draw on a combination of the limited available research and best practice. While being cognisant there will be a level of variability between reports, there are common aspects about youth reports that are outlined below.

Purpose

An essential aspect of undertaking youth reports is that psychologists are aware of why the report is requested and subsequently make sure that this is addressed in the report (Cruise, 2006); this will also inform the nature of the material included. If the referral question is unclear, psychologists should go back to the referrer to clarify this before commencing the assessment.

Even though the therapeutic potential of psychologists' interactions with youth and their families/caregivers are constrained by the context within which the assessment takes place (i.e. limiting the level of privacy and confidentiality of the assessment), these interactions can also provide an opportunity for therapeutic processes (Goldberg and Dimond, 2005). For example, assisting young people and their families/caregivers/supporters to be willing and open to therapeutic options (Goldberg and Dimond, 2005). It is up to the psychologist to make the most of this, while also being mindful of the limitations imposed by his/her role of providing information to the court.

Style and clarity of report

Psychologists should write comprehensive and detailed reports (Christy et al., 2004) that are well-structured, clear and concisely written, so they are easily understood (Thomson and Webster, 2003). For example, making use of section headings and subheadings helps organise content and assists with the flow of the report (Thomson and Webster, 2003). Other approaches that will assist include ensuring the content is logically and objectively reasoned and flagging any data that is discrepant and/or contrary to other information. Related to this, is avoiding or minimising the use of technical jargon or difficult to understand words (Griffith et al., 2010).

Central to working with children and youth is the emphasis placed on the participation of children/youth and their parents/caregivers (Roose et al., 2009). There are a wide variety of ways that report writers reflect this, including: (1) the choice of words that can influence the report and the messages it conveys (explicitly as well as implicitly) to the reader (Roose et al., 2009); and (2) giving youth, family members and caregivers voice through the use of direct quotes (Griffith et al., 2010; Roose et al., 2009). How we incorporate these things is important, as the narrative we create can humanise the examinee 'without regard for which side of the legal case requested the examination; the psychiatrist [and psychologist] writes to explain a complex life' (Griffith et al., 2010, p. 38). Such an approach goes some way to ameliorating the power differential that exists between youth, their families and the professionals involved.

Information sources

As part of taking a developmentally appropriate approach, psychologists must consider the young person within the context of their broader system – family, school/work, peers and community (Thomson and Webster, 2003). Therefore, it is good practice to use multiple data sources and assessment methods including interviews, instruments, self-report and file review (Christy et al., 2004). Psychologists must then ensure a report is more than just a written record of the information gathered during the assessment process and organise information from various sources into a coherent narrative. Third party/collateral information should be included with statements and claims clearly attributed to their source(s) (Christy et al., 2004; Cruise, 2006; Hecker and Steinberg, 2002; Thomson and Webster, 2003).

In addition to an interview with the young person, it is common to include additional interview sources, while also accessing one or more documents (Thomson and Webster, 2003). Typical information sources include parents, caregivers, legal guardians, teachers, lawyers, probation officers or social workers. Documentation should include a thorough review of the youth's file (Hecker and Steinberg, 2002) and a variety of other documents (Cruise, 2006) typically including:

1   police reports
2   court history

3   predisposition reports and comprehensive social histories prepared by youth justice services
4   documentation in relation to responses to previous terms of probation/supervision
5   history of institutional behaviour
6   previous psychiatric and psychological evaluations
7   medical history
8   summaries of previous treatment and current treatment progress
9   school records such as academic reports, history of suspensions and expulsions, educational assessments and interventions, including their outcomes
10 child protection/welfare records

Content

Effective reports should provide a comprehensive description of the youth's functioning across relevant contexts and domains that help inform decision making and address the appropriate legal issues (Christy et al., 2004; Hecker and Steinberg, 2002). Reports should cover a breadth of areas common to standard clinical assessments as these issues have the capacity to impact treatment responsivity and inform recommendations around disposition and/or treatment targets. These include evaluations of personality, cognitive skills/functioning, aptitude/ability testing, psychosocial functioning (Cruise, 2006; Hecker and Steinberg, 2002; Romaine et al., 2011) and mental status examinations (Christy et al., 2004). Areas that should be covered broadly include: (1) individual factors, (2) family, and (3) resources external to the family but within the community, which are also important to assess in order to determine the nature and quality of community services and treatment options if community placement is an option (Christy et al., 2004; Hecker and Steinberg, 2002). In the youth justice arena there are specific areas that require a psychologist's attention, including clinically relevant behaviours (e.g. violence towards others; Christy et al., 2004) and an increasing expectation that reports will consider issues of risk to others and of reoffending (Christy et al., 2004).

Psychometrics

We should use psychological and forensic assessment tools that are appropriate to the setting, issue(s) and client (Christy et al., 2004) and are pertinent to the assessment issues. They should also be well validated on the appropriate age group (Christy et al., 2004). As very few forensic assessment instruments have been normed on youth (Christy et al., 2004), clinicians may need to use their clinical judgement when making decisions about which instrument to use, if at all. Justification for their use should be given. For youth who may be transferred into the adult system, think about the ongoing assessment and monitoring of their needs as they get older. No matter what tools are used, psychologists must ensure they infer from the psychometric 'only what can be empirically substantiated' (Hecker and Steinberg, 2002, p. 300).

Conclusion/formulation/opinion

In youth reports, the formulation (see Chapter 4) should explain the event of interest (e.g. index offence[s]) within the broader contexts of the youth's life (Griffith, Stankovic and Baranoski, 2010), including highlighting the most pertinent factors from his/her history that have contributed to this across developmental, family, psychosocial and cultural domains (Griffith et al., 2010), mental health and functional capacity (Cruise, 2006). It is important that psychologists clearly outline their decision-making processes and the rationale for their conclusions and subsequent recommendations (Cruise, 2006; Hecker and Steinberg, 2002), for example, clearly describing the relationship between psychopathology and the young person's functional deficits in relation to the required legal abilities (Christy et al., 2004; Hecker and Steinberg, 2002; Ryba et al., 2003).

Recommendations

Recommendations must be relevant to the referral question, should be clear and reasonable and address the key issues, including the offending behaviour, that were identified in the course of the assessment (Christy et al., 2004; Cruise, 2006; Hecker and Steinberg, 2002). Thompson and Webster (2003) found that the average number of recommendations made in psychological forensic reports for youths was four, which is appropriate in light of the complex range of risk factors and needs. Consider multisystemic interventions that address that range of issues with which young people present; specify the treatment type and length, when appropriate, or what is required for the restoration of competence (Christy et al., 2004; Thompson and Webster, 2003). The most frequent recommendations made in youth reports are counseling to address alcohol and drugs problems, family counseling, mental health issues and educational/vocation counselling. Other common recommendations include medical or psychiatric follow-up or further psychological assessment (Thompson and Webster, 2003). Psychologists should also consider issues such as engagement, coordination and monitoring when making their recommendations in order to ensure the young person (and their support system) is motivated to change (Thomson and Webster, 2003).

Outline of report

Youth reports typically have three main parts: I) Introduction, II) Presentation data and III) Discussion/Conclusion (Griffith et al., 2010).

Part I: Introduction

This lays out basic information such as identifying information for the young person (name, age, date of birth), referral agent, referral question and nature of confidentiality as explained to the young person. Interviews typically occur with the young person, family members, youth justice officers, other youth justice staff and also, less frequently, school personnel and other agencies (Thompson and Webster, 2003). Documents accessed typically include existing youth justice reports, but also, though less frequently, psychiatric and psychological reports, youth justice background information and other agency and police information/reports (Thompson and Webster, 2003). Therefore details of the documents reviewed (date, author, organisation/affiliation) and interviews (including name of interviewee, relationship to the youth, date, organisation/affiliation) and psychological tests undertaken should be clearly listed (Griffith et al., 2010; Thompson and Webster, 2003).

Name: Jonathan Smith
Date of Birth: 14 April 2000

Referral: Jonathan Smith was referred by the West County Youth Court due to concerns about his offending behaviour and possible mood issues. The court requested a psychological assessment to determine if he had any current mental health and, if so, how his mental health might relate to his offending.

Interviews:
- *Jonathan Smith was interviewed by Jane Morrow, Clinical Psychologist, on 01 and 06 July 2015*
- *May Smith, Mother, was interviewed by Jane Morrow, Clinical Psychologist, on 01 July 2015*
- *Robert McDonald, Principal of West County High School, was interviewed by telephone on 02 July 2015*

Documents utilised in the preparation of the report:
- *School reports from West County Primary School from 2006-2010*
- *School reports from West County High School from 2012-2015*
- *Previous youth court plans dated 1 February 2014 and 18 October 2014*
- *Psychological report written by Dr. J. Gold, Registered Psychologist, Child and Adolescent Community Mental Health Service dated 12 March 2015*

Psychologists must be clear with young people that our interactions with them as psychologists within the youth justice system do not follow the normal client-practitioner relationship. Be aware of the developmental context of our clients and how this might impact their understanding. The section on confidentiality therefore must outline confidentiality and its limitations as it was explained to the young person, including specifying the steps that were taken not only to inform the young person about the limitations associated with confidentiality but also ensuring they understood it (Cruise, 2006).

Part II: Presentation data

Although the content of this section is similar to normal clinical reports, they are often more complex in forensic settings. Information from multiple sources should be synthesised and data presented in a coherent manner so the report is readable by a non-clinically trained audience. Grouping information under key sections can assist with this, though the exact headings and order of presentation may vary between reports.

There are some areas that are specific, or certainly require psychologists to take a more developmentally appropriate approach for youth reports:

> *Family history*: Family factors can help identify potential issues associated with the onset and maintenance of the youth's antisocial behaviour and explore the level of support that may be available for the youth within the family. A range of topics can be covered in this section, including family functioning, family involvement, parenting style and approach, stability of parental figures, level of monitoring and supervision, quality of relationships (e.g. with parents/caregivers and siblings), psychiatric and criminal histories of family members, loss of significant others and any other family stressors (e.g. parental health difficulties, substance use and/or unemployment).
>
> *Developmental history*: An overview should be included if possible covering topics such as pregnancy, labour and birth, early attachment experiences, information on key milestones during infancy and early childhood including eating solids, sleep patterns, walking and talking, childhood temperament and coping with transitions and separations from their parent/caregiver – for example, when the child started at preschool and school.
>
> *Behavioural history* (including offending): This section may be a separate section or incorporated with the offending section (see below). Many youth justice systems, certainly initially, deal with youth informally, e.g. through cautions and warnings, rather than formally charge them. Thus for youth it may be more appropriate to take a broader view of their behavioural histories and not simply limit it to their official criminal records that may not adequately reflect their behaviour over their developmental spans. This should include the onset of behavioural problems, progression over time, age of first police contact (which may be different from first charge), contact with justice, including youth justice systems, and completion of prior sentences and youth justice plans. Behaviours of interest may include general antisocial behaviour as well as violence and/or sexualised behaviour.
>
> *Social history*: Delinquent peers are an important risk factor for antisocial behaviour in youth and, developmentally, peers are important during adolescence, so consideration of the youth's social skills, their past and current friends and acquaintances, role of peer influence, etc., are important.

There are a number of areas that are similar to those that are included in adult forensic reports and thus are only briefly mentioned here. Some of these sections may be combined with other sections.

Offending/Criminal history (may be combined with the behavioural history section described above): Provides an overview of the current/index offence(s) as well as past offending by the youth. It should include details on the state's and youth's version of events (Griffith et al., 2010).

Educational history: Covers information on such issues as their academic achievement and behaviour problems at school, including suspensions and expulsions and changes in schools. For older youth this section may be expanded to include a discussion of the age they left school and their job training and/or employment history.

Substance use history: Youth generally have quite high levels of substance use so it is important to include a discussion of past and current alcohol and other drug use specifying the type(s) of substance used, age of onset, frequency and duration of use for each substance, change in patterns of use, experiences of intoxication and withdrawal and any treatment that has been sought (Hecker and Steinberg, 2002).

Mental health history: Prior and current mental health, including areas of difficulty and/or diagnosis, duration and frequency of the difficulty, prior involvement with mental health services and course of treatment (medication and/or therapy; Hecker and Steinberg, 2002). Information on mental health history may help guide recommendations around disposition and/or treatment needs (Cruise, 2006).

Risk to self: Information on past and current periods of suicidal ideation, suicidal plans and attempts and self-harm.

Trauma and its related symptomatology may impact on the youth's functioning across multiple domains (Romaine et al., 2011). Consider experiences of child sexual, physical and psychological abuse and neglect, exposure to domestic violence and other significant traumatic events.

Health history: An overview of their medical history, instances of hospitalisation or serious illness and occasions of broken bones or head injuries should be noted.

Other sections on specialised assessment areas can be covered depending on the referral question including: (1) cognitive functioning; (2) personality functioning, including use of standardised measures (Hecker and Steinberg, 2002); and (3) a summary of any assessment around competency issues.

Risk

Risk of reoffending is frequently left out of the youth reports (Thompson and Webster, 2003), but there is an increasing expectation that this should be considered (Christy et al., 2004), as it is relevant to central issues including intervention and level of service (Thomson and Webster, 2003). Risk assessment should be based on theories of youth delinquency and incorporate risk factors that have been identified in the literature as being associated with antisocial behaviour and/or reoffending

(Cruise, 2006). Cruise (2006) recommends that when making statements about risk the report writer also notes the following key issues:

1 Explicitly link risk to the various environments the youth interacts with.
2 Include a plan for the management and intervention which will address the identified risk.
3 Specify the time frame for the risk assessment.
4 Specify when a reassessment of risk level should occur to determine changes in risk and protective factors and review the effectiveness of the intervention(s) implemented.

Psychological testing

This section provides a summary of psychological testing including a description of the psychometric tools used and presentation of results in clear and coherent language. This may be woven in with other sections (e.g. mental health section), but can appear in a separate section.

Part III: Discussion/conclusions

There are different aspects to this part though the most common are:

> *Formulation* – which involves the 'weaving together of information into a structure that is scientifically sound, truthful, respectful to person, and understandable to the law' (Griffith et al., 2010, p. 36) in order to present a coherent formulation, and diagnoses that answer the question raised. This may involve making a clear statement about the psychologists' options on the key issue, such as the legal issue of competency.
> *Diagnosis* – states relevant diagnoses (if not included in the formulation).
> *Recommendations* – which address the risks and needs identified during the assessment and remedy issues of competency if relevant.

Common difficulties/confusion

Too often we see youth reports that do not consider the developmental context of the young person, done by clinicians with inadequate specialised training. Most legal professionals (e.g. judges and lawyers) are not trained in differentiating between good and poor quality reports (Hecker and Steinberg, 2002). Thus we have a professional responsibility to make sure that we are monitoring the quality of psychological reports and ensuring we maintain at least an adequate level of ongoing professional development to keep up-to-date with the current knowledge and best practice in the areas of assessment and reporting for youths.

Clinicians often do a better job of addressing the issue of legal capacities than they do providing information on clinical functioning (Christy et al., 2004) and an adequate developmental context in their reports. Inadequate coverage occurs of the young person's adjustment and functioning, failure to document important aspects of their behaviour or report on aspects of the mental status examination, e.g. covering psychotic symptoms, orientation and mood (Christy et al., 2004). Developmental history should be strongly integrated into youth justice reports; this should occur in the developmental history section but also in other sections, such as behavioural/offending and family history where we are interested in the developmental trajectory of their problematic behaviour, gaining insight into maintaining factors and using information that will inform our formulation and treatment recommendations. Alongside this we see the inclusion of inadequate collateral information (Duit et al., 2012) and failure to identify a variety of sources of information, such as interviews with family members or looking at existing reports (Christy et al., 2004). In order to provide a good understanding of a youth's history, collateral information should be included in the report.

There is also inconsistency in the psychometric assessment instruments used (Christy et al., 2004) and often a lack of a clear rationale for including a specific psychometric measure (Thomson and Webster, 2003). If including psychometric test results, see Chapter 1 for guidance.

Risk information is not always reported. On the flip side, when information about vulnerabilities are reported, there can be a lack of information about a youth's strengths presented alongside them. It is important to remember to include both risk factors and strengths in the report (Thomson and Webster, 2003).

Furthermore, clinicians must be clear about their role and '[k]now the difference between [a] forensic and therapeutic assessment' (Christy et al., 2004, p. 386). When preparing youth justice reports, we are not involved for therapeutic purposes, but are there to provide information to the legal system; our 'client' is often not the young person sitting before us during the assessment but the court or some other party in the justice system (Christy et al., 2004).

Other common difficulties include failure to pay adequate attention to report structure and content, poor grammar, punctuation errors, typographical errors, the use of unclear language and poor reasoning about how conclusions were reached. These can all contribute to undermining the effectiveness of the report (Duits et al., 2012; Griffith et al., 2010; Thomson and Webster, 2003). A range of other issues that often arise include unsubstantiated or subjective expert opinions; consideration of irrelevant data; failure to consider alternative hypotheses; failure to acknowledge limitations of the report or evaluation; and failure to relate psychopathology to the experts' opinions regarding the psycho-legal abilities (Duits et al., 2012). Finally, some reports do not actually address the question that was raised. Psychologists should therefore aim for a report that is carefully considered and well written.

Review task

Too often youth reports provide little or no developmental context or fail to consider the youths' broader functioning and systems (e.g. family). Read the following extract from a hypothetical report:

> ***Offending history*** – *Jonathan is appearing before the youth court on charges of aggravated robbery and assault. He has been previously convicted of theft and driving without license.*

Now think about the issues with this approach. How might it be improved? How descriptive is it? How might it help inform your formulation and treatment recommendations? Does it consider developmental aspects of the youth? What kind of offending trajectory do you think Jonathan might be on – is he likely to be adolescent limited or a chronic/persistent offender? Does this information help inform any risk assessment you might do? The answer is 'no' to most of these questions. How might this be improved? An alternative is suggested below:

> ***Offending history*** – *Jonathan is a 15-year-old who is appearing before the youth court on charges of aggravated robbery and assault. His first contact with the Police occurred at 9 years of age after he and a group of friends were found doing graffiti in a local park. He had regular contact with the Police for a range of incidents between the ages of 10 and 13 years including further instances of graffiti, joyriding and drinking alcohol in a public park. At age 14 years he was first arrested for driving a stolen vehicle while under the influence of alcohol and marijuana. He has had two previous youth justice plans which he has failed to complete. Jonathan was unable to say why he had not completed them although his mother and social worker reported this was because . . .*
>
> ***Behavioural history*** – *Jonathan's mother reported struggling to manage his behaviour since he was a toddler. She reported a range of behaviour problems including tantrums until approximately age 5 years, hitting his siblings since he was a toddler, not doing as he was told. . . . She reported attending various parenting programmes. . . . School reports indicated ongoing difficulties managing his behaviour since Jonathan started school. His current school principle reported ongoing issues managing Jonathan's behaviour including . . . .*

This latter version provides much more detail about the progression of Jonathan's behavioural issues, not just his official record, and indicates a persistent pattern of problematic behaviour throughout Jonathan's development. This developmental approach, which provides further details about his behaviour in a range of contexts, will help inform a psychologist's formulation, treatment planning and assessment of his risk of reoffending.

Checklist of steps/advice

1   Ensure you have adequate knowledge, training and skill in the range of relevant domains, including skills for undertaking clinical assessments with youth, knowledge of youth development and theories of youth delinquency, et cetera.
2   Make sure the report is well written and clearly structured.
3   Include information on the youth's developmental history and ensure this is integrated throughout other sections – e.g. the development of the behavioural difficulties.
4   Check you have sought information from multiple sources and integrated this information into your report, clearly identifying the source(s).
5   Check you addressed the referral question.
6   Finally, proofread your report.

Further reading

Cruise, K.R. (2006). Special issues in juvenile justice. *Applied Psychology in Criminal Justice*, *2*(3), 177–204.

Kruh, I. and Grisso, T. (2009). *Evaluation of juveniles' competence to stand trial.* Oxford, UK: Oxford University Press.

Hecker, T. and Steinberg, L. (2002). Psychological evaluation at juvenile court disposition. *Professional Psychology: Research and Practice*, *33*, 300–6.

Thompson, A. and Webster, M. (2003). *An analysis of psychological forensic reports for juvenile offenders.* CRU Monograph Series – Number 3. New South Wales, Sydney, Australia: Collaborative Research Unit, Department of Juvenile Justice. Unpublished government report. Retrieved from www.juvenile.justice.nsw.gov.au/Documents/Monograph3_2004.pdf.

References

Borum, R. (2000). Assessing violence risk among youth. *Journal of Clinical Psychology*, *56*(10), 1263–88.

Christy, A., Douglas, K.S., Otto, R.K. and Petrila, J. (2004). Juveniles evaluated incompetent to proceed: Characteristics and quality of mental health professionals' evaluations. *Professional Psychology: Research and Practice*, *35*, 380–8.

Cruise, K.R. (2006). Special issues in juvenile justice. *Applied Psychology in Criminal Justice*, *2*(3), 177–204.

Duits, N., van der Hoorn, S., Wiznitzer, M., Wettstein, R.M. and de Beurs, E. (2012). Quality improvement of forensic mental health evaluations and reports of youth in the Netherlands. *International Journal of Law and Psychiatry*, *35*, 440–4.

Goldberg, D. and Dimond, C. (2005). Can adolescent court reports be used to facilitate therapeutic change? *Clinical Child Psychology and Psychiatry*, *10*, 575–85.

Griffith, E.E.H., Stankovi, A. and Baranoski, M. (2010). Conceptualizing the forensic psychiatry report as performative narrative. *Journal of the American Academy of Psychiatry and the Law*, *38*, 32–42.

Hecker, T. and Steinberg, L. (2002). Psychological evaluation at juvenile court disposition. *Professional Psychology: Research and Practice, 33*, 300–6.

Romaine, C.L.R., Sevin Goldstein, N.E., Hunt, E. and DeMatteo, D. (2011). Traumatic experiences and juvenile amenability: The role of trauma in forensic evaluations and judicial decision making. *Child Youth Care Forum, 40*, 363–80.

Roose, R., Mottart, A., Dejonckheere, N., van Nijnatten, C. and De Bie, M., (2009). Participatory social work and report writing. *Child and Family Social Work, 14*, 322–30.

Ryba, N.L., Cooper, V.G. and Zapf, P.A., (2003). Juvenile competence to stand trial evaluations: A survey of current practices and test usage among psychologists. *Professional Psychology: Research and Practice, 34*, 499–507.

Thompson, A. and Webster, M. (2003). *An analysis of psychological forensic reports for juvenile offenders*. CRU Monograph Series – Number 3. New South Wales, Sydney, Australia: Collaborative Research Unit, Department of Juvenile Justice. Unpublished government report. Retrieved from www.juvenile.justice.nsw.gov.au/Documents/Monograph3_2004.pdf.

9

REPORTING ON FEMALE CLIENTS

Susan Cooper and Kelley Blanchette

Introduction

It is vital to understand and report on female clients in a way that is sensitive to gender issues, recognising the elevated rates of historical trauma amongst female offenders. Gender-sensitive approaches to assessment and trauma-informed interventions (Covington, 2014; Grella, 2008; Messina, Grella, Burdon and Prendergast, 2007) should be recognised and the gendered context (or 'pathways') of female offending (Salisbury and Van Voorhis, 2009; Simpson, Yahner and Dugan, 2008) considered.

Over recent years, there has been a greater recognition of gender differences in the pathways to offending and the unique needs of female offenders. In a unique study examining gendered pathways, Salisbury and Van Voorhis (2009) used interview and survey data to assess various gender-responsive needs with an intake cohort of more than 300 female probationers. Three gendered pathways to women's incarceration were identified:

1 childhood victimisation as a precursor to mental illness and substance abuse;
2 women's dysfunctional intimate relationships enabled adult victimisation, reduced self-efficacy and current mental illness and substance abuse; and
3 women's needs in the areas of education, family support and self-efficacy, as well as relationship dysfunction, contributed to employment/financial difficulties and, ultimately, imprisonment.

Prevalence studies lend support to this work, as research indicates that female offenders often have a history of emotional, physical or sexual abuse during childhood (Norman and Barron, 2011). Furthermore, female clients with a history of trauma and abuse often have overlapping problems with mental and physical health, have been victims of crime and engage in self-harming behaviour (Bloom, Owen and Covington, 2003; Corston, 2007; Covington, 2014). Major mental illness has been found to be more prevalent in women than in men (Corston, 2007). These are important considerations when preparing reports on female clients and should serve to guide the content of the report.

Further supporting the notion of gendered pathways into offending, research indicates gender specific motivations underlying criminogenic and offending behaviour. For example, some research suggests that women's patterns of drug abuse are more socially embedded than men's and primarily revolve around interpersonal relationships (Bloom, Owen and Covington, 2003). Other research likewise indicates that male offenders' motivation for maintaining substance abuse is often pleasure and peer pressure, whereas women are more likely to continue using/abusing substances as a coping mechanism (Inciardi, Lockwood and Pottieger, 1993).

Best practice

In this section we will highlight the importance of considering women's pathways into offending, utilising gender sensitive theories of offending behaviour and gender sensitive tools in report writing.

Consideration of pathways to offending in report writing

When reporting it is therefore important to consider a woman's pathway into offending, including the role of trauma. Psychologists and other professionals can be blind to thinking about women's trauma (Chu, 1988), therefore engaging in contra-therapeutic dynamics such as colluding with denial. Focusing only on offending behaviour without considering the traumas and experiences that have led to offending will result in an incomplete case formulation that is not meaningful for the client. However, although consideration of women's past trauma is a critical clinical consideration, it can also be easy to fall into stereotyped views of women as victims, and that is not helpful. Both research evidence and clinical experience of working with justice-involved women support the need to consider the duality of the client as both a victim and a perpetrator. Too much emphasis on the woman's experience of victimisation and denial of her capacity to harm others will impede the psychologist's analysis of the offending behaviour and formulation of a comprehensive risk assessment. Indeed, it is sometimes necessary to 'think the unthinkable' (Motz, 2010) and overcome stereotypes of women (especially mothers) as wholly nurturing carers of others.

Adshead (2011) explained how techniques are frequently used that reduce women's agency and responsibility for violence compared to their male counterparts, and compared to non-offending women. Similarly, Eldridge and Saradjian (2000) suggested that because violence in the form of sexual abuse by women is such a transgression of our expectations of female behaviour, it has been difficult to understand why women behave in this way. If report writers consider, where relevant, women as both perpetrators and victims of abuse, this would lead to the most balanced reports.

Gender sensitive models and theories of offending behaviour

When reporting on female clients, it is important not to rely on models developed for male offenders; rather, report writers should consider models of offending behaviour that are applicable to females. Over recent years there have been developments in typologies and theoretical models of female offending that are gender sensitive. For example, Gannon, Rose and Ward (2008) have developed a Descriptive Model of Female Sexual Offending based on interviews with females imprisoned for sex offences. Unfortunately, the state of research specific to women's offending lags far behind that for men. However, based on the available evidence, it is argued here that integrating gender-informed theories and methodologies into assessment and interventions for females will yield the best results.

Relational theory (Miller, 1986) is a highly salient perspective for incorporation into correctional services for women. Briefly, relational theory suggests that connection to other human beings is necessary for healthy human development in both genders but is particularly important for women. Further, relational theorists note that healthy relationships are characterised by empathy, empowerment and mutuality. It is argued that these criteria promote zest and vitality, empowerment to act, knowledge of self and others, self-worth and a desire for increased connection (Bloom et al., 2003). The emphasis on healthy relationships, connectedness, empowerment and self-worth makes relational theory very compatible with the pathways perspective.

Research provides support for the relevance and influence of a variety of relationships in women's offending behaviour, or their decision to desist from crime. For instance, research shows that women express aggression differently than men (Dittmann, 2003) and use more indirect (relational) aggression such as gossiping, spreading rumours or other ways of damaging a person's sense of self (de Vogel, 2012). Women are more prone than men to be aggressive within the context of a relationship and within the family (Monahan et al, 2001; Motz, 2010), again highlighting gender differences in the experience and expression of aggression and violence.

Studies highlighting gender differences in motivations for committing offences also lend support to relational theory. For instance, in a study including a cross-national sample of 227 women arrested for a sexual offence, approximately half acted with another person (Vandiver, 2006). This raises questions about this group of women's motivations to offend, the extent to which they are influenced by a male offending partner and why they might offend only within the context of a relationship. When thinking about this, however, it is important not to become influenced by stereotyped views of women as passive victims who are coerced by men.

Related to this, Welldon (2012) wrote about malignant bonding where perverse, enmeshed relationships normalise abuse and cruelty, within which women are active in this process, not passive.

Strengths-based approaches, such as those proposed by Van Wormer (2001), suggest that the woman's strengths need to be recognised and integrated into assessments and interventions in corrections. More specifically, when writing treatment plans, outcome reports and risk assessments for women, assessors should consider and leverage the offender's strengths in order to help her heal and reintegrate into the community.

Gillham and Seligman (1999) discussed the origins, benefits and costs of 'negative psychology' and highlighted that prominent psychological theories have often failed to focus on people's capacities to demonstrate resilience and have underestimated the relevance and power of general well-being. Gillham and Seligman argued for the development of a science of 'positive psychology', a psychology capable of providing individuals with knowledge on 'how to build virtues like creativity, hope, future-mindedness, interpersonal skill, moral judgment, forgiveness, humor and courage, and how to enhance happiness and life satisfaction'.

An effective paradigm for conceptualising components of positive psychology is the Good Lives Model for offender rehabilitation. Ward (2002) suggested that typical rehabilitation efforts presuppose the conception of possible 'good lives' for offenders; in turn, the understanding of the necessary internal and external conditions for living such lives are not always implicit. Ward (2002) refers to 'good lives' as methods of living that are beneficial and fulfilling for individuals, arguing that any conception of a possible 'good life' requires an understanding of an offender's capabilities, temperament, interests, skills, values and support networks. Ward argues that a requisite condition for the reduction of offending is the instillation of ways of living that are more fulfilling and coherent. Accordingly, effective re-integration efforts should integrate perspectives that will contribute to the 'good lives' of female offenders.

In one's efforts to understand the contribution of gender-specific variables, gendered pathways, relational theory, positive psychology and other constructs and theories outlined in this chapter, it is critical to recognise that measuring change and outcomes related to these areas is prudent (see Chapter 7). For some, this may require a systematic paradigm shift with acknowledgement that understanding women's crime requires awareness of much more than an understanding of outcomes related to reoffending. Data related to reoffending are treated as the 'gold standard' in outcome research with limited recognition of the impact of interim outcomes.

Hedderman, Palmer and Hollin (2008) provided a framework for measuring change related to gendered pathways; this model recognises the contribution of gender sensitive variables to the crime process. Such a framework may contribute to consistency in measurement, thereby, strengthening related research outcomes both nationally and internationally.

Importantly, until this knowledge base grows, report writers will continue to struggle with carefully distinguishing between: (1) gender-specific needs that directly predict criminal behaviour; (2) those that are in essence precursors to established criminogenic needs but are not criminogenic in and of themselves; and, (3) those that should be treated as responsivity factors. As highlighted by Hollin and Palmer (2006), in dealing with women, we are dealing with 'interacting adverse life events' and need to ensure that assessments do not artificially, or inadvertently, reduce or elevate risk while at the same time avoiding a mistranslation of women-specific needs into criminogenic needs.

Our capacity to move beyond the traditional focus on criminogenic needs and a pure risk reduction framework (e.g. Andrews, Bonta and Hoge, 1990) toward the enhancement of female offenders' well-being will inevitably be facilitated by: (1) the consideration of gendered pathways; (2) the recognition of the critical nature of healthy relationships for women; and (3) the incorporation of strengths-based perspectives and positive psychology. Accounting for all of these components in an integrated model of assessment and intervention for female offenders will optimise case formulation and successful reintegration into the community.

Gender sensitive tools

Just as it is important to draw on gender informed theories and models, it is also important to use gender sensitive tools. Standardised, structured risk assessment tools (see Chapters 3 and 5) have largely been developed using male samples, and some authors argue that it is not appropriate to use standardised tools with women if they have not been developed specifically for women (de Vogel, de Vries Robbé, van Kalmthout and Place, 2012). There is little debate that, as a group, women are less violent than men and that the context of women's violence differs. Therefore, classification systems designed for men might not be appropriate for the female offender population (Blanchette and Brown, 2006; Brennan, 1998; Hardyman and Van Voorhis, 2004; Harer and Langan, 2001; Van Voorhis and Presser, 2001).

More recently there has been a drive to address this with gender sensitive risk assessment tools such as the Female Additional Manual (FAM [de Vogel et al, 2012]). The FAM provides additional guidelines to the HCR-20 for assessing risk for violence in women. Similarly, Van Voorhis and colleagues (2010), in partnership with the National Institute of Corrections (NIC), developed a 'trailer' to the (gender-neutral) Level of Service Inventory-Revised (LSI-R [Andrews and Bonta, 1995]). The gender-responsive trailer incorporates risk factors that are particularly salient to women (e.g. self-esteem, relationship dysfunction, parental stress, housing safety, current mental health factors, victimisation) and has shown superiority over the 'gender neutral' assessment alone.

Even when using female specific tools, it is important to think carefully about the individual client. For example, one of the issues with using structured risk assessment tools with women who perpetrate offences within the family is that recognised risk factors do not always apply in the same way as they do with other groups of offenders. For example, 'failure to comply with treatment' is a recognised risk factor in many tools, yet a woman with Factitious Disorder Imposed on Another, a condition in which a person deliberately produces, feigns or exaggerates physical symptoms in a person in his/her care (often a child), might seemingly comply with treatment. She might perversely thrive on professional contact, attending all appointments offered, but this might actually be indicative of high risk behaviour rather than an indication of a reduction in risk. For such reasons, it is important not to rely on risk assessment tools without careful consideration of the population(s) for which the tool has been developed and validated, and case-specific variables unique to the individual being assessed. With atypical offences or very complex cases, the assessor may choose to abandon the use of structured tools. Rather, clinical judgement and formulation (see Chapter 4) might need to be relied upon when conducting assessments for anomalous cases.

Likewise, when using psychometric tests (see Chapter 1) ensure they have been validated on an appropriate female population. Assessment of 'psychopathy' is commonly used for the evaluation of risk for offender populations (see Chapter 6). However, there has been controversy in terms of how well the construct of psychopathy applies to females. The debate about the PCL-R (Hare, 1991, 2003) highlights the need to think carefully about the appropriateness of tools with female clients, even when they are widely used in forensic practice.

It is important to consider the implications of using diagnostic tools that might stigmatise the client. Female clients can be complex and might appear to meet the criteria for a number and range of diagnoses; to report this might be confusing or of little utility. In such cases, a case formulation approach is recommended (Chapter 4). Likewise, when reporting on the results of psychometric and personality tools using an overall score might be misleading and lack in meaning. For example, an IQ score of 80 might be reflective of very diverse profiles. Wherever possible, psychometric test results should be explained in a clear narrative and considered alongside other information such as interview and observation data (see Chapter 1).

The terms 'high', 'medium' and 'low' risk are commonly used to classify risk of reoffending, but these terms need to be carefully considered in female clients. Some researchers have argued that when assessors use tools developed on males with women offenders, it results in women's over-classification (Bloom, 2000; Hannah-Moffat, 2000; McMahon, 2000; Shaw and Hannah-Moffat, 2000). As noted earlier, it is critical that assessors take into consideration women's social context and pathways into the criminal justice system (Bloom, 2000; Hannah-Moffat, 2000; McMahon, 2000; Shaw and Hannah-Moffat, 2000) when reporting on women's risk.

Outline of report

When preparing reports on female clients it is necessary to understand and formulate the offending behaviour (see Chapter 4). The formulation with female clients should be gender sensitive; relevant issues from the woman's personal history need to be included in the early section of the report. Consideration should be given to the role of trauma (if any) in explaining current difficulties. Experiences of abuse have been linked to an increased risk of committing violent offences in men and women (de Vogel et al., 2012). For example, victimisation is a risk factor for future criminal activity, drug use and relationship difficulties. These, in turn, are directly related to offending. It is important to consider the extent to which any history of trauma or mental health problems are criminogenic (related to offending) for the individual.

When reporting on any client it is important to ensure reports are written to a high standard. The client and other professionals need to understand exactly what is being communicated. To avoid poor quality reports, it is of course important to ensure that the assessor works within her/his area of competence and adheres to psychological theory. Reports should be clear, relevant, informative and defensible. It is helpful to formulate and plan before starting to write the report to ensure the report is well structured. It is essential to explain why the chosen assessment measure(s) has been used in order to justify relevance to the report. The report writer needs to be aware of the limitations of any tests used with female clients and communicate information that makes such limitations clear.

Technical jargon should be avoided unless carefully explained, perhaps in a glossary of terms at the end of the report. Emotive or pejorative terms should also be avoided. Typographical errors can be distracting for the reader and might undermine the report, so it is therefore worthwhile to ask a colleague to proofread the report before it is submitted. A report is more defensible if it includes evidence to support opinions. As a general rule it is recommended that facts are outlined in the body of the report and opinions articulated in the concluding section. The formulation needs to be trauma-informed and reflect the female client's life experiences, including the links between these experiences and subsequent offending behaviour. Indeed, it is important that report writers provide clearly formed conclusions and opinions. If appropriate, treatment options should flow logically from the main body of the report; there should be no surprises in the conclusions and opinions section of the report.

Like the assessments and formulations, treatment recommendations need to be gender sensitive. Offending behaviour programmes for perpetrators are often designed for male offenders and focus on the offender taking responsibility for the offence and empathising with the victim. This can be difficult for female offenders when there are complicated victim/perpetrator issues related to offending. It has been argued that interventions for female offenders should attend to the client's experiences as a survivor of abuse as well as a perpetrator (Stalans, 2009). A recent meta-analytic study showed that, when including only high quality outcome research, gender-informed programmes are more effective than traditional 'gender neutral' programmes for women (Gobeil, Blanchette and Stewart, 2016). The authors suggested that gender-informed programmes might be especially effective at reducing recidivism for those who followed a gendered pathway to crime. Finally, it is recommended that the details from risk assessments, psychometric tests and other tools are placed in an appendix at the end of the report.

It is helpful to ensure reports are written in collaboration with the client and that the report is shared with the client in a timely manner. Of course, collaboration can be difficult in some situations, for example, if the client lacks insight into her offending behaviour or is in denial of the offence. During the feedback process, it is important to be willing to listen to the views of the client. Finally, it is important to think about report disclosure and how this can be achieved in the most helpful way, particularly if the report contains information that is difficult for the client to hear. Examples of good practice include setting aside two or more sessions for report disclosure and amending the report based on information shared during the disclosure process, if appropriate.

Common difficulties/confusion

When conducting assessments and reporting on female clients, it is important to be aware of engagement issues. There might be intense feelings of shame and failure and the interview process can reinforce these feelings and sometimes lead to problematic behaviour, such as self-harm and disengagement. It might be difficult for women to disclose problematic aspects of themselves, so it is essential to spend time to build rapport. Some clients might present as callous and unfeeling, not caring about their victims, but this might reflect a coping mechanism of emotional detachment, rather than a psychopathic callous lack of empathy for others. By developing rapport, it can become possible to break through such defences. However, it should be considered that developing a positive relationship actually might hinder disclosure if this heightens the client's sense of shame about her experiences or behaviour.

Consideration should be given to how the interpersonal relationship with the interviewer might parallel or replicate earlier relationships. For example, a female client with a history of sexual abuse might become overly compliant in the relationship with the report writer and replicate a dynamic from previous unhealthy relationships. A client with a history of manipulating professionals may well try to do the same with the report writer, perhaps minimising any ongoing problems of offending behaviour. It would be important to reflect on the therapeutic relationship and address such issues, if appropriate. It is also important to consider how dynamics in relationships with professionals can influence the level of engagement in the assessment process, and the likely influence of those dynamics on treatment.

It is equally important that the report writer processes his or her own thoughts and feelings about the client and her offending behaviour so this does not impact on the therapeutic relationship. This is particularly significant when the client has committed serious offences that might be viewed as abhorrent, such as offences against a child or other vulnerable person. Ashfield, Brotherston, Eldridge and Elliott (2010) highlighted the importance of a positive therapeutic relationship in order to work effectively with female sex offenders. Relational theory would also suggest that social reinforcers of an interpersonal nature, such as verbal praise and warm therapeutic relationships, may be particularly salient for females.

There might be inconsistencies across reports or interviews, which need to be understood. There can be problems relying on information in the files, as this may be based on the client's previous self-report or unreliable sources such as the client's relatives. It is important to consider the information cited in the report and weigh this accordingly when drawing conclusions and professional opinions.

Review task

When reporting on female clients it is critical to understand the uniqueness of the female forensic population and adhere to gender sensitive models and tools. Consider the tools that you use frequently in your assessments and identify the extent to which the tools are appropriate for use with women in forensic contexts. The RATED resource on the Risk Management Authority, Scotland website (http://rated.rmascotland.gov.uk/) is a good place to start to review risk assessment tools, or if you do not yet use a range of tools and wish to complete this task.

When reviewing each tool, consider the following questions:

1   Was the tool developed on a male or female population?
2   Has the reliability of the tool been tested on female populations? If so, does the tool meet acceptable levels for reliability?
3   Has the validity of the tool been tested on female populations? If so, is the tool valid for use with women?
4   Has the predictive validity of the tool been demonstrated for female populations?
5   How representative are the female populations identified in answering the questions above? Are these populations similar to the females with which you work?

As highlighted in this chapter, this task is likely to have clearly revealed a number of limitations in many tools in respect to demonstrated reliability and validity for females. Hence, it is important that the strengths and limitations of any chosen tools for each individual female client is made clear in each report.

Checklist of steps/advice

1   Reports need to be defensible and grounded in psychological theory; attention should be given to theories and models of female offending behaviour.
2   There must be a consideration of the pathways into offending for female clients. This will provide a context for their current risk and need factors.
3   Psychological tools used for risk appraisals should be selected because they are reliable, valid and applicable to female clients. When there is an absence of appropriate tools, a clinical case formulation approach is recommended.

4 Information needs to be clearly and effectively communicated to the client and other professionals. The report should be logical and well-structured.

5 Within the report, there needs to be a clear explanation of arguments and evidence to support the opinions and conclusions drawn.

6 Reports need to be shared with clients in a sensitive and timely manner.

Further reading

See * items in reference list below.

References

*Adshead, G. (2011). Same but different: Constructions of female violence in forensic mental health. *International Journal of Feminist Approaches to Bioethics, 4*, 41–68.

Andrews, D.A. and Bonta, J. (1995). *Level of service inventory,* revised. North Tonawanda, NY: Multi-Health Systems.

Andrews, D.A., Bonta, J. and Hoge, R.D. (1990). Classification for effective rehabilitation: Rediscovering psychology. *Criminal Justice and Behaviour, 17*, 19–52.

*Ashfield, S., Brotherston, S., Eldridge, H. and Elliott, I. (2010). Working with female sexual offenders: Therapeutic process issues. Cited in Gannon, T.A. and Cortoni, F. (eds.), *Female sexual offenders: Theory, assessment and treatment.* Chichester, UK: John Wiley and Sons.

*Blanchette, K. and Brown, S. L. (2006). *The assessment and treatment of women offenders: An integrated perspective.* Chichester, UK: Wiley.

Bloom, B.E. (2000). Beyond recidivism: Perspectives on evaluation of programs for female offenders in community corrections, in McMahon, M. (ed.), *Assessment to assistance programs for women in community corrections* (pp.107–38). Arlington, VA: American Correctional Association.

Bloom, B., Owen, B. and Covington, S.S. (2003). *Gender-responsive strategies: Research, practice, and guiding principles for women offenders.* Retrieved from www.nicic.gov accessed 1 December 2016.

Brennan, T. (1998). Institutional classification of females: Problems and some proposals for reform, in Zaplin, R.T. (ed.) *Female offenders: Critical perspectives and effective interventions* (pp. 179–204). Gaithersburg, MD: Aspen Publishers.

*Chu, J.A. (1988) Ten traps for therapists in the treatment of trauma survivors. in Adshead, G. and Jacob, C. (2009), *Personality disorder: The definitive reader.* London: Jessica Kingsley Publishers.

*Corston, B. (2007). *The Corston Report.* London: Home Office.

Covington (2014) Creating gender-responsive and trauma-informed services in the justice system. *The Magistrate,* Oct/Nov 2014, 70(5), 2–3. The London: Magistrates' Association.

*de Vogel, V., de Vries Robbé, M., van Kalmthout, W. and Place, C. (2012). *Female additional manual: Additional guidelines to the HCR-20 for assessing risk for violence in women.* Utrecht, Netherlands: Van der Hoeven Stichting.

Dittmann, M. (2003). Anger across the gender divide. *Monitor on Psychology, 34*, 52.

*Eldridge, H.J. and Saradjian, J. (2000). Replacing the function of abusive behaviours for the offender: Remaking relapse prevention in working with women who sexually abuse children, in Laws, D.R., Hudson, S.M. and Ward, T. (eds.), *Remaking relapse prevention with sex offenders: A sourcebook* (pp. 402–26). Thousand Oaks, CA: Sage.

★Gannon, T.A. and Cortoni, F. (eds.). (2010). *Female sexual offenders: Theory, assessment and treatment*. Chichester, UK: John Wiley and Sons.

Gannon, T.A., Rose, M.R. and Ward, T. (2008). A descriptive model of the offence process for female sex offenders. *Sexual Abuse: A Journal of Research and Treatment, 20*, 352–74.

Gillham, J.E. and Seligman, M.E. (1999). Footsteps on the road to a positive psychology. *Behaviour Research and Therapy, 37*(Supplement 1): S163–S173.

★Gobeil, R., Blanchette, K. and Stewart, L. (2016). A meta-analytic review of correctional interventions for women offenders: Gender-informed versus gender-neutral approaches. *Criminal Justice and Behavior, 43(3)*, 301–22.

Grella, C. (2008). From generic to gender-responsive treatment: Changes in social policies, treatment services, and outcomes of women in substance abuse treatment. *Journal of Psychoactive Drugs, 5*, 327–43.

Hannah-Moffat, K. (2000). Re-forming the prison: Re-thinking our ideals. In Hannah-Moffat, K. and Shaw, M. (eds.), *An ideal prison? Critical essays on women's imprisonment in Canada* (pp. 30–40). Halifax, Canada: Fernwood Publishing.

Hardyman, P. and Van Voorhis, P. (2004). *Developing gender-specific classification systems for women offenders*. Washington, DC: U.S. Department of Justice, National Institute of Corrections.

Hare, R.D. (1991). *The Hare psychopathy checklist*, revised. Toronto, Canada: Multi-Health Systems.

Hare, R.D. (2003). The *Hare psychopathy checklist,* revised. 2nd ed. Toronto, Canada: Multi-Health Systems.

Harer, M.D. and Langan, N.P. (2001). Gender differences in predictors of prison violence: Assessing the predictive validity of a risk classification system. *Crime and Delinquency, 47*, 513–36.

Hedderman, C., Palmer, E. and Hollin, C. (2008). *Implementing services for women offenders and those 'at risk' of offending: Action research with together women*. Ministry of Justice Research Series 12/08. Retrieved from www.justice.gov.uk/publications/research.htm accessed 14 September 2010.

Hollin, C.R. and Palmer, E.J. (2006). Criminogenic need and women offenders: A critique of the literature. *Legal and Criminological Psychology, 11*, 179–95.

Inciardi, J., Lockwood, D. and Pottieger, A.E. (1993). *Women and crack-cocaine*. New York: MacMillan.

McMahon, M. (ed.). (2000). *Assessment to assistance: Programs for women in community corrections*. Arlington, VA: American Correctional Association.

Messina, N., Grella, C., Burdon, W. and Prendergast, M. (2007). Childhood adverse events and current traumatic distress: A comparison of men and women drug-dependent prisoners. *Criminal Justice and Behavior, 34*, 1385–1401.

Miller, J.B. (1986). *What do we mean by relationships? Work in progress no. 33*. Wellesley, MA: Stone Center, Working Paper Series.

Monahan, J., Steadman, H.J., Silver, E., Appelbaum, P.S., Robbins, P.C., Mulvey, E.P., Roth, L.H., Grisso, T. and Banks, S. (2001). *Rethinking risk assessment: The MacArthur study of mental disorder and violence*. Oxford, UK: Oxford University Press.

★Motz, A. (2010). *The psychology of female violence: Crimes against the body*. London: Routledge.

Norman, N. and Barron, J. (2011). *Supporting women offenders who have experienced domestic and sexual violence*. Bristol, UK: Women's Aid Federation of England.

Salisbury, E. and Van Voorhis, P. (2009). Gendered pathways: A quantitative investigation of women probationer's paths to incarceration. *Criminal Justice and Behavior, 36*, 541–66.

Shaw, M. and Hannah-Moffat, K. (2000). Gender, diversity and risk assessment in Canadian corrections. *Probation Journal, 47*, 163–73.

Simpson, S.S., Yahner, J.L. and Dugan, L. (2008). Understanding women's pathways to jail: Analyzing the lives of incarcerated women. *The Australian and New Zealand Journal of Criminology, 41,* 84–108.

Stalans, L.J. (2009). Women's offending behavior: Evidence-based review of gender differences and gender responsive programs. *Victims and Offenders, 4,* 405–11.

Vandiver, D.M. (2006). Female sex offenders: A comparison of solo offenders and co-offenders. *Violence and Victims, 21,* 339–54.

Van Voorhis, P.V. and Presser, L. (2001). *Classification of women offenders: A national assessment of current practices.* Washington, DC: U.S. Department of Justice, National Institute of Corrections.

Van Voorhis, P., Wright, A., Salisbury, E., and Bauman, E. (2010) Women's risk factors and their contributions to existing risk/needs assessment: The current status of a gender-responsive supplement. *Criminal Justice and Behavior, 37(3),* 261–88.

★Van Wormer, K. (2001). *Counseling female offenders and victims: A strengths-based approach.* New York: Springer.

Ward, T. (2002). Good lives and the rehabilitation of offenders: Promises and problems. *Aggression and Violent Behavior, 7,* 513–28.

Welldon, E.V. (2012). The malignant bonding, in Adlam, J.A. (ed.), *The therapeutic milieu under fire.* London: Jessica Kingley Press.

10

REPORTING ON VULNERABLE CLIENTS INCLUDING THOSE WITH COGNITIVE IMPAIRMENTS

Robin J. Wilson and Brandie Stevenson

Introduction

Attention to science and a dedication to implementing evidence-based practices over the past 30 or so years has led to both increased public safety and better assessment, treatment and risk management regarding people who get into trouble with the law. Some of these gains were fuelled by heightened public concerns about community safety leading to changes in legislation and risk management procedures, but we should not ignore the key roles played by probation and parole officers and treatment providers. Nonetheless, although foundational research (e.g. Bonta and Andrews, 2016) has provided a road map regarding important principles that must be followed when working with clients who have transgressed social conventions; the aforementioned legislative and risk management aspects have not always stayed true to the recommended path.

Generally, interventions with people who have offended are more likely to succeed when the intensity of the intervention applied is in keeping with the assessed level of risk and the focus of the intervention is on those factors that are scientifically demonstrated to increase the chance of recidivism (i.e. the *risk* and *need* principles of the Bonta and Andrews (2016) Risk-Need-Responsivity framework). Additionally, however, interventions must also attend to the individual nature of the clients to whom they are offered (i.e. the *responsivity* principle). For instance, efforts must be made to instill and maintain motivation to change, attention must be paid to learning abilities and style, and other idiosyncratic aspects of clients that could threaten treatment success must be considered. In a 2009 review of the application of the RNR model to programmes for people who have sexually offended, only 4/23 programmes adhered to all three principles (see Hanson, Bourgon, Helmus and Hodgson, 2009).

It has been our observation that programmes often have difficulty in offering services that fully take into consideration the individualised aspects of the clients they seek to serve. Indeed, nowhere has this been more apparent than in service delivery to people who might be seen as vulnerable – often described in the literature as 'special needs' clients (see Wilson and Prescott, 2014; Wilson, Prescott and Burns, 2014). Operationally, for the purposes of this chapter we will define vulnerable/special needs clients as those who are intellectually disabled, severely mentally ill, cognitively limited (due to head injury, age-related cognitive decline or other brain-based difficulties), elderly, and other less common presentations that would render clients both vulnerable and hard to serve. The aforementioned increase in knowledge and expertise regarding assessment, treatment and risk management has certainly led to the implementation of greater technologies and a better understanding of the dynamics of offending for 'typical', non-disabled clients; however, these advances have been slower in regard to services for those clients we are defining as vulnerable or special needs.

Best practice

Writing risk/needs assessments for vulnerable clients

Psychological assessments, by definition, are likely to be highly specialised documents, replete with lots of jargon and technical language. However, it is critically important to recognise that our clients will often read what we write. For clients with compromised intellectual or language abilities, this means that we should endeavour to make our reports as 'readable' as possible. Of course, reports of this sort will need to provide an evaluation of risk to reoffend or engage in other problematic behaviours, highlight areas to be addressed in treatment and provide recommendations for supervision and risk management related interventions.

Psychological reports are used variously for sentencing, consideration of alternatives to incarceration, community placement decisions, suggestions regarding support requirements and information for supervision/risk management frameworks. As it has often been said, assessment forms the foundation of any subsequent intervention, so it is important to be sure that the necessary data are compiled. Equally important, those data must be used to both increase overall public safety and inform a process that allows for skill-building opportunities, greater personal understanding and, to the greatest extent possible, the development of balanced, self-determined lifestyles for the clients we serve.

Conducting assessments of any sort with clients with special needs can be complicated, requiring careful consideration of multiple factors, such as the client's ability to provide relevant and accurate information, memory, verbal abilities and understanding of past events. Problems in any or all of these factors can affect the quality of the information obtained. Corroboration via information gathered from collateral contacts is often critical in understanding the client's history. These data may come in the form of third party reports, such as prior written reports and verbal information from staff, family members and other supports with information valuable to the overall risk management enterprise. Clients with special needs have often interacted with multiple service providers over the course of their life-time, meaning that accessing all of the pertinent information may be difficult. File reviews should include a full analysis of the client's social history, clinical presenta-tion, problematic behaviours (including inappropriate and criminal conduct), sexu-ality and intimate relationships, and their interaction with mental health assessment and treatment personnel.

It would be our perspective that all assessment reports must start with a clear statement about what it is the report intends to address. Often termed the 'presenting problem', this statement gives the reader a clear image of what it is you intend to address in the report. Following this statement, it is important to give a descrip-tion of the client's presentation during the assessment, so as to assist the reader in understanding how client attributes might impact his/her ability to participate in the assessment, as well as his/her attitude and understanding of the purpose of the assessment. The client's capacity to consent to the assessment must be assessed and documented. If the client does not have the capacity to provide informed consent, as may be the case for many special needs or otherwise vulnerable clients, a substi-tute decision maker's consent to the assessment and the assessment process must be obtained and documented.

Testing and assessment

A range of standardised and clinical tools are used to examine special needs clients in a variety of domains, both in regard to general personal and interpersonal function-ing, as well as specialised assessment of issues and problems related to inappropriate behaviour. The materials referenced below are not intended to be comprehensive with respect to the range of tools available; rather, we will highlight several instru-ments and methods that we have found useful in our work with special needs clients. Of course, not all the assessment tools referred to in this chapter are required and, in keeping with the prescriptions of the RNR model, focus should be based on areas of concern.

Some degree of clinical judgement will need to be employed as to whether the client was open and truthful during the assessment, and evaluators will need to attend to factors that may have impacted the client's ability to fully partic-ipate (e.g. fatigue, limited verbal abilities, attention difficulties, etc.). In forensic evaluations or assessments, there is a greater than average tendency for clients to respond according to the demand characteristics of the process (Orne, 1962) and how they perceive information given might limit their lifestyle options. There are many ways to assess response set tendencies with respect to impression management and self-deceptive enhancement. We have tended to report scores on the Paulhus Deception Scales (PDS – Paulhus, 1998), which provide a measure of the client's potential level of Impression Management (IM) and Self-Deceptive Enhancement (SDE) during the assessment process. Given that few people are 'perfect', high scores on IM suggest that the client is attempting to make him/herself look better than (s)he actually is by either endorsing highly unlikely traits/tendencies (e.g. 'I never swear') or denying all aspects of negative traits/tendencies that most people possess (e.g. 'I sometimes lie if I have to'). High scores on SDE suggest that the client tends to overstate positive qualities while minimising faults in an attempt to increase self-esteem or have others view them as being generally more capable than they actually are (e.g. 'I am a completely rational person').

Mental status exam

It is usually a good idea to conduct a screening of the client's mental state and potential for cognitive impairment during the beginning phase of a clinical interview related to behavioural or mental health services. There are many assessment tools available for such purposes (e.g. Mini-Mental State Exam – MMSE [Folstein, Folstein and McHugh, 1975]), although many clinicians have their own methods to screen for such issues. Typically, it is important to evaluate the client's orientation to time and space, receptive and expressive language capabilities, comprehension, memory and gross indications of psychiatric difficulties. Any difficulties noted during this screening process may provide the first window into the nature of the client's special needs issues, to be explored in greater detail during further evaluation.

A psychological assessment typically provides a summary of the client's social history, including current and past diagnoses, learning history (academic and otherwise) and the client's developmental and behavioural histories. We often find that the semi-structured interview provided in the Level of Service Inventory – Revised (LSI-R; see Andrews and Bonta, 2001, or other tools in the LS series) is a helpful framework. Information pertaining to the client's specific learning needs, developmental stages and any behavioural and learning challenges must be documented and considered as these will figure prominently in the client's ability to succeed in both treatment and supervision. Understanding whether the client was raised by their biological parents or was exposed to various foster care and group home living environments is relevant in understanding the client's supports and experiences, as many clients with special needs will have disproportionately higher experiences of spending time in care facilities. Unfortunately, it is in these settings where they are often subjected to sexual, physical or psychological abuse. Hingsburger (1995; see also Sobsey and Doe, 1991) has reported that as many as 90 per cent of intellectually disabled clients in care will be abused before age 18, and that a significant percentage will suffer ongoing sexual and other abuse into their adulthood. As such, this information can speak to their learning history regarding sexual behaviours, potentially as an explanatory precursor to adolescent and adult reactive sexuality.

Intellectual abilities, activities of daily living (ADLs) and general functioning

Many clients with special needs demonstrate difficulties in regard to intellectual and memory capabilities, either as a consequence of developmental difficulties, acquired brain injuries, mental health processes or age-related cognitive decline. In assessing clients with special needs, it is important to know their current level of functioning, as well as areas of strength and weakness. Some clients may have a current psychological assessment on file in which specialised testing is documented and, in such cases, it may not be necessary to repeat testing. Information obtained from tests in this domain provide a framework for not only understanding the client's perception of their current circumstances (including criminal charges or behavioural consequences) but also their ability to make reasonable decisions. In some situations, testing of this sort may also help in understanding whether the client was capable of engaging in a process of planning and organising regarding offences and other problematic behaviours. These data are useful in distinguishing intent, impulsivity, opportunistic or circumstantial elements, or poor judgement. Information obtained in assessing these domains can also assist with treatment planning and understanding risk from the perspective of the client's ability to incorporate information learned and use it in a meaningful way. In considering the Risk-Need-Responsivity model we referred to above, the client's cognitive abilities – both strengths and weaknesses – should be considered when making treatment and supervision recommendations (see also Marshall, Marshall, Serran, and O'Brien, 2011). Treatment and supports need to not only reflect the client's risk and need but must be provided and organised in a manner to which the client is able to respond.

One of the more common tools used to assess intellectual capacity and memory is the Wechsler Adult Intelligence Scale (WAIS-IV [Wechsler, 2006]; although in some instances, a more comprehensive measure of memory abilities may be required). However, it is important to note that some clients may be too disabled to respond adequately to questions on these measures, necessitating use of tools relying less on verbal abilities (e.g. TONI – Test of Nonverbal Intelligence [Brown, Sherbenou and Johnsen, 2010]). Although the fourth edition of the Diagnostic and Statistical Manual of Mental Disorders (text revision – DSM-IV-TR [American Psychiatric Association, 2000]) differentiated the degree of mental retardation according to IQ ranges, the DSM-5 (APA, 2013) codes current severity of intellectual disability 'defined on the basis of *adaptive functioning and not IQ scores*' (emphasis added), because it is adaptive functioning that determines the 'level of supports' that the individual will require (p. 33).

In regard to general and adaptive functioning, we are fond of the Achenbach system (Adult Behaviour Checklist and Adult Self-Report – ASEBA [Achenbach and Rescorla, 2003]). ASEBA items are designed to identify aspects of a client's functioning and specific problem areas that are potentially relevant to a person's need for help. It should be noted that the ASEBA has not been standardised on clients with intellectual disabilities or other cognitive limitations and, therefore, caution should be exercised in interpreting results. Generally, it is important to consider the extent to which a special needs client is able to understand and complete psychological tests and other measures. Depending on the extent of the client's limitations, it may be unwise to rely on self-report data in the absence of corroboration from other sources (e.g. parents, caregivers, social service workers, etc.). However, notwithstanding this caution, results obtained using this assessment tool highlight clinical areas that may require intervention which, ultimately, may assist practitioners in interpreting client behavioural challenges. For example, a comparison of the client's self-report scores with scores obtained from a support person can reveal the degree of self-awareness the client has into their problems and whether they are more likely to internalise or externalise their difficulties.

An important consideration in completing assessments of special needs clients, beyond highlighting areas of risk or concern, is the degree to which clients will be able to function independently – now or in the future. Activities of daily living include grooming, self-regulation, interpersonal skills, and other routine functions and behaviours in which all people engage in the natural course of life. One tool that has been specifically designed for clients with intellectual disabilities is the Adaptive Behaviour Rating Scale (ABAS-III [Harrison and Oakland, 2015]). This tool is intended to provide a diagnostic assessment of clients who present with difficulties in the sort of daily adaptive skills necessary to function effectively, given the typical personal and environmental demands placed on clients of the same age. Typically a support person or someone familiar with the client would complete this scale. There is a self-report option, which we have sometimes used with higher functioning clients, but in order to minimise issues of impression management, we tend to rely on ratings from a primary support person.

Many of the tools noted above provide some information regarding emotion regulation; however, some special needs clients will require more precision in assessing potential problem areas. There are a number of tools that may be used to assess such domains, including personality inventories (e.g. Personality Assessment Inventory – PAI [Morey, 1991]), and shorter, more targeted scales, such as the Beck Depression, Anxiety, and Helplessness Scales (see Beck and Steer, 1993; Dozois and Covin, 2004). These latter instruments are self-report questionnaires that provide helpful screening data as to whether further, more comprehensive evaluation might be required. As these scales have not been specifically validated for clients with all of the special needs we are highlighting in this chapter, some caution should be exercised in interpreting results. For special needs clients with histories of engagement in sexual and other violence, it may also be necessary to examine the degree to which strong emotions (e.g. anger; see Spielberger, 1999) may have played a role in their problematic conduct. For special needs clients – who often have low frustration tolerances – better understanding of the experience and expression of anger may be critical to ensuring programme success.

Education and employment history, recreation and leisure

In this section of the report, it is important to document the client's educational experience, including reference to any suspensions and expulsions, as well as the type of educational programme (e.g. special education) and highest level of completion. Employment history speaks to the client's skills and abilities regarding maintaining employment, respecting levels of authority, and following instruction. This information can also be helpful in determining client competencies in employment-related skills, as well as limits to the client's capacities, so as to assist in setting realistic goals.

The client's participation in structured and non-structured activities outside of employment also provides helpful information as to his ability to join a community, engage in meaningful activities and explore opportunities to meet and make friends. Lack of participation in recreational activities or isolation from his/her community can suggest a lack of connectedness and meaning in his/her life, which may also be important in assessing risk and protective factors. Current treatment methods for people who engage in problematic behaviour focuses on self-regulation and the pursuit of balanced, self-determined lifestyles. Accordingly, what clients do in their spare time, or when they have are not involved in structured activities, is an important consideration.

Evaluation of sexuality and intimate relationships

It is often important to obtain relevant information regarding the client's sexuality, including sexual experiences (abusive and non-abusive), onset and course of puberty, sex education (i.e. where and what did the client learn about sexuality and from whom) and attitudes concerning sex and intimacy. In comparison to their non-disabled or neurotypical peers, clients with special needs are often less likely to have been married or to have experienced intimate relationships. To the extent that some clients may have had such opportunities, it is important to document who the relationship was with, how long it lasted, whether the relationship was healthy or unhealthy and the degree to which physical intimacy was a component.

Because clients with special needs will often have had limited opportunities for sexual and relationship intimacy as a consequence of being in care facilities or living with parents well into adulthood, it may be necessary to explore how they think about sex and what they know about it. This limited knowledge base may manifest as ignorance, prudishness or some mix of squeamishness or bashfulness. Some of this is due to a lack of education, but it is also likely that influences from others also play a role (including an unfortunately pervasive belief that sex should not occur in special needs populations). Regardless of the origins of these difficulties, there is little doubt that many of our clients yearn for the sort of emotional and physical closeness that they observe in others without disabilities or limitations. Before special needs clients can safely negotiate such behaviours or relationships, it is often important to assess the degree to which they can give and receive consent for sexual activities. The Verbal Informed Sexual Consent Assessment Tool (VISCAT [YAI National Institute for People with Disabilities, available at www.yai.org]) was designed by the Young Adult Institute and has been recognised by Canadian and American courts as a valid assessment of consent. Although the VISCAT is not a standardised assessment tool, it provides a useful framework to determine a client's knowledge and understanding in five key areas: (1) sexual choices, sexual intercourse and whether they understand they have a choice in whether to engage in sexualised behaviour or not; (2) pregnancy, pregnancy prevention and sexually transmitted infections; (3) public and private behaviour and boundaries around sexual behaviours; (4) sexual behaviours that are against the law and potential consequences; and (5) abuse, sexual exploitation and their ability to formulate a safe response to various situations. Overall, the VISCAT provides important information as to whether clients can make responsible decisions concerning sexual activity, but it also assists evaluators in understanding the degree to which the client fully understood and appreciated that their behaviours were offensive or whether their behaviours represent a lack of understanding and appreciation for consent rules.

Evaluating inappropriate and criminal behaviour and the risk of future incidents

Evaluating special needs clients requires a thorough overview of all problematic behaviours, including any criminal inquiries and/or charges that may have resulted. This review must include the client's behavioural history, triggers or precipitating events, and a functional analysis of problem behaviours. Indeed, it is sometimes helpful to chart the frequency and persistence of inappropriate behaviours as a means to better understand patterns or linkages to precipitating events or conditions. Understanding the function of the problematic behaviour assists in understanding what need the behaviour served.

When evaluating special needs persons who have engaged in socially inappropriate behaviours, it is important to make a distinction between that conduct which may be problematic versus that which would be considered criminal. Whatever responses were made to those behaviours should be noted and considered when developing hypotheses regarding antisocial propensities and intervention strategies; however, evaluators may wish to consider that many clients with special needs are often not charged or convicted due to the courts' reluctance to issue sanctions to people with such presentations. Consequently, evaluators may need to look for other 'sanctions' or responses to inappropriate conduct that would be considered relevant in assessing risk for future similar behaviours.

The influence of alcohol and drug abuse on behaviour is well documented in the forensic clinical literature. Although some special needs clients may reside in facilities or other accommodations where access to such disinhibiting agents is less likely, it is very important to consider the effects of alcohol and drugs on problem-solving abilities in clients who likely already experience considerable difficulties in this domain. There are a number of useful screening tools that may be employed in evaluating the degree to which alcohol (Michigan Alcohol Screening Test – MAST [Selzer, 1971]) or drug abuse (Drug Abuse Screening Test – DAST [Skinner, 1982]) may have played a role in client misconduct or other problems.

Specialised risk assessment procedures

Formal risk assessment for clients with special needs is an area of emerging understanding. That is, there is much research left to be completed in predicting future criminal or socially inappropriate behavior in this client group. As such, it is important to note that caveats must be made. Primarily, many of the tools used to predict risk were composed and standardised with a non-special needs population in mind. Although some research has been conducted to explore the utility of these tools with persons outside of the standardisation sample, such studies are far from comprehensive. Accordingly, readers are encouraged to exercise caution in interpreting risk assessment information.

The past 15–20 years has been witness to consider innovation and refinement with respect to the methods we use to assess risk for future engagement in problematic and criminal conduct. Whereas risk assessment processes were once quite subjective and reliant on clinical judgement (see Monahan, 1981), most seasoned evaluators now anchor their judgements using actuarial risk assessment instruments (ARAIs) augmented by measures of dynamic risk potential (see Frize, undated; Hanson, Harris, Scott and Helmus, 2007). One of the more widely used ARAIs for assessing risk of reoffending is the LSI-R (see Andrews and Bonta, 2001); however, while this tool appears reasonable for use with special needs clients, there has been little research completed to specifically address validity with these populations.

Although research clearly demonstrates the critical utility of ARAIs in assessing risk for known offenders (Quinsey, Harris, Rice and Cormier, 2005), a comprehensive evaluation of risk potential also requires examination of the client's current circumstances and presentation. Several measures of risk according to dynamic predictors are available; however, while the normative samples for many of these instruments will have included subgroups of special needs offenders, most were not specifically designed for use with special needs offenders (NB: the Static-99 appears to be valid for clients with intellectual disabilities – see Hanson, Sheahan and VanZuylen, 2013). The Assessment of Risk and Manageability with Intellectually Disabled Individuals who Offend Generally (ARMIDILO-G [Frize, undated] – an adaptation of the ARMIDILO-S for sexual offenders – see Boer, Haaven et al., 2012) is a measure of dynamic risk potential designed to be used in conjunction with a static factor ARAI. The ARMIDILO-G is based on structured professional judgement and considers stable and acute dynamic risk factors, separated into client and environmental domains. All aspects of the client's dynamic risk potential are then assessed as to whether they are exacerbating or mitigating (i.e. risk vs. protective factors). Combining ratings on ARMIDILO-G factors with scores on a static ARAI ultimately gives a comprehensive rating of risk. Of cautionary note, it is important that the ARMIDILO-G not be used alone in assessing risk, as would be true of any risk assessment tool.

Final steps: summary and recommendations

An effective risk management plan must adhere to the general principles of effective correctional interventions: (1) intensity of treatment/management/supervision must be in line with level of risk; (2) criminogenic needs must be specifically targeted; and (3) treatment/interventions must be offered in a manner that is sensitive to the personal characteristics and abilities of the offender.

Using data gathered regarding a client's presenting issues, risk and protective factors, and needs *vis-à-vis* treatment and supervision, it will be important to chart where the client has been, where he/she is now, and where he/she (and we) hopes to be in the future. In this regard, we are particularly fond of Jim Haaven's (2006) 'old me/new me' framework. Confirmation of diagnoses, clinical concerns and ratings with respect to risk to reoffend should be offered with clear recommendations, which should not only include risk management strategies for levels of supervision and access to the community but also concern whatever treatment recommendations flow from the assessment findings. Recommendations include directives specific to a particular client's risk and needs profile and may include any combination of the following not-necessarily-comprehensive listing:

- housing options, with differential levels of structure and supervision able to reinforce healthy boundaries and expectations;
- socials skills and relationship skills training;
- education regarding sexuality, consent and responsible sexual decision making;
- treatment (group or otherwise);
- programming focusing on emotions management and regulation;
- individual counseling for client-specific issues (e.g. developmental abuse, general psychotherapy);
- behavioural programming to assist in modifying maladaptive behaviours.

These are only a few recommendations, and depending on the assessment, there may be a number of other clinical areas requiring intervention.

Closing remarks

In this chapter, we have provided information regarding the assessment of clients with intellectual disabilities and other cognitive limitations, mental health issues and other presentations leading to vulnerability – collectively described as special needs offenders. We have emphasised throughout that this client population demonstrates complex needs, leading to difficulties in accurately assessing risk and ensuring optimal responsivity in treatment and supervision. As such, comprehensive, multidisciplinary and flexible are key descriptors of any assessment protocol for special needs clients. To that end, we have suggested a variety of processes and assessment tools that readers might find helpful in their own practice. Of course, there may be times when individual practitioners will need to explore their own creativity in devising evaluation and intervention schemes, but that is the nature of innovation and it is what has driven our field to seek evidence-based methods and best practices over the past 30 years. Working together, we can balance the needs of the community to feel safe while ensuring that clients have opportunities to learn from their mistakes and reclaim their lives. We end with this quote from Judge Trueman (cited in Chartrand and Forbes-Chilibeck, 2003):

> *The cognitively challenged are before our courts in unknown numbers. We prosecute them again and again and again. We sentence them again and again and again. We imprison them again and again and again. They commit crimes again and again and again. We wonder why they do not change. The wonder of it all is that we do not change.*

Review task

We have frequently referred to the RNR Model (Bonta and Andrews, 2016) throughout this chapter as being important in developing best practices in both assessment and intervention. With vulnerable/special needs clients, likely that most important aspect is responsivity – in this instance, making sure that the processes fit the clientele. What personal and environmental factors will you likely have to consider in completing a comprehensive assessment of a special needs client?

Checklist of steps/advice

1 Establish the purpose of the evaluation. What is the presenting problem?
2 What aspects of the client's presentation are likely to impede your evaluation process and how might you need to adapt that process?
3 Ensure you have the necessary consents. Keep in mind that many vulnerable clients have substitute decision makers.
4 Pick your tools and schedule your evaluation.
5 Be non-adversarial and remember to speak clearly without too much use of jargon, etc.
6 Be comprehensive and consider multiple possibilities – especially regarding functional behavioural assessment (i.e. there may be various reasons why the client engaged in the behaviour – what was (s)he trying to accomplish?).
7 Write a report that will be understandable to both experts and clients/family.

Further reading

Please review the references list below. Those materials marked with an * may provide particularly good assistance in understanding this client group.

References

Achenbach, T. and Rescorla, L. (2003). *Manual for the ASEBA adult forms and profiles: An integrated system of multi-informant assessment.* Washington, D.C.: Library of Congress.

American Psychiatric Association. (2000). *Diagnostic and statistical manual of mental disorders,* 4th ed., text revision. Washington, DC: American Psychiatric Association.

American Psychiatric Association. (2013). *Diagnostic and statistical manual of mental disorders,* 5th ed. Washington, DC: American Psychiatric Association.

Andrews, D. and Bonta, J. (2001). *The level of service inventory,* revised. Toronto, Canada: Multi-Health Systems.

Beck, A. and Steer, R. (1993). *Beck anxiety inventory: Manual.* San Antonio, TX: Harcourt Brace and Company.

Boer, D.P., Haaven, J.L., Lambick, F., Lindsay, W.R., McVilly, K., Sakdalan, J. and Frize, M. (2012). *ARMIDILO-S Manual: Web Version 1.0.* Retrieved at www.armidilo.net

★Bonta, J. and Andrews, D. (2016). *The psychology of criminal conduct,* 6th ed. Cincinnati, OH: Anderson.

Brown, L., Sherbenou, R.J. and Johnsen, S.K. (2010). *Test of nonverbal intelligence (TONI-4),* 4th ed. San Antonio, TX: Pearson/PsychCorp.

Chartrand, L.N. and Forbes-Chilibeck, E.M. (2003). The sentencing of offenders with fetal alcohol syndrome. *Health Law Journal, 11,* 35–70.

Dozois, D.J.A. and Covin, R. (2004). The Beck Depression Inventory-II (BDI-II), Beck Hopelessness Scale (BHS) and Beck Scale for Suicide Ideation (BSS). In M.J. Hilsenroth and D.L. Segal (eds.), *Comprehensive handbook of psychological assessment,* Vol. 2: *Personality assessment* (pp. 50–69). Hoboken, NJ: John Wiley and Sons.

Folstein, M., Folstein, S.E. and McHugh, P.R. (1975). 'Mini-Mental State', a practical method for grading the cognitive state of patients for the clinician. *Journal of Psychiatric Research, 12,* 189–98.

★Frize, M. (undated). Assessing short term risk of reoffending for intellectually disabled offenders: The predictive and ecological validity of the ARMIDILO-G. Powerpoint presentation retrieved from www.psychdd.com.au/wp-content/uploads/wordpress/ARMIDILO.pdf (accessed 29 July 2016).

Haaven, J. (2006). Suggested treatment outline using the Old Me/New Me Model, in G. Blasingame (ed.), *Practical treatment strategies for forensic clients with severe and sexual behavior problems among persons with developmental disabilities.* Oklahoma City, OK: Wood 'N' Barnes/Safer Society Press.

Hanson, R.K., Bourgon, G., Helmus, L. and Hodgson, S. (2009). The principles of effective correctional treatment also apply to sexual offenders: A meta-analysis. *Criminal Justice and Behavior, 36,* 865–91.

Hanson, R.K., Harris, A.J.R., Scott, T.L. and Helmus, L. (2007). *Assessing the risk of sex offenders on community supervision: The dynamic supervision project* (User Report 2007-05). Ottawa, Canada: Public Safety Canada.

Hanson, R.K., Sheahan, C.L. and VanZuylen, H. (2013). Static-99 and RRASOR predict recidivism among developmentally delayed sexual offenders: A cumulative meta-analysis. *Sexual Offender Treatment, 8*(1).

Harrison, P. and Oakland, T. (2015). *ABAS-3 adaptive behavior assessment system,* 3rd ed. Torrance, CA: Western Psychological Services.

★Hingsburger, D. (1995). *Just say know! Understanding and reducing the risk of sexual victimization of people with developmental disabilities.* Angus, Canada: Diverse-City Press.

Marshall, W.L., Marshall, L.E., Serran, G.A. and O'Brien, M.D. (2011). *Rehabilitating sexual offenders: A strength-based approach*. Washington, DC: American Psychological Association.

*Monahan, J. (1981). *Predicting violent behavior: An assessment of clinical techniques*. Thousand Oaks, CA: Sage.

Morey, L. (1991). *The personality assessment inventory: Professional manual*. Lutz, FL: Psychological Assessment Resources, Inc.

Orne, M. (1962). On the social psychology of the psychological experiment: With particular reference to demand characteristics and their implications. *American Psychologist, 17,* 776–83.

Paulhus, D. (1998). *Paulhus Deception Scales (PDS): The balanced inventory of desirable responding – 7*. Toronto, Canada: Multi-Health Systems.

*Quinsey, V.L., Harris, G.T., Rice, M.E. and Cormier, C.A. (2005). *Violent offenders: Appraising and managing risk*, 2nd ed. Washington, DC: American Psychological Association.

Selzer, M.L. (1971). The Michigan Alcoholism Screening Test (MAST): The quest for a new diagnostic instrument. *American Journal of Psychiatry, 3,* 176–81.

Skinner, H.A. (1982). The drug abuse screening test. *Addictive Behavior, 7,* 363–71.

Sobsey, R. and Doe, T. (1991). Patterns of sexual abuse and assault. *Sexuality and Disability, 9,* 243–59.

Spielberger, C. (1999). *STAXI-2: State-Trait Anger Expression Inventory-2*. Lutz, FL: Psychological Assessment Resources.

Wechsler, D. (2006). *Wechsler Adult Intelligence Scale*. 4th ed. Pearson.

Wilson, R.J. and Prescott, D.S. (2014). Understanding and responding to persons with special needs who have sexually offended, in K. McCartan (ed.), *Sexual offending: Perceptions, risks and responses*. Basingstoke, UK: Palgrave-MacMillan.

Wilson, R.J., Prescott, D.S. and Burns, M. (2014). People with special needs and sexual behaviour problems: Balancing community and client interests while ensuring effective risk management, in K. McCartan and H. Kemshall (ed., special issue). Sex offender (re)integration into the community: Realities and challenges, *Journal of Sexual Aggression, 21,* 86–99.

YAI National Institute for People with Disabilities. The tool for assessing informed sexual consent through an evaluation of responsible sexual behavior. Retrieved from www.yai.org.

11

REPORTING ON RELATIONSHIPS

Wendy Morgan and Erica Bowen

Introduction

Intimate partner violence and abuse (IPVA) causes significant psychological, physical and financial damage to those affected both during and after the relationship. Risk of harm (including lethal abuse) substantially increases during separation and divorce (Kelly and Johnson, 2008). Much abuse occurs in the presence of children, with those below the age of 6 at greater risk of exposure (Fantuzzo and Fusco, 2007). In addition to the effects of direct abuse, children who live in abusive households are harmed by living in a tense and anxious household (Geffner, Conradi, Geis and Aranda, 2009).

Essential to a robust assessment of risk in this context is an understanding that IPVA encompasses a range of behaviours. The focus should not be solely on physical violence; other forms of abuse (such as psychological abuse) are important to understanding risk trajectory. Effective risk assessment requires knowledge of the literature in relation to a range of risk factors, offence patterns, potential victims (including children/other family members) and relationship dynamics. A hypothesis–testing approach to assessment will help the report writer detect and control for biases, such as those caused by a failure to incorporate all information or an uncritical acceptance of previous assessments.

Best practice

Intimate partner violence and abuse includes a range of different behaviours

IPVA can include psychological, sexual, financial or physical abuse. More than one form of abuse is likely to be present (Gordon, 2000) and may not include physical violence. This wider conceptualisation of IPVA is not always fully understood, and defining IPVA remains contentious (see Dutton, 2015). For example, lawyers and other professionals and practitioners sometimes mistakenly consider IPVA to refer only to physical violence (Olagunju and Reynolds, 2012). Report writers should therefore be aware of the potential for misunderstanding about definitions of abuse and articulate the criteria they have used for assessment (see example below) and ensure this fits with the requirements of the authority that has requested the report.

> The definition of Intimate Partner Violence or Abuse (IPVA) used within this report is taken from the Centre for Disease Control and Prevention (CDC; Breiding et al., 2015). The CDC defines IPVA as behaviour by a partner or ex-partner which causes physical, psychological or sexual harm. This definition was derived from a comprehensive review of the literature and an expert panel discussion. The definition has been designed to assist with violence surveillance, identification of harm, and risk assessment and prevention between partners regardless of gender or sexual orientation.

Patterns in behaviours are significant

The significance of abusive acts may be missed if they are considered in isolation (Johnson, 2008; Stark, 2013). Coercive controlling abuse is exemplified by a pattern of behaviour (see Figure 11.1). A desire for power and control, located at the 'hub' of this model, reflects the effect of the abuse as well as the motivation for it. Sexual or physical violence (located at the rim of the wheel) need not be frequent or recent. Such behaviour reinforces, and is reinforced by, other forms of abusive behaviour (the 'spokes' of the wheel). Direct violence does not need to have occurred; threat of violence, or deliberate destruction of property, may be sufficient to intimidate the victim. Actual or threatened violence towards the victim's close friends or family members, or strangers perceived to have 'offended' the perpetrator, can also be considered within a framework of IPVA when the violence has an effect on the perpetrator's partner.

Because the pattern of abusive behaviours is significant, a reduction in the severity of assaults, or evidence that the most recent assault was non-injurious, should not automatically be taken as evidence of a reduction in risk (see Stark, 2013). Consequently, practitioners must be open-minded as to how IPVA is presenting. A detailed assessment of the nature, onset, duration, variation and interplay between different forms of IPVA should be documented. Escalation of the abuse, such as an increase in the intensity of abuse episodes (i.e. decreasing time between episodes) or severity (i.e. a shift from non-physical to physical, or from minor acts of physical violence to more serious and injurious acts) should be reported. When the perpetrator retains control over the victim through the use of minimal force, escalation may not be seen. However, the potential for escalation should the victim resist the control (e.g. through separation) should be considered, and where appropriate, carefully managed.

DOMESTIC ABUSE INTERVENTION PROJECT
202 East Superior Street
Duluth, Minnesota 55802
218-722-2781
www.duluth-model.org

FIGURE 11.1 The Power and Control Wheel (Pence and Paymar, 1993)

IPVA has different patterns and manifestations

The power and control wheel can lead to a misunderstanding of the nature of IPVA (Wangmann, 2011). The literature describes a number of different forms of abuse (Kelly and Johnson, 2008) that have different intersections with gender in heterosexual relationships.

Researchers who espouse the power and control wheel model tend to consider IPVA in relation to sociocultural considerations that systematically disempower women and socialise men to be violent (see Gondolf, 2012). Within this framework IPVA is a specific form of gender-based violence. Evidence from a range of studies suggests gender inequality is associated with higher rates of violence against women by their partners (Archer, 2006; Johnson, 2011). High rates of violence against women are reported across the globe (García-Moreno et al., 2015) and women consistently report higher rates of severe victimisation than men (Hamby, 2015).

Other theorists consider that violence within relationships results from interactions between situations and risk concerns. Highly patriarchal views are a potential risk indicator but other factors (e.g. poor resolution skills, inability to cope constructively with conflict, inappropriate responses to stress) also appear relevant (Finkel and Eckhardt, 2013). For example, when all forms of IPVA (not just the most serious) are considered, men and women report approximately equal rates of violence perpetration (Archer, 2002). Thus, family violence researchers argue that domestic violence should be considered outside of the framework of gender (Finkel and Eckhardt, 2013).

In an attempt to bring these diverse views together, Johnson (2008) suggested a typology which incorporated gendered (coercive control) and non-gendered (situational violence) abuse:

- The power and control wheel reflects *Coercive Controlling Violence* (CCV). Perpetrators of CCV hold unhealthy attitudes towards relationships and gender roles. Risk of CCV continuing, even after separation, is high. The power imbalance between the victim and the abuser means that some intervention strategies, such as mediation, are cautioned against (Ver Steech, Davis and Fredrick, 2011). Studies have repeatedly shown that coercive controlling violence is more commonly perpetrated by men against women (Johnson, 2011). However, when interpreting this finding, report writers should consider that: (a) there is evidence that women do engage in CCV; and (b) men who have experienced abuse within relationships encounter barriers to disclosing this (see Williamson, 2014). Hence the current literature and evidence may not accurately capture male victimisation.
- *Situationally determined abuse* is triggered by specific events and neither party feels controlled by the other. This form of abuse appears related to perpetrators' poor coping skills and inabilities to respond appropriately to conflict (Kelly and Johnson, 2008). Either of the partners can be the perpetrator and the abuse may be uni- or bi-directional. The harm associated with this form of abuse tends to be less significant than for CCV, although it can still be severe. Situational abuse should not automatically be considered less significant than CCV (Johnson, 2008). In particular, the effect on children of living in a household characterised by conflict and violence should not be underemphasised.
- *Separation instigated violence* is described by Kelly and Johnson (2008) as a form of situational violence. Individuals who have not previously demonstrated IPVA may react violently during a relationship breakdown. They may destroy photographs, shout or assault their partners or their partners' lovers. Violence may be minor or severe, but abuse of this nature is characterised by a small number of relatively isolated incidents at the beginning of, or during, the separation. Such abuse is characterised by relatively low risk of continuing violence.

- Dutton (2008) described a *more serious form of separation-instigated violence*. Men who have fears of abandonment, or who are overly enmeshed within their relationships, may experience lethal rage at the point of separation. Standardised risk assessment tools may have relatively little to offer in such cases and hence should not be relied upon (Dutton, 2008). A careful analysis of the individual's background, early experiences and personality will help the risk assessment process.

Psychological abuse is significant

Psychological abuse is a recognised component of IPVA. The power and control wheel (Figure 11. 1) includes some examples but other forms exist (Starke, 2015). Psychological violence appears to exacerbate the effect of physical partner abuse (Pico-Alfonso, 2005). For example, Krantz and Vung (2009) found the odds of reporting physical pain/discomfort increased from 3.75 to 15.4 when physical violence was combined with coercive, controlling behaviours. The odds of suicidal thoughts in relation to physical or sexual violence also increased from 4.64 to 10.8 under these circumstances.

Recently the effect of psychological abuse in the absence of physical violence has been discussed (Winstok and Sowan-Basheer, 2015). However, difficulties arise through the lack of a clear, accepted definition of psychological abuse. It is recommended that report writers consider Shorey et al.'s (2012) conceptualisation to define this their reports:

> Shorey and colleagues (2012) defined psychological abuse as behaviours designed to erode self-esteem, resilience and confidence and to increase distress, isolation and doubt. These characteristics are associated with poor mental health and therefore offer a potential explanation for the impact of this form of abuse upon victims.

Men can be victims of abuse

The role and function of violence by women against their partners presents a challenge to report writers. It is a source of much contention within the IPVA literature. Some researchers have concluded that female perpetrated IPVA is predominantly situational violence or violent resistance (violence used by a victim of controlling abuse to defend themselves) (Bair-Merritt et al., 2010). Because CCV does not need to include physical abuse (incipient coercive control), it is possible that the female victim may be the only partner to be physically violent within the relationship (Johnson, 2008).

However, more recently the role of women as coercive controlling abusers has been discussed (Morgan and Wells, 2016). Generally, less is known about the role and dynamics of these abusers although the following conclusions can be drawn at this stage:

1   Women are predominantly the victims of CCV (see Kelly and Johnson, 2008). However, this tells us little about the characteristics of individual relationships. It is important to make an independent assessment of the risk within the couple you have been asked to assess (Geffner et al., 2009). It is possible for women to engage in CCV (Johnson, 2011).

2   Women who use violence to protect themselves from abuse (violent resistance) present a reduced risk of harm once they are safe. However, where the violence relates to conflict or stress management deficits (situational violence), or reflects CCV, their risk remains even after the relationship has ended.

3   Given the vigorous debate over the role, purpose and function of female perpetrated IPVA, report writers need to be explicit about the basis on which they have made their decisions (see example below). They will need to be prepared to defend their positions with regard to the literature and the basis for their conclusions.

> Both Mr and Mrs X acknowledged that they had engaged in violence towards each other during the course of the relationship. Both individuals reported they only used violence in response to the controlling behaviour of the other. When asked about the abuse, Mr X was able to describe a range of abusive behaviours he had experienced (isolation, reputational damage, emotional abuse) in rich detail. He was able to describe the context in which the abuse occurred, a pattern of abuse, his emotional reactions and his decision making. He was also able to describe in detail how he attempted to cope with the abuse (including through the use of force). In contrast, Mrs X's account was lacking in detail. She tended to provide general and unspecific examples of abuse she had experienced. She was not able to articulate how she had responded to the pattern of abuse. She reported that she "felt controlled" but was unable to explain further when asked to do so. One possible explanation for this could be that her victimisation had resulted in trauma, or stress, which affected her ability to process information. However, no evidence for this was identified within the assessment. Based on the available data I have concluded that Mrs X used coercive controlling violence within the relationship. She did experience abuse herself, but this was in the form of violent resistance by her partner. While most coercive controlling abusers are men, it is possible for women to use this form of violence (Johnson, 2011).

There are a variety of reasons why victims do not report

It is not uncommon to conduct assessments with individuals who discuss the presence of abuse only when the relationship has broken down (Saunders, 2015). Assessors should keep an open mind about possible explanations for this. In cases of separation instigated violence, the abuse will only have occurred during the relationship breakdown. In other cases, abuse may have occurred but not been disclosed for reasons of embarrassment, fear (Geffner et al., 2009) or because of how the question was asked. Higher rates of abuse are detected when victims are asked about specific behaviours rather a general question about 'being the victim of abuse'. Focusing on examples of specific behaviours or incidents allows the assessor to make an independent judgement about the presence and extent of the abuse. Indeed, it is sometimes useful to administer self-report measures of physical and non-physical IPVA.

It is not uncommon for other professionals to fail to detect abuse when it is present (Saunders, 2015) or conclude that violence has occurred when it has not. Mackay (2014) drew the following conclusions: (1) false accusations do occur; however, because of methodological, ideological and conceptual variations in studies we know little about their frequency; (2) when false accusations occur, they damage children's mental health and their relationships with parents; (3) false accusations are not always detected by other professionals (necessitating a thorough and independent review of the evidence by each new assessor).

The risk factors for IPVA are not necessarily the same as those for other forms of violence

Intimate partner abusers are heterogeneous (Holtzworth-Munroe et al., 2000). Some have an entrenched history of violent conflict with their propensity for violence revealed within a number of settings inside and outside of the home. These generally violent antisocial offenders show a number of risk factors (such as early onset of violence, antisocial attitudes) associated with general violence risk assessment, and are likely to engage in instrumental, coercive IPVA (Day and Bowen, 2015). However, the absence of such risk concerns does not imply a lack of risk. Some offenders only demonstrate violence within the home and have few risks associated with general criminality. When assessing such cases, it is useful to consider the degree and role of psychopathology within the perpetrator.

Higher levels of risk, in terms of frequency and severity of abuse, tend to be seen within those individuals with higher levels of social, emotional and psychological dysfunction. Such individuals (referred to as borderline dysphoric) frequently have a history of depression, substance abuse and may have a history of childhood abuse. They often have poor attachments to significant others. Abusers with this profile tend to respond poorly to concerns (actual or perceived) about abandonment. Reactions may include threats to harm themselves or others (Holzworth-Munrore et al., 2000; Dutton, 2008). In addition, IPVA perpetrators with this profile are more likely to engage in post-separation stalking (see Dixon and Bowen, 2016 for a review of IPVA and stalking) and child abuse (Herron and Holtzworth-Munroe, 2002).

IPVA risk assessment tools offer some value

A number of risk assessments for assessing IPVA perpetrators can be used in forensic practice (see Table 11.1 and Bowen, 2011a). Selecting the most appropriate one for the forensic task at hand requires consideration of a number of factors

TABLE 11.1 Summary of available IPVA risk assessments for perpetrators

Tool	Focus of assessment	Approach	Validation samples	Measurement properties
DVSI-R	Perpetrator; physical violence	Actuarial	Williams and Houghton (2004): US 1465 arrested men; 18-month follow-up	$\alpha = 0.71$ Concurrent validity with SARA r = 0.54 ROC AUC = 0.61 (domestic violence); 0.65 (general reoffending)
ODARA	Perpetrator; physical violence	Actuarial	Hilton et al. (2004): 589 Canadian male perpetrators; average 4.79 years follow-up; cross-validation sample of 100 offenders	ROC AUC= 0.77 Concurrent validity with SARA r = 0.60
			Hilton et al. (2014): 30 female incarcerated Canadian perpetrators; 9-year follow-up	ROC AUC = 0.72
DVRAG	Perpetrator; physical violence	Actuarial	Hilton et al. (2008): Male Canadian perpetrators; average 5-year follow-up; independent sample 346 males	ROC AUC = 0.71 ROC AUC = 0.70 Inter-rater reliability r = 0.92
SARA	Perpetrator; physical violence	SPJ	Kropp and Hart (2000) 2861 Canadian males (probation n = 1671; prison n = 1010)	Inter-rater reliability r = 0.80
			Grann and Wedin (2002) 88 Swedish males; 7-year follow-up; file review only	6-month AUC: 0.49 (part 1); 0.54 (part 2); 0.52 (Total) 5-year AUC: 0.59 (Part 1); 0.62 (Part 2); 0.65 (Total)
			Hilton et al. (2004) Canadian sample 589 perpetrators	ROC 0.64

(see Chapters 3 and 5). The tool selected should enable the practitioner to most directly address the forensic question being asked. General best practice in conducting risk assessments needs to be followed here (Chapters 3 and 5). However, given the scepticism with which the self-reports of IPVA perpetrators are viewed, the input of victims and other professionals is of paramount importance. Best practice requires multiple informants (e.g. perpetrator, victim, probation officers, social workers, psychiatrists where relevant), and the collation of a range of information using appropriately validated measures where available (e.g. personality, psychopathology, addiction, relationship history, IPVA history and recent behaviour, criminal history and record).

What are you assessing?

Despite literature suggesting that in some relationships IPVA may be 'mutual', most forensic contexts require the identification of a primary perpetrator or primary victim. In relationships where mutual violence has been documented, both parties need to be interviewed in order to determine more fully the nature of the IPVA within the relationship. Current risk assessment tools focus on appraising the likelihood of future physical IPVA. Consequently, if you are required to focus on assessing the likelihood of non-physical forms of IPVA, a formulation-based approach (Chapter 4), informed by the available research examining relevant risk factors, may be of most use.

Who are you assessing?

Much attention has been diverted towards understanding risk for IPVA in adult (age 18 and older) heterosexual couples. Within these relationships, most research has explored situations where men are perpetrators and women are victims. Moreover, the literature is biased largely towards European-American samples and the majority of tools have only been validated in a small number of countries. Consequently, it is imperative to understand whether the risk assessment tool that you are using is valid in the context of the relationship that you are assessing. The main parameters to consider are victim or perpetrator gender, age, ethnicity and sexuality. Currently, there exist no IPVA risk assessment tools validated on samples younger than 18 years (Bowen and Walker, 2015), or on LGBTIQ samples. In addition, the extent to which the models of IPVA adequately account for behaviours in these populations or in older adults or those with learning disabilities is unclear.

The selection of the tool must be clearly justified in the final report and any weaknesses in the 'fit' between the tool, the client and the forensic question need to be clearly stated. Conclusions should be appropriately cautioned in light of any limitations. In some circumstances it may be inappropriate to use a risk assessment tool and the reasons for this need to be made clear.

Victim-based risk assessments

There is one validated assessment for victims – the Danger Assessment (Campbell, 1995). This was designed to assess female IPVA victims' risk of being seriously or lethally injured by a current or former partner. It can also be used to assess the woman's risk of killing her abusive male partner (Campbell, Webster and Glass, 2009). So far it has only been validated in North America.

It is important to try to incorporate victim perspectives in risk assessments as this offers valuable information (Bowen, 2011a). Studies show that regardless of how it is phrased (e.g. what do you think the likelihood is that you will experience severe violence from your partner in the next year on a 10 point scale?), the predictive validity of these perceptions is good; with approximately 66 per cent of victims being able to accurately predict future violence. Validity is less good for women with PTSD symptoms who tend to overestimate their risk of physical and psychological violence (Bennett Cattaneo et al., 2007; Bell et al., 2008). Victim perceptions have also been found to significantly add to the predictive validity of other perpetrator-based risk assessments (Heckert and Gondolf, 2004).

A hypothesis-testing approach is required

Report writers should ensure their conclusions are based on the scientific evidence in relation to the phenomenon of concern (APA, 2013). Reporting on risk of violence within relationships presents particular challenges in this regard. Debates and divisions in the IPVA literature contribute towards biases in the assessment of individual cases. In order to control for this, assessors should collect as much critical data as they can, from a range of sources (Saunders, 2015). Tentative hypotheses should be formed before confirmatory and disconformity evidence is actively sought. Formulating alternative hypotheses can help in countering confirmatory and anchoring biases during an assessment process (Rodgers, 2016). Developing hypotheses about the role of trauma may be helpful in understanding the role of irritable, angry or hostile responses by respondents (Saunders, 2015).

Common difficulties/confusion

For over 40 years, researchers and victim advocates have fiercely debated whether violence by men against their female partners is more prevalent, dangerous and frequent than violence by women against men (Anderson, 2013). Report writers need to consider their own position on this and reflect upon how this may result in biases during assessment processes. For example, some legal professionals consider only coercive control violence to be 'true' IPVA, meaning that those who use situational violence are not considered 'batterers' (Wangmann, 2011).

Report writers need to appreciate that most empirical papers discuss general patterns. These should inform, but not dictate, your assessment, which needs to consider the individual characteristics of the relevant parties (Saunders, 2015). There are notable gaps in the current literature base. For example, the Serious Crimes Act (2015) created a new criminal offence of coercive control within England and Wales. However, appraising risk of this is complicated. The majority of research has focused on defining IPVA in terms of physical violence in heterosexual relationships (Bowen, 2011b). The extent to which coercive control has the same or unique risk factors in other populations (e.g. see Greenberg, 2012) is less well understood. Even within heterosexual relationships the intersections of gender, culture, ethnicity, immigration status and violence are not clear (Morgan and Omuku, 2016).

Review task

Sally applied for a divorce after 10 years of marriage. She was diagnosed with depression last year. Sally reports no violence prior to asking Ben for a divorce, but then he became angry, smashed property and shook her. The neighbours called the police, who observed bruises on Sally's arms where she'd been held. Sally reports that Ben liked a quiet house. When the children (aged 9 and 7) were too loud he would smash their toys as punishment. Following this he would 'sulk' and blame Sally, telling her she was bad mother.

During the assessment Ben was distressed and angry about the divorce. He felt Sally was only divorcing him because she was depressed. He said he always loved her and worked hard to be a good provider and father. He acknowledged he could be 'grumpy' when he got in from work. This was because while he was working Sally used to spend all her time 'gossiping' with friends and neighbours. He acknowledged that he did not approve of this. He made visitors to the house feel uncomfortable in the hope they would not come round and 'distract' Sally.

Questions for reflection

- What other information would you like?
- What is the evidence of IPVA? What are the exact behaviours of concern?
- What is the evidence Ben has shown separation-instigated violence?
- What other hypothesises about his behaviour could be developed and tested?
- What conclusions would you draw?
- What recommendations would you make?

Checklist of steps/advice

1 Be familiar with the IPVA literature, in general and in relation to the characteristics of the couple you are assessing.
2 Collect independent evidence. Do not rely on one party's description or previous assessments by other professionals.
3 Identify and test possible hypotheses to explain the evidence.
4 Identify the characteristics and nature of the IPVA within the relationship.

5   Consider risk factors, potential victims (including children), impact and trajectory of abuse.
6   Develop realistic options for intervention, risk management and reduction as appropriate to the referral question.

Further reading

See * references below.

References

American Psychological Association. (2013). Specialty guidelines for forensic psychology. *The American Psychologist, 68*, 7–19.

Anderson, K.L. (2013). Why do we fail to ask 'why' about gender and intimate partner violence? *Journal of Marriage and Family, 75*, 314–18.

Archer, J. (2002). Sex differences in physically aggressive acts between heterosexual partners: A meta-analytic review. *Aggression and Violent Behavior, 7*, 313–51.

Archer, J. (2006). Cross-cultural differences in physical aggression between partners: A social-role analysis. *Personality and Social Psychology Review, 10*, 133–53.

Bair-Merritt, M. H., Crowne, S. S., Thompson, D. A., Sibinga, E., Trent, M. and Campbell, J. (2010). Why do women use intimate partner violence? A systematic review of women's motivations. *Trauma, Violence and Abuse, 11*, 178-89.

Bell, M.E., Bennett Cattaneo, L., Goodman, L.A. and Dutton, M.A. (2008). Assessing the risk of future psychological abuse: Predicting the accuracy of battered women's predictions. *Journal of Family Violence, 23*, 69–80.

Bennett Cattaneo, L., Bell, M.E., Goodman, L.A. and Dutton, M.A. (2007). Intimate partner violence victims' accuracy in assessing their risk of re-abuse. *Journal of Family Violence, 22*, 429–40.

*Bowen, E. (2011a). An overview of partner violence risk assessment and the potential role of female victim risk appraisals. *Aggression and Violent Behavior, 16*, 214–26.

*Bowen, E. (2011b). *The rehabilitation of partner-violent men*. Chichester, UK: Wiley-Blackwell.

Bowen, E. and Walker, K. (2015). *The psychology of violence in adolescent romantic relationships*. London: Palgrave-MacMillan.

Breiding, M.J., Basile, K.C., Smith, S.G., Black, M.C. and Mahendra, R.R. (2015). *Intimate partner violence surveillance: Uniform definitions and recommended data elements, Version 2.0*. Atlanta, GA: National Center for Injury Prevention and Control, Centers for Disease Control and Prevention.

Campbell, J.C. (1995). *Assessing dangerousness*. Newbury Park, CA: Sage.

Campbell, J.C., Webster, D.W. and Glass, N. (2009). The danger assessment validation of a lethality risk assessment instrument for intimate partner femicide. *Journal of Interpersonal Violence, 24*(4), 653–74.

Day, A. and Bowen, E. (2015). Offending competency and coercive control in intimate partner violence. *Aggression and Violent Behavior: Special Issue 20*, 62–71.

Dixon, L., and Bowen, E. (2016, in press) Intimate partner violence and stalking. In Beech, A.R. and Davies, G. (eds.) *Forensic Psychology*, 2nd ed. Malden, MA: Wiley-Blackwell.

Dutton, D.G. (2008). Caveat assessor: Potential pitfalls of generic assessment for intimate partner violence, in Baldry, A.C., Winkel, F.W., (eds.), *Intimate partner violence prevention and intervention: The risk assessment and management approach* (pp.125–31). Hauppauge, NY: Nova Science Publishers.

Dutton, D.G. (2015). The gender paradigm and custody disputes. *International Journal for Family Research and Policy*, *1*(1). Retrieved from http://ijfrp.journals.yorku.ca/index.php/ijfrp/article/view/39579

Fantuzzo, J.W. and Fusco, R.A. (2007). Children's direct exposure to types of domestic violence crime: A population-based investigation. *Journal of Family Violence*, *22*, 543–52.

Finkel, E.J. and Eckhardt, C.I. (2013). Intimate partner violence, in Simpson, J.A. and Campbell, L. (eds.), *The Oxford handbook of close relationships* (pp.452–74). Oxford: Oxford University Press.

García-Moreno, C., Zimmerman, C., Morris-Gehring, A., Heise, L., Amin, A., Abrahams, N., Montoya, O., Bhate-Deosthali, P., Kilonzo, N. and Watts, C. (2015). Addressing violence against women: A call to action. *The Lancet*, *385*, 1685–95.

Geffner, R., Conradi, L., Geis, K. and Aranda, M.B. (2009). Conducting child custody evaluations in the context of family violence allegations: Practical techniques and suggestions for ethical practice. *Journal of Child Custody*, *6*, 189–218.

Gondolf, E.W. (2012). *The future of batterer programs: Reassessing evidence-based practice*. Boston, MA: Northeastern University Press.

Gordon, M. (2000). Definitional issues in violence against women: Surveillance and research from a violence research perspective. *Violence Against Women*, *6*, 747–83.

Grann, M. and Wedin, I. (2002). Risk factors for recidivism among spousal assault and spousal homicide offenders. *Psychology, Crime and Law*, *8*, 5–23.

Hamby, S. (2015). A scientific answer to a scientific question: The gender debate on intimate partner violence. *Trauma, Violence and Abuse*, DOI: 1524838015596963.

Heckert, D.A. and Gondolf, E.W. (2004). Battered women's perceptions of risk versus risk factors and instruments in predicting reassault. *Journal of Interpersonal Violence*, *19*, 778–800.

Herron, K. and Holtzworth-Munroe, A. (2002). Child abuse potential: A comparison of subtypes of maritally violent men and nonviolent men. *Journal of Family Violence*, *17*, 1–21.

Hilton, N.Z., Harris, G.T., Rice, M.E., Lang, C., Cormier, C.A., an Lines, K.J. (2004) A brief actuarial assessment for the prediction of wife assault recidivism: The Ontario domestic assault risk. *Psychological Assessment*, *16* (3), 267–73.

Hilton, N.Z., Harris, G.T., Rice, M.E., Houghton, R.E. and Eke, A.W. (2008). An in-depth actuarial assessment for wife assault recidivism: The domestic violence risk appraisal guide. *Law and Human Behavior*, *32*, 150–63.

Hilton, N.Z., Popham, S., Lang, C. and Harris, G.T. (2014). Preliminary validation of the ODARA for female intimate partner violence offenders. *Partner Abuse*, *5*, 189–203.

Holtzworth-Munroe, A., Meehan, J.C., Herron, K., Rehman, U. and Stuart, G.L. (2000). Testing the Holtzworth-Munroe and Stuart (1994) batterer typology. *Journal of Consulting and Clinical Psychology*, *68*, 1000.

Johnson, M.P. (2008). *A typology of domestic violence: Intimate terrorism, violent resistance, and situational couple violence*. Boston, MA: Northeastern University Press.

Johnson, M.P. (2011). Gender and types of intimate partner violence: A response to an anti-feminist literature review. *Aggression and Violent Behavior*, *16*, 289–96.

Greenberg, K. (2012). Still hidden in the closet: Trans women and domestic violence. *Berkeley Journal of Gender Law and Justice*, *27*, 198–251.

Kelly, J.B. and Johnson, M.P. (2008) Differentiation among types of intimate partner violence: Research update and implications for interventions. *Family Court Review*, *46* (3), 476–99.

Krantz, G. and Vung, N.D. (2009). The role of controlling behaviour in intimate partner violence and its health effects: A population based study from rural Vietnam. *BMC Public Health*, *9*, 143–52.

Kropp, P.R. and Hart, S.D. (2000). The Spousal Assault Risk Assessment (SARA) guide: Reliability and validity in adult male offenders. *Law and Human Behavior, 24*, 101–18.

MacKay, T. (2014). False allegations of child abuse in contested family law cases: The implications for psychological practice. *Educational and Child Psychology, 31*(3), 85.

Morgan, W. and Omuku, A. (2016). Help-seeking by abused women: Experiences of the Ugandan community in the UK. Unpublished manuscript, London Metropolitan University.

Morgan, W. and Wells, M. (2016) 'It's deemed unmanly': men's experiences of intimate partner violence (IPV). *The Journal of Forensic Psychiatry and Psychology, 27* (3), 404–18.

Olagunju, A. and Reynolds, C. (2012). Domestic violence. *Georgetown Journal of Gender & Law, 13*, 203.

Pico-Alfonso, M.A. (2005). Psychological intimate partner violence: The major predictor of post-traumatic stress disorder in abused women. *Neuroscience and Biobehavioral Reviews, 29*, 181–93.

Saunders, D.G. (2015). Research based recommendations for child custody evaluation practices and policies in cases of intimate partner violence. *Journal of Child Custody, 12*(1), 71–92.

Shorey, R.C., Temple, J.R., Febres, J., Brasfield, H., Sherman, A.E. and Stuart, G.L. (2012). The consequences of perpetrating psychological aggression in dating relationships: A descriptive investigation. *Journal of Interpersonal Violence, 27*, 2980–98.

Stark, E. (2013) Coercive control, in N. Lombard and L. McMillan (eds.). *Violence against women: Current theory and practice in domestic abuse, sexual violence and exploitation*, pp. 17–33.

Rogers, R. (2016). An introduction to insanity evaluations, in Jackson, R.L. and Roesch, R. (eds.), *Learning forensic assessment*, 2nd ed. New York: Routledge.

Ver Steech, N., Davis, G. and Frederick, L. (2011). Look before you leap: Court system triage of family law cases involving intimate partner violence. *Marquette Law Review 95*, 955.

Wangmann, J.M. (2011). *Different types of intimate partner violence – An exploration of the literature*. Sydney: Australian Domestic and Family Violence Clearinghouse.

Williamson, E. (2014). Heterosexual men as victims of domestic violence and abuse, in N. Aghtaie, N. and Gangoli, G. (eds.), *Understanding gender based violence: National and international contexts* (pp.147–59). New York: Routledge.

Williams, K.R. and Houghton, A.B. (2004) Assessing the risk of domestic violence reoffending: a validation study. *Law and Human Behavior, 28* (4), 437–43.

Winstok, Z. and Sowan-Basheer, W. (2015). Does psychological violence contribute to partner violence research? A historical, conceptual and critical review. *Aggression and Violent Behavior, 21*, 5–16.

SECTION 3:

Considerations when reporting in specific contexts

Introduction to Section 3

This section examines the reporting requirements of secure settings (Chapter 12), parole/hearings (Chapter 13) and finally, non-custodial, community settings (Chapter 14).

Chapter 12 explores secure settings where people are detained or held in custody. This is an environment that provides specific challenges which requires the Practitioner Psychologist to consider to ensure that his or her reports are both clear and defensible. The chapter points to the accomplishments of the prison systems in England and Wales, where forensic reports in one secure setting can cross-reference to practice in other legislatures and jurisdictions. Not surprisingly, issues of engagement with clients are a strong consideration, as are issues of approach (i.e. Practitioner Psychologists need to be clear in their obligations both to the authority and the service user, and at the same time consistent in their practice across situations and cases).

Chapter 13 addresses reports to parole boards and other decision makers regarding release. These can take the form of assessment or treatment reports, and arise from a variety of circumstances that the authors discuss in detail. The chapter describes many of the uncertainties that professionals are likely to encounter in these situations, and offers guidance in what to include and how to structure reports. To this end, the authors provide examples from sample reports.

Finally, Chapter 14 addresses community treatment reports. This is another area that has received very little attention in the literature. The authors note that community treatment reports 'provide valuable information related to a client's ongoing functioning, management of their risk factors and response to intervention. Given risk management is not static, ongoing consideration, review and reporting of a client's participation and progress in treatment and management of identified risk factors are critical. The authors next discuss treatment intake reports, treatment progress reports, post–suspension/treatment closure reports and treatment completion reports. Each of these areas includes specialised considerations. The authors discuss the importance of confidentiality, balancing the sharing of information with privacy, case conceptualisation and the opportunity for reports themselves to be therapeutic. This last point can include the possibility of reports involving collaboration of those involved. To this end, the authors note that the style of the report matters. The authors provide helpful discussion on the organisation and contents of these reports.

12

REPORTING IN SECURE SETTINGS

Martin Fisher, Kerry Beckley and Jo Bailey

Introduction

Forensic reporting in secure settings is comprised of two principal and primary contexts: Prisons and Secure Hospitals. Each has its own internal set of subsystems based on the age of those persons incarcerated, their perceived threat levels to the public and each other, and to the stability of the estates in which they are held. In providing reports in secure settings Practitioner Psychologists need to carefully balance and manage various issues; this chapter considers these in a series of process and content reflections and considerations, before drawing the various aspects together into a composite view of report writing in secure settings which forms the conclusion.

Looking at each of these settings as operating circumstances will assist in identifying and describing the common processes that overlay both contexts. This chapter will enable the exploration of reporting structure, application of research and theory to the specific case, stylistic issues, and issues arising from confirmatory bias, authority in reporting and how the needs of the client hierarchy can best be met. These areas are covered under the headings of 'Issues of Engagement', 'Issues of Approach' and 'Issues of Role'.

Assessment in prison settings

Using the UK England and Wales Prison System[1] as an exemplar for the content of forensic reports in secure settings enables clear cross-referencing to practice in other legislatures and jurisdictions. Although the statutory process may vary, the application of forensic report writing principles discussed here applies.

Primarily, the reports written by Practitioner Psychologists are provided to the Parole Board of England and Wales within the auspices of the Parole Board

Rules (2011). Generally, reports to the parole board are requested where an indeterminate sentence prisoner has his or her case referred for consideration of suitability for progression or release under supervision into the community. The position in respect of indeterminate sentencing in England and Wales is well summarised in R. (Haney, Kaiyam and Massey) v. Secretary of State for Justice (UKSC, 2014).

It is within this framework of sentencing that practitioner psychologist reports in secure prison settings are positioned. The report writer must seek to assist the parole board in deciding if the imprisoned offender subject to review should be recommended for a move to conditions of reduced security, or be released from custody under supervision to live in the community. Equally the assessor may conclude and recommend that the risk to public safety is best managed by the retention of the imprisoned offender in more secure conditions.

In terms of instruction then, for the practitioner psychologist in a secure setting, subject to specific direction from the parole board, the requirement is consistent and specific with four potential outcomes: no change, higher security, reduced security or release. This is contrary to circumstances in non-custodial forensic settings where the forensic assessor is in receipt of particular and specific areas of instruction. That is, the importance of a specific reason for referral, which varies case by case, is less important (e.g. Wolber and Carne, 2002). That notwithstanding, the requirement for a clear set of recommendations arising from clear argument and reasoning retains its importance, given the potential for reputational damage to the criminal justice system and those working within it, as well as potential new victims, when errors of judgement arise (Needs, 2010). The impact on those suffering the consequences of further criminal actions on the part of the released offender in such situations is immeasurable (e.g. *The Guardian*, 2006).

Reports provided by practitioner psychologists in prisons (acting on behalf of the Secretary of State for Justice) follow a pre-set format within prisons in England and Wales and the structure is a requirement for submission to the parole board. Practitioner psychologists reporting under the instruction of an imprisoned offender's legal representative, or the offender, must respond to the same parole board instruction as those reporting on behalf of the Secretary of State, but need not be constrained by the same structured formatting.

The parole board review process is not described as an adversarial process (Parole Board Rules, 2011), but an inquisitorial one in which opinion is submitted to assist the parole board in arriving at its conclusion(s) in any given case, rather than favouring one argument over the other. The interests of public safety are paramount, but the obligation on the state to rehabilitate imprisoned offenders, thus enabling a successful outcome from a parole board referral (defined as release from the prisoner's perspective) increases in its importance as successful challenges to existing circumstances in prisons continue (R. [Morales] v. Parole Board, the Secretary of State for Justice, Staffordshire Probation Service (EWHC, 2011).

Assessment in secure hospital settings

There are a number of overlapping principles which would be common to assessments undertaken in a hospital with those noted above for prison settings. All offenders placed in a secure hospital are detained under the Mental Health Act (1983), which requires the person to be diagnosed as suffering from a 'mental disorder'. This is a complex issue as many individuals who are managed within the prison estate have a mental disorder and there are often diverging opinions regarding the most suitable setting for such individuals to be located. Individuals being treated in a hospital setting will be detained under different parts of the legislation. An individual can be directed to a hospital by the court for a pre-sentence assessment (MHA 1983 S.35) or at the point of sentencing to be treated under a hospital order (MHA 1983 S.37) with or without a restriction order (MHA 1983 S.41), the latter being without limit of time. Alternatively, a sentenced prisoner can be transferred to the hospital for treatment under MHA 1983 S.47/49 and may be returned to prison at any point during his/her sentence. It is important to understand the legal context as this may have a bearing on the purpose of the assessment. For example, when the person is detained under MHA 1983 S.35 or MHA 1983 S.47/49, there may be greater emphasis on the person's anticipated response to treatment in a hospital, as returning to prison remains an alternative.

Although hospital settings may differ in the types of psychological assessments undertaken, there are, as in the case of prison assessments for the parole board, core themes. The admission assessment addresses the psychological aspects of a person's mental disorder and their functional link to offending behaviour. Structured clinical judgement tools broadly cover the key areas of assessment (see Chapter 5), but there is often a greater emphasis on the person's mental health than may be seen in custodial settings. A typical assessment would involve taking a history, specific assessments of mental health difficulties or personality, risk factors, core beliefs/schemas, co-morbid conditions such as other mental health conditions or neuropsychological assessment, a consideration of behaviours likely to interfere with the treatment process and behaviours that may mirror or parallel offending behavioural patterns (Willmot, 2011).

Diagnostic tools such as the International Personality Disorder Examination (IPDE [Loranger, 1999]) or the Structured Clinical Interview for DSM Disorders (SCID [First et al., 1997]) can be used, albeit with the caveat that diagnosis can have limited utility in understanding the individual. Psychological formulation (see Chapter 4) should always be used alongside diagnostic assessments to capture the links between mental disorder and offending behaviour. All behaviour, however challenging and extreme, has a valid function. Within offenders with mental health problems, the meaning may be understood as part of a delusional belief system or in the context of early traumatic experiences. The person may engage in offending or self-injury in an attempt to meet his/her own needs if (s)he has limited, whether perceived or in reality, alternative methods of doing so. The formulation should identify treatment goals, which address the underlying reasons for problematic behaviours, not just the behaviours themselves (see Chapter 4).

Practitioner psychologists are also required to provide reports on a person's engagement with interventions. These usually have a structured format, comment upon motivation and engagement in the treatment and address how the risk factors have changed in response to treatment (see Chapter 7). All interventions are considered 'offence focused' if they explicitly target those factors. Discharge reports (MHA 1983 S.117) are required when the person returns to prison or progresses to a less secure hospital environment or community. As with treatment reports, these should reflect how treatment has addressed the person's risk factors, with recommendations to address outstanding needs, if there are any. As such, secure hospital assessments have a less structured format requirement but the context of assessment remains to be one in which the benefit from treatment and/or hospitalisation needs to be balanced with the assurance of public safety.

Issues of engagement

Whilst various authors have sought to distinguish between the differing requirements of clinical, forensic and counseling psychology reports (Grisso, 2010; Karson and Nadkarni, 2013; Ownby, 1997, for example), the secure setting provides for some specific issues that cross professional domains. Not least of these is that in the assessment paradigm the primary service user is less clearly defined than in a purely clinical setting and the reporting situation is not necessarily one of choice.

All service users in secure settings ('service user' will be used henceforth to describe prisoners, offenders and detained patients about whom or for whom reports are prepared in secure settings) are brought together with the reporting Practitioner Psychologist by either their location in the prison or hospital estate or on the instruction of a legal representative, rather than by choice per se. As such, in many cases the assessment interaction, which will ultimately lead to reporting, is not necessarily one arising from service user choice. The willingness and degree, therefore, to which service users engage will vary in the authors' experience contingent upon the service users' perceptions and expectations of the assessment process. The authority (be that the Parole Board, Mental Health Review Tribunal, etc.) will require the assessment to inform decision making about the future of the service user irrespective of the level of engagement. This provides for issues of consent and consequent considerations of beneficence to the service user where engagement is less than complete, or is seen as under some form of obligation by the service user. Whilst the practitioner needs to operate within the requirement of the Health and Care Professions Council (HCPC) Standards of Proficiency (SoP) (HCPC, 2015) by whom all Practitioner Psychologists are regulated[2], the requirement to report to the authority must take legislative precedence. Rest (1982) describes a helpful model of ethical conduct that assists in the practitioner's management of engagement in secure settings to assure service user benefit and provide for defensible practice, which is a critical component of report writing in secure settings. The model has been adopted by the British Psychological Society (BPS) in its guidance on the teaching of ethics in psychology (BPS, 2015a) and as such can assist in issues of engagement to assure effective practice. Figure 12.1 below describes the basis of the model.

Where a service user is unwilling, or unable (e.g. due to mental disorder or location in special accommodation) to fully engage, the practitioner needs to moderate his/her approach such that it is adapted and responsive to the presenting circumstances, being mindful of the need for service user beneficence. In secure settings, when a service user is not fully engaged in the report writing process, or is adversarial to it, this can not only impact upon the quality of the ensuing report but also potentially on the Practitioner Psychologist's view of the service user.

The impact of the degree and style of engagement by the service user in secure settings on the Practitioner Psychologist's assessment can specifically affect how heuristics, or confirmatory biases, come into play in the process. Karson and Nadkarni (2013) noted particularly the heuristics of 'anchoring' and 'availability' (Kahneman, 2011; Tversky and Kahneman, 1974). 'Anchoring' refers to potential biasing of numerical information based on the way in which the information is presented. For example, if a service user declines a meeting for the preparation of a report, then there may be a tendency to see this as an indicator of increased risk, when in fact it is not per se leading the practitioner to adjust their rating. Adjusting actuarial measures based on clinical experience should be approached with extreme caution (Campbell and De Clue, 2010). 'Availability' refers to making judgements based on familiar scenarios that may not be representative of the presenting situation. As Karson and Nadkarni (2013) observed, it is much easier to think of service users in secure settings behaving badly than ex-service users leading successful lives in the community, especially when one is reporting on a service user refusing to participate in an assessment process, ultimately aimed at assisting them to progress.

It is also critical to effective report writing in secure settings to be mindful of influencing the reader, either positively or negatively, in terms of how information is framed (Kahneman, 2011), be it in terms of full and willing engagement or little if any engagement. When a report writer experiences an apparent open, willing and motivated service user there may be a tendency to report more positively than when engagement is minimal, or adversarial. For example, the phrase 'fatally injured 6 victims under the age of 10 years in the context of sexual assault' will frame the event of an offence differently than 'murdered and sexually molested 6 children'. How the same facts are reported can be influenced by the report writer's experience of meeting the service user. Slovic and Monahan (1995) found that

- Ethical Sensitivity: *Interpreting the situation, and identifying the presence of an ethical issue.*
- Ethical Reasoning: *Formulating the morally ideal course of action by identifying the relevant ethical issues and using these principles to consider appropriate actions.*
- Ethical Motivation: *Deciding what one actually wishes and intends to do.*
- Ethical Implementation: *Executing and implementing what one intends to do.*

FIGURE 12.1   Four component model of ethical thinking (Rest, 1982)

judging likelihood of harm as a probability, as opposed to on a ranking scale of dangerousness, led to clinicians' judgements being affected in such a way that the probability scale was treated as a ranking scale: participants seemed unable to consider probability in a 'consistent quantitative way' (p. 62). This is to say, in practice a linear relationship is assumed when in fact it is not linear, leading to inaccurate judgements of risk.

Aside from the willingness of the service user to engage with the assessment process for reasons associated with perceptions of the intent of the process, or bias towards the Practitioner Psychologist (service users being just as susceptible to heuristics as report writers), one also needs to consider cultural, socio-economic and affiliated issues. For example, Elbogen (2002) reported that female assessors of male patients reported a higher level of violence risk than their male counterparts. More broadly than the sex of Practitioner Psychologists (the majority of Clinical and/ or Forensic Psychologists are female), completing reports in secure settings needs to consider the Equalities Act (2010) in which there are eight protected characteristics[3], in which incarcerated or detained service user groups are over-represented when compared with the community population in England and Wales. These are predominantly in terms of disability (mental disorder), but also race and religion or belief. Practitioner Psychologist report writers should therefore be sensitive to responsivity issues for service user engagement given these, and other, affiliated group identities. Taking account of the idiographic as well as the nomothetic and choroplethic aspects of the service user, and his/her potential societal and personal affiliations, can be a critical aspect of successful engagement in secure settings.

Issues of approach

Given that reports prepared (ideally in an active dialogue) with service users in secure settings have a common set of instructions, parameters and service user outcomes that underpin their purpose and therefore preparation, Practitioner Psychologists need to be clear in their obligations both to the authority and the service user, and at the same time consistent in their practice across situations and cases. The relevant authority relies on a consistent approach, which follows a set and legislative process in seeking to provide defensible and proper outcomes from its activities, and the report writer in secure settings needs to be responsive to that.

Various authors have described approaches to the structure of reports, and within legislatures, requirements are duly stipulated (for example BPS, 2015b; Grisso, 2010 for a summary review; Ownby, 1997; Wolber and Crane, 2002). In a more general sense, however, in secure settings the principles of approach can be more important to the purpose of report writing than specific content per se. In that sense, reports in secure settings, being provided in the contexts of prisons and secure hospitals as described above, benefit from an effective 'first principles' approach. Lichtenberger et al. (2004), after Ownby (1997), described four desired outcomes as shown in Figure 12.2. This approach to the provision of reports in secure settings ensures that the Practitioner Psychologist retains clarity of purpose, which should supersede specific aspects of the service user's particular case to ensure that consistency in practice is sustained, given the consistency in the context of the reporting.

1   Answer the referral question as explicitly as possible.
2   Provide the referral source with additional information when it is relevant.
3   Create a record of the assessment for future use (the report).
4   Recommend a specific course of action.

FIGURE 12.2   Desired outcomes from a psychological assessment report (Lichtenberger et al., 2004; after Ownby, 1997)

As the requirements placed on Practitioner Psychologists will often include specific directions for comment or particular assessment approaches that are ancillary to the primary purpose of the report, maintaining a clear grounding is critical. In the authors' experience, review processes external to the host organisation (health or prison) will often seek named assessments that they believe will assist in their decision-making processes, or in some instances for the Practitioner Psychologist's view of other information submitted in the service user's case.

In line with these requests for specific information, believed to be pertinent to the service user's progression, Grisso (2010) noted that 'the content is often different (*in forensic reports*) because of the need to address forensic questions that require different data than most clinical reports' (p. 103 – italics added). It is also of note that Jackson (1989) found that there were no substantial differences in perceptions of a person's dangerousness between mental health professionals and laypersons. Therefore, the Practitioner Psychologist providing a report on a service user in a secure setting needs to be mindful that whilst being specific in his/her response to instruction, there is also a need to consider those for whom the report is being provided and their expectations. As a consequence of the need for consistency in submitted reports, templates are usually provided for submission that the report writer is expected to follow, adapting his/her preferred style to match the requirement. Whilst formal court directed reports have minimum requirements, reports in secure settings require greater formalised structure. A further approach issue is, therefore, ensuring that the information provided, as indicated, is geared towards the reviewing authority. Practitioners need to recognise the ability of the instructing authority to require information, the value of which may not be immediately apparent in the first instance. Assisting the authority in its deliberations is always the primary aim of the practitioner's report.

Karson and Naskarni (2013) noted that when faced with rules that are either confusing or not clear in their purpose to the clinician, report writers manage their anxiety by ignoring the rules and following a preferred behavioural pattern. Personal motives are viewed as just and minimise any consequences of not following the requirement on the basis that they are experts in their field. Additionally, report writers need to be mindful of gaps in their competence and knowledge and acknowledge these. This links directly to issues of engagement in terms of biases discussed in that section above: the likelihood that report writers will be biased towards the service user is only matched by the likelihood that the report writer believes they know more than they actually do.

In this regard, Practitioner Psychologists preparing reports in secure settings need to be mindful of, and reflect upon, the issues of authority and competence. The approach should not be speculative (as might be the case in a more clinically oriented report), but rather a clear exposition of the risk management issues presenting in the case. The completion of the report and the formulation of the case is in itself the work of the forensic assessor. The reports prepared in secure settings are open to scrutiny by a range of other professionals and staff involved in the management of the case, as well as the authority completing the review. Therefore, Practitioner Psychologists need to ensure their conclusions are informed by data and sound theory, more so than in a purely clinical context (Karson and Nadkarni, 2013). In terms of approach then, the need to avoid emotion-driven report writing is paramount to not only manage the biasing factors described in the engagement section above but also to manage the report writer's credibility and professional standing with those scrutinising the work. Critically, avoidance of taking an advocacy position and following the legislative framework in meeting requirements must underpin an effective approach. Practitioners need to be mindful in such scenarios of managing the tension between the needs of the authority and the service user effectively.

In summary then, when writing reports in secure settings Practitioner Psychologists need to establish their role with both the authority and the service user at the outset. That is, that they are seeking to provide a clear response to the referral question and adopting an objective (as far as that is possible, as has been discussed) position, which does not advocate for one position or another (that of the authority or the service user). Rather the provision of information (analysed and interpreted data) which will inform the authority in making decisions about the service user's future progression – as set out in relevant statute and legislation, in a fair, evidenced and defensible way with due beneficence to the service user – is the role to adopt. In professional and ethical practice terms this sets the authority and the service user in parity, with overall public safety as the leading outcome.

Conclusions

The preparation and delivery of forensic reports in secure settings provides a particular set of challenges to the Practitioner Psychologist. Setting out an overly prescriptive approach is not helpful as it detracts from the primary function of the reports and cannot ever accommodate all service users in their myriad complexities, nor account for the potential requirements of the authority seeking advice (Grisso, 2010; Ownby, 1997). Clear principles that support practice in this area are, however, helpful and this chapter has sought to describe some of those in the framework of the three principal areas of issue that arise in the authors' experiences.

Common difficulties/confusion

The role of the Practitioner Psychologist in providing reports in secure settings is a multi-faceted one, and managing these competing tensions effectively is a cornerstone of good practice in this context. As observed above, service users in secure settings are by definition incarcerated against their will, be it under prison sentence handed down by the courts, or through the provisions of the MHA (1983). The behaviour that led to the service user's presenting situation is, therefore, at least antisocial if not also criminal, and may have elements that involved direct physical and/or emotional harm to the victim(s). The likelihood of harm, be it physical or psychological, on the Practitioner Psychologist is increased as a consequence of this. Therefore, Practitioner Psychologists must also be mindful of their own well-being, whilst maintaining their professional and ethical duty to act at all times with beneficence to the service user (HCPC, 2015). The service user's view of the reporting Practitioner Psychologist may be hostile due to the group the report writer is perceived to represent, or does represent by virtue of their sex, for example. Issues of approach noted above may assist in moderating potential threats, but the Practitioner Psychologist cannot ignore the role that the service user perceives the report writer represents and needs to make active efforts to successfully manage the interaction so that safety is assured to the optimal level and interfering factors arising are minimised. Maintaining a non-adversarial, focussed position on the purpose of the report will assist in this process.

The role of the Practitioner Psychologist in preparing reports in secure settings is one of both professional witness and expert in the field. This dual role can present challenges to the way in which information on service users is presented, and referring back to Figure 12.2, the provision of additional information when relevant is particularly pertinent in this context. Practitioner psychologists have a high level of knowledge, skill and competence in their field of expertise. In preparing reports in secure settings though, as a part of a multidisciplinary team carrying out assessment and reporting work on service users, there is a need to be clear about the distinction between competence and authority (Karson and Nadkarni, 2013). Whilst practitioner psychologists may have a good and thorough knowledge of a particular aspect of forensic practice, if it is not their primary and registered area of competence, they should not consider themselves to have the appropriate authority to comment in formal reports. For example, in working with men who have offended sexually, practitioner psychologists may become particularly familiar with the application and management of anti-libidinal medication in risk management. A Forensic Psychiatrist is, however, the authority on the use of such medicated approaches and any assessments completed by a Practitioner Psychologist should remain within his/her boundary of competence – i.e. evidenced and assessed approaches using psychological theory and practice that are complementary to the application of medication. Conversely, whilst psychiatrists will often refer to the outcomes of psychometric assessments, practitioner psychologists are the appropriate authority in this field.

Review of the task and key points to consider when preparing and writing reports in a secure setting

This chapter has outlined the main contexts in which practitioner psychologists may be asked to provide reports and highlights the main similarities and differences between the prison and hospital environments. Writers of reports such as this need to be mindful of and reflect on some key issues in this area of practice – primarily, the ability to effectively engage with the service user in terms of the relevant aspects of their case and presentation that are most likely to enable an effective dialogue. What are the drivers of this for both the service user and the practitioner, and will the therapeutic relationship in the assessment process be one that is of benefit to the service user and maximise the practitioner's expertise?

In that engagement process, how has the consent been validated and is it sufficiently inclusive from the outset to enable a thorough and needs driven assessment to be completed to meet the needs of all the stakeholders, not just the practitioner and the service user?

How the practitioner prepares for engagement in terms of managing their own heuristics and biases (their reflexive position) and being clear in what it is they are seeking to achieve through the assessment process? Does it meet the authority's instruction? Is this realistic in the time scale provided? If as a Practitioner Psychologist you feel unsure about or unable to answer these questions for yourself, then the report you deliver is likely to be less good than it could be. Report writing can be a complex and challenging process and is one core to the profession: it is essential to perform to the highest possible standard.

Checklist of steps/advice

Grisso (2010) described the outcomes from a systematic review of the 10 most common errors made in forensic reports: if the reader takes time to consider the process of their practice, as advocated here, then the majority of these are easily avoided.

1   Providing opinion without sufficient explanation
2   Purpose of the report is unclear
3   Information not being presented in an organised format
4   Irrelevant data being included
5   A failure to consider a range of interpretations of the data
6   Relying on inadequate evidence
7   Mixing interpretation with data (fact and opinion)
8   An overreliance on a single source of data (i.e. self-report)
9   Inappropriate language (jargon, pejorative language)
10 Inappropriate use of tests or interpretation of tests

Further reading

The starred references below are of particular use and provide for additional extensive coverage of the points made in the current chapter. Those working directly in secure services are recommended to access firsthand, read and understand through peer discussion and shared practice with other members of multidisciplinary teams the particular requirements of their working context as a secure setting.

Notes

1 NOMS: The National Offender Management Service is responsible as a UK government agency for the management of prisons and probation services in England and Wales.
2 Standard 2 applies here: 'be able to practise (sic) within the legal and ethical boundaries of their profession' (p.7).
3 These are: age, disability, gender reassignment, marriage and civil partnership, race, religion or belief, sex, sexual orientation.

References

British Psychological Society. (2015a). *Psychologists as expert witnesses,* 4th ed. Leicester, UK: BPS.

British Psychological Society. (2015b). *Guidance on teaching and assessment of ethical competence in psychology education.* Leicester, UK: BPS.

Campbell, T.W. and DeClue, G. (2010) Maximizing predictive accuracy in sexually violent predator evaluations. *Open Access Journal of Forensic Psychology, 2,* 148–232.

Elbogen, E.B. (2002). The process of violence risk assessment: A review of descriptive research, *Aggression and Violent Behavior, 7,* 501–604.

Equalities Act. (2010). Retrieved from www.legislation.gov.uk/ukpga/2010/15/contents (accessed 11 August 2015).

Grisso, T. (2010). Guidance for improving forensic reports: A review of common errors. *Open Access Journal of Forensic Psychology, 2,* 102–15.

The Guardian. (2006). Killer should not have been freed, says report. Retrieved from www.theguardian.com/uk/2006/may/11/topstories3.ukcrime (accessed 22 April 2015).

Health and Care Professions Council. (2015). *Standards of proficiency.* Retrieved from www.hcpc-uk.org/assets/documents/10002963SOP_Practitioner_psychologists.pdf (accessed 10 August 2015).

First, M.B., Gibbon, M., Spitzer R.L., Williams, J.B.W. and Benjamin, L.S. (1997). *Structured clinical interview for DSM-IV Axis II personality disorders* (SCID-II). Washington, DC: American Psychiatric Press.

Jackson, M. (1989). Psychiatric decision-making for the courts: Lay people, judges or psychiatrists? *International Journal of Law and Psychology, 9,* 507–20.

Kahneman, D. (2011). *Thinking fast and slow.* New York: Farrar, Strauss and Giroux.

*Karson, M. and Nadkarni, L. (2013). *Principles of forensic report writing.* Washington, DC: APA.

*Lichtenburger, E.O., Mather, N., Kaufman, N.L. and Kaufman, A.S. (2004). *Essentials of assessment report writing.* Hoboken, NJ: John Wiley and Sons.

Loranger, A.W. (1999). *IPDE: International personality disorder examination DSM-IV and ICD — 10 interviews.* Lutz, FL: Psychological Assessment Resources.

Mental Health Act. (1983). Retrieved from www.legislation.gov.uk/ukpga/1983/20/contents (accessed 10 August 2015).

Needs, A. (2010). Systemic failure and human error, in Ireland, C.A. and Fisher, M.J. (eds.), *Consultancy and advising in forensic practice: Empirical and practical guidelines*. Chichester, UK: John Wiley and Sons.

★Ownby, R.L. (1997). *Psychological reports: A guide to writing in professional psychology*. New York: John Wiley and Sons.

Parole Board Rules. (2011). Retrieved from www.legislation.gov.uk/uksi/2011/2947/part/1/made.

Rest, J. (1982) A psychologist looks at the teaching fo ethics. *The Hastings Center Report, 12* (1), 29–36.

R. (Haney, Kaiyam and Massey) v. Secretary of State for Justice, R. (Robinson) v. Secretary of State for Justice UKSC 66 (2014). Retrieved from www.bailii.org/uk/cases/UKSC/2014/66.html (accessed 25 July 2015).

R. (Morales) v. Parole Board, Secretary of State for Justice, Staffordshire Probation Service EWHC 28 (Admin) (2011). Retrieved from www.bailii.org/ew/cases/EWHC/Admin/2011/28.html (accessed 10 August 2015).

Slovic, P. and Monahan, J. (1995). Probability, danger, and coercion: A study of risk perception and decision making in mental health law. *Law and Human Behavior, 19*, 49–65.

Tversky, A. and Kahneman, D. (1974). Judgement under uncertainty: Heuristics and biases. *Science, 185* (4157), 1124–31.

Willmot, P. (2011). Assessing personality disorder in forensic settings, in Willmot, P. and Gordon, N. (eds.), *Working positively with personality disorder in secure settings*. Chichester, UK: John Wiley and Sons.

★Wolber, G.J. and Carne, W.F. (2002). *Writing psychological reports: A guide for clinicians*, 2nd ed. Sarasota, FL: Professional Resource Press.

13

REPORTING FOR THE PAROLE BOARD OR OTHER RELEASE DECISION MAKERS INCLUDING MENTAL HEALTH REVIEW TRIBUNALS

Michael Daffern, Jessica Mooney, Kylie Thomson and Gabrielle Klepfisz

Introduction

Release decisions are important junctures within the criminal justice and forensic mental health systems during which determinations are made regarding a person's suitability for release into the community following a period of imprisonment or hospitalisation. It requires board members to consider a myriad of factors and review multiple sources of information. Despite the increase in mandatory sentencing structures and the automatic release of some offenders over recent decades, a discretionary decision-making approach is still adopted to varying degrees by multiple authorities internationally (Kinnevy and Caplan, 2008). In jurisdictions where a discretionary process is maintained, members are typically provided with decision-making guidelines. However, these guidelines may be broad, contain an extensive list of variables for consideration and provide limited or no guidance regarding how factors should be weighed and integrated to produce the ultimate release judgement (Gobeil and Serin, 2009). Therefore, for the most part, the factors considered are at the discretion of board members. Research suggests that a range of individual, contextual and legal factors are taken into account. Factors frequently considered include offender demographic characteristics such as age (Kinnevy and Caplan, 2008); criminal history and offence-related variables (Huebner and Bynum, 2006; Morgan and Smith, 2005); factors related to an offender's parole plan and risk for future violence (Hood and Shute, 2000); general and aggressive misconduct during confinement; and mental health status. Also critical are the person's participation and performance in offender rehabilitation programmes. Unfortunately, methods for determining change in treatment are poorly developed, and this is a much-needed topic for further research. In this chapter we recommend consideration of reliable and clinically significant change indices (see Klepfisz, O'Brien and Daffern, 2014), structured measures of risk (e.g. the Violence Risk Scale or HCR-20^{v3}) and protective factors (e.g. the Structured Assessment of Protective Factors for violence risk) to assist with the appraisal of change and risk for recidivism. A neglected area of consideration is the positive changes offenders make during their period of incarceration.

Best practice

There is a lack of research into the impact of psychologists' reports on release decision-making boards and uncertainty as to why reports are requested. Anecdotally, they appear to be requested most commonly when there is a perception that there is something unique or troubling about the offender, when the person's offending is unusual or when the offences are intuitively associated with psychological aberration (e.g. exhibitionism, fire setting, sexual offences against children), and finally, when people appear to have a mental illness or a history of mental health treatment.

A critical first task is determining what the parole board requires. Unless this is undertaken, there is a very real risk that the report writer will prepare a misguided report that is of little use. At the same time, it is important to request from the board the information that will be required to conduct the assessment. This may include previous psychological assessments and reports on performance in treatment and behaviour in the prison or hospital. Without these the report is limited; these limitations should be noted. In many instances, boards will know the person's personal background in great detail. There may be little value in providing another extensive summary; instead clarify with the board what information they would like and direct the board to other reports if they provide a valid and comprehensive summary of the person's background. Of course, if discrepancies with other reports are identified, then these should be noted.

For a comprehensive report, the assessment will need to include the following:

- a brief family history;
- a personal history that includes the person's social and personal development;
- any significant medical history as it pertains to psychosocial functioning and offending;
- mental health history (of not only his/her use of treatment but also of experienced illness) including substance use (our preference is to locate the person's substance use history within the mental health section since it is a mental disorder);
- forensic history (including an analysis of the index offence, paying particular attention to the offender's account and any discrepancies with official records);
- relevant psychometrics; and
- anything else relevant to the case.

Collateral information should be sought to verify the person's account of his/her history. Educational, vocational, medical and mental health records, and perceptions of the offender offered by knowledgeable third parties (with clients' consent), can be helpful. These should be requested in the first instance from the referrer (parole board or mental health review board).

Outline of report

The report best commences with a description of the offender, including their age, date of birth and date of assessment. The presenting problem or reason for the assessment should be stated and details of the request should be listed. Sources of data used to prepare the report also need to be included. The following sections provide a structure for the report.

* Introduction
* Presentation and mental state
* Personal history
* Mental health history
* Forensic history
* Risk assessment and identification of treatment needs
* Conclusions/opinion/recommendations

This list may vary according to the needs of the board and the characteristics and situation of the person being assessed. The aforementioned list does not include a separate psychometric test results section. Although some will prefer a separate section, it is our view that psychological test results are best integrated into the relevant section alongside other descriptions and impressions of the person. When the assessment includes psychological testing, introduce the test, comment on its relevance and validity and then present the results and your interpretation. Keep this section concise and avoid jargon. Developing your own vocabulary is one of the hardest parts of report writing and something that clinicians do differently. You may change the way you say things as you become more experienced. Reading others' reports is a key way of learning what sounds good and what is confusing.

> *Mr. Adam presented as open and honest although to assist appraisal of his response style I also administered the Paulhus Deception Scales (PDS). The PDS is designed to assess a client's self-reporting style. When self-reporting, some people provide accurate, insightful self-descriptions, while others purposely attempt to manage the impression they create by describing themselves in overly positive terms. Still others try to be honest, yet exaggerate their virtues as a result of self-deception. Mr. Adam's scores on the PDS were all within the normal range, suggesting that he was not presenting himself in an overly favourable light. As such, his responses to other self-report inventories completed during the interview were likely not skewed by the situational demands of the interview.*

Introduction

Begin with a general statement about the reason for the referral:

> *This report has been prepared at your request, dated 3 January 2015. According to the request Mr. Smith was convicted of assault, during which he stabbed another man*

with a knife. You note that Mr. Smith has no prior criminal history but he has a recent history of drug use and depression. He has been incarcerated for the last two years and is eligible for parole on 12 June 2015. You asked whether there is a need for ongoing counseling to address his anxiety, which is purportedly related to his substance use and therefore his offending.

Include a brief statement describing: (a) the circumstances of the referral (this should orient the reader to the report and the types of issues that will be discussed. It should elaborate or refine the referral statement if it is inappropriate); (b) the date and nature of your clinical contacts; (c) the sources of information made available to assist in the preparation of the report; and (d) an outline of the assessment procedure. This is necessary so that the court, board or tribunal knows how reliable your report is, how you arrived at your conclusions and what information was available/unavailable for your assessment. Describe any information that you did not have access to that might have been useful and how this limits the conclusions that can be drawn.

You provided copies of the following: Criminal History, dated 20 November 2014, Summary of Charges, Sentencing comments, dated 1 March 2013, a letter from Mr. J. Johnson, Psychologist, addressed to Mr. G. Brown, Solicitor, Solicitors R Us, dated 3 November 2005, and a substance use treatment programme completion report dated 3rd December 2014.

Mr. Smith was interviewed at the Armidale Correctional Centre for one and a half hours on Wednesday morning, the 29th January 2015. In addition to a clinical interview he was administered the following psychometric tests: the Paulhus Deception Scale (PDS), an instrument to assess whether a respondent is attempting to create an overly favourable impression at interview, the Beck Depression Inventory-11 (BDI-11), a standardised self-report measure used to assess symptoms of depression, the State-Trait Anger Expression Inventory-11 (STAXI), a standardised self-report instrument used to assess the experience and expression of anger, and the Level of Service Inventory-Revised (LSI-R), an observer-rated measure used to assess the level of risk for general criminal recidivism and to identify treatment needs. The HCR-20, an instrument designed to appraise risk for violent behaviour was also scored.

In your report, state how you obtained informed consent. This shows that you have discussed with the person the limits to confidentiality, who may have access to the information gathered during the assessment process and the person's response to this information.

The nature and purpose of the assessment and the limits to confidentiality were outlined to Mr. Smith at the commencement of the interview. He was made aware that the information he gave during the assessment, and the results from psychometric testing, could be included in the final report and presented to the Parole Board. Mr. Smith stated that he understood this and agreed to proceed.

Presentation and mental state

This can be a very important section, since it gives you a chance to convey qualitative features of the assessment, as well as comment on how valid you think your assessment was. The presentation section should be structured like the psychiatric Mental Status Examination, which proceeds from a description of the person, through interpretation of mood and affect, and then to aspects of form and content of thought. It typically concludes with a comment on cognition. Try to be descriptive in this section rather than interpretative. Do not merely say that the person appeared depressed. Describe the behaviours that indicated that the person was depressed; for example, that they were slow, sad and often made self-critical statements. Avoid jargon. When it is necessary to communicate using language that is rarely used outside of professional mental health contexts, provide a definition (e.g. his affect [the outward expression of immediately experienced emotion] was normal in terms of range, intensity, reactivity and appropriateness).

> *Mr. King is a 19-year-old man. He was well groomed, had an earring in each ear, a tattoo on his right arm and was dressed in clean, casual clothing. He was attentive and maintained good eye contact throughout the interview. He seemed mildly uncomfortable at the outset of the interview but appeared to gain confidence during the process. There were no obvious signs of a severely disturbed mood; his range of emotional responsivity was considered to be within the normal range. His verbal communication skills were adequate, although he did require prompting on occasion for more detail in his responses. His speech was of normal rate, quantity and tone. There were no reported symptoms or overt signs of any psychotic processes (e.g. formal thought disorder, hallucinations). Although not formally tested, he was fully alert and oriented, his memory appeared intact and his level of intellectual functioning is likely to fall in the Low-Average range. Mr. King was compliant with the interview process. He was open in his responses to questions regarding his offence, although appeared confused about what had led to his offending.*

Personal background

The key here is relevance. This is one section where people tend to write too much, as they are unsure what is relevant and what is not; this can be clarified through a discussion with the referrer and consultation with a supervisor. You do not need to present the individual's whole life history. Ask yourself whether it really contributes to your analysis of the case or not (cite another report if you know the referrer has this). You may include:

- family background, including composition and early childhood and adolescent experiences;
- significant life events such as loss, abuse, history of emotional and behavioural disturbances;

- physical health;
- education (academic performance, relationship with peers, relationship with teachers, whether they were expelled or suspended from school);
- employment history;
- relationship history;
- psychosexual development (for sexual offenders);
- relationships; and
- social circumstances.

Information needs to be presented in a logical and coherent manner. It should be descriptive rather than evaluative. Keep in mind that this is a description of a person's life and they may read your report. Although the assessment report should not be biased and the assessment interview is not therapy, it is important that the experience and product of the assessment is not aversive for the person being assessed and does not limit the possibility of future consultation with a psychologist.

Mental health history

In this section describe the person's mental health background and his/her history of mental health treatment, including his/her response to treatment. Include here a description of his/her substance use history. Establish the nature of the relationship between his/her mental health problems and his/her criminal behaviour (if a relationship exists).

Forensic history

In this section describe the development of the person's criminal behaviour (when criminal behaviours were initiated, how they were maintained and their developmental course). For example, when there is a problem with aggression, consider early exposure to violence, victimisation (neglect, sexual and other violent behaviour), attitude towards violence, acquisition of the aggressive repertoire, anger, the functions of aggression and factors inhibiting aggression (protective factors). For sexual violence, consider early sexual abuse, sexual development, relationship history, assess for paraphilia(s), sexual history, current sexual behaviour and the repertoire of sexual interests and past sexual behaviours.

For the index offence, prepare a thorough analysis including a description of the person's behaviour and mental state at the time of the offence. This section incorporates an official offence history, conveys the offender's account of his/her offence and that portrayed by official sources (e.g. witness statements, summary of charges). It should point out discrepancies where relevant. In general, when describing the person's account consider writing 'Peter stated . . .' or 'Peter reported . . .' when the veracity of self-report is unclear. If you write, for example, 'Peter was abused as a child', this sounds like it is factual and you do not necessarily know that it is. Be clear if you have any doubts about the accuracy of the information that you present.

Risk assessment and identification of treatment needs

The assessment of risk for future offending behaviour is a critical task. Whilst risk may not be the focus of every assessment (e.g. where the board is interested in the nature of the mental health problem and the appropriate treatment), it is relevant because risk issues may impact where treatment should occur and the level of assertiveness in which it should be offered. Risk assessment procedures have seen marked advancements over recent decades, resulting in the development of actu-arial (see also Chapter 3) and structured professional judgement (SPJ) measures (e.g. HCR-20 [Webster, Douglas, Eaves and Hart, 1997]; VRS [Wong and Gordon, 2000]; see also Chapter 5). Actuarial and SPJ measures have comparable predictive accuracy (Yang, Wong and Coid, 2010) that is considered stronger than unaided clinical approaches (Ægisdóttir, White, Spengler, Maugherman, Anderson, Cook, Lampropoulos, Walker and Cohen, 2006). However, the latter may facilitate the reappraisal of violence risk and inform the treatment and management of violent offenders (Douglas and Kropp, 2002; Yang et al., 2010). This reappraisal of risk is often of great importance for release decision makers, and recent evidence suggests that some SPJ assessments may be administered before and after treatment, or at the start and conclusion of a period of incarceration, to determine whether dynamic risk factors have changed (lessened or increased) over time (de Vries Robbé, de Vogel, Douglas and Nijman, 2014; Olver, Beggs Christofferson and Wong, 2015).

Risk and treatment change measures

The measurement of intra-individual within-treatment change has received increasing attention in recent years, including how such change should be mea-sured (see Chapter 7). One method of calculating change with clinical appeal is the clinically significant change method (CSC). The CSC approach categorises an individual's response to treatment based on whether they have made reliably significant treatment gains (using the Reliable Change Index) and his/her level of functioning following rehabilitation. Notably, an individual's post-treatment score on a psychological test must fall below a calculated cut-off between what is con-sidered 'dysfunctional' and 'functional' (Jacobson and Truax, 1991). By combining post-treatment scores and the amount of change achieved, researchers have created descriptive subgroups to differentiate and communicate an individual's response to treatment (recovered, improved, already okay, unchanged and deteriorated) (Bowen, Gilchrist and Beech, 2008; Olver et al., 2015). With the primary goal of offender treatment being reduced criminal behaviour, there is a fundamental assumption that an individual's treatment-related changes will be related to future offending. As such, knowing whether someone has changed during treatment, and the direction and magnitude of this change, may be essential in making decisions regarding release and further supervision and/or treatment need.

Risk assessment in secure environments: Special considerations

Contemporary researchers have encouraged a shift toward prevention-based approaches to the assessment and management of violence risk (Douglas and Kropp, 2002). Emphasis has been placed on the development and validation of assessment methods incorporating dynamic factors that capture an individual's 'risk state' (Douglas and Skeem, 2005) and case-formulation driven (see Chapter 4) approaches (Daffern, Jones, Howells, Shine, Mikton and Turnbridge, 2007; Hart, Sturmey, Logan and McMurran, 2011). Against this background, various methodologies for incorporating institutional behaviour into risk assessment and risk reduction procedures have emerged. One such approach is the so-called Offence Paralleling Behaviour (OPB [Jones, 2004; Daffern et al., 2007]) framework, which has emerged as a potential supplement to structured risk assessment methods. The OPB framework provides suggestions for identifying idiographic patterns of behaviour that manifest within custodial environments and are functionally similar to an individual's offending behaviour (Daffern et al., 2007). These OPBs are critical to appraisals of dynamic risk factors for people in custody since these manifestations may be altered by the prison environment (e.g. prisoners may not express their risks in typical offence type behaviour such as physical aggression due to a fear of being caught, rather they may isolate in their cell or engage in noncompliant behaviour). Correctional environments are designed to minimise the occurrence, and facilitate the detection, of aggressive (including sexually aggressive) behaviour. Researchers have highlighted the potential for this unique environment to suppress or alter an offender's aggressive behaviour (Daffern, 2010; Jones, 2004) by way of removing some antecedents that typically precede an individual's aggression in the community, or prompting offenders to develop skills to avoid the detection of their aggressive behaviour (detection evasion skills; Jones, 2004). Certain aspects of the institutional environment may also provoke aggression, such as overcrowding (Porporino, 1986), high turnover rates and problematic interpersonal interactions between custodial staff and prisoners (Bottoms, 1999). Any analysis of the relevance of misconduct within an institution should consider these issues.

A key task for clinicians is understanding the purpose of the index offending behaviour – delineating the sequence of behaviour, thoughts and emotions that preceded and followed the offending – and then comparing these behaviours with the person's present behaviour to determine whether there is functional similarity. The frequency of these sequences of behaviour may be monitored to help assess risk and treatment need, and may provide more nuanced scoring of SPJ tools within secure settings. A similar procedure through which institutional behaviour may be incorporated into the process of assessing risk and determining treatment change is by looking for behavioural indicators of criminogenic needs within the custodial environment. For this purpose, Gordon and Wong (2010) developed the Offence

Analogue and Offence Reduction Behavior Rating Guide. This rating guide was designed to supplement violence risk assessments in custodial environments conducted using the Violence Risk Scale (VRS [Wong and Gordon, 2000]). The rating guide directs clinicians to look for behavioural manifestations of each dynamic VRS factor, referred to as Offence Analogue Behaviours (OABs). Clinicians are also required to look for prosocial behaviours said to indicate risk reduction (Offence Reduction Behaviours – ORBs). A decrease in the frequency of OABs and an increase in the frequency of ORBs on a risk factor relevant for the offender is said to indicate a reduction in violence risk. Mooney and Daffern (2013) showed that prisoner behaviours (OABs and ORBs) linked to five dynamic VRS factors were significantly associated with the length of time between an offender's release and to the commission of violence; of these five VRS factors more were ORBs, reflecting prosocial rather than antisocial behaviours.

These approaches broaden the focus from overt aggressive and violent behaviour (e.g. verbal abuse or physical violence) to include behavioural representations of dynamic risk factors, and in this way may provide a useful mechanism for incorporating institutional behaviour into risk assessments of incarcerated offenders. Recent research conducted by Lewis, Olver and Wong (2012) illustrated the dynamic nature of the VRS dynamic risk factors and showed that change in these factors from pre- to post-treatment corresponded to reductions in violent recidivism. This suggests that OABs and ORBs, said to represent behavioural manifestations of these risk factors, may act as treatment targets for interventions designed to address violent offending. They are also valid indicators of risk that, when altered, may indicate a reduction in criminal propensity.

These findings also suggest that the development and use of prosocial skills over the course of imprisonment may play an important role in reducing an offender's risk for future violence and show the importance of looking beyond the absence of antisocial behaviour when assessing violence risk. Similarly, de Vries Robbé et al. (2014) has shown that an increase in protective factors as well as a reduction in dynamic risk factors is associated with reduced propensity for violent behavior. As such we recommend SPJ tools that permit measurement of change in risk and protective factors to assess risk and change in treatment.

In any risk assessment section introduce the risk assessment instruments, outline the rationale for their selection and define the benefits and limitations of the instrument (see Chapters 3 and 5). Make explicit the limitations of the test and your interpretations. If terms like *high*, *moderate* and *low risk* are invoked, then define these terms and state the source of the definition (if it is not your own), as clinicians use these terms differently.

Conclusions/opinion/recommendations

This is undoubtedly the most important part of your report, where you get to use your specialist knowledge and offer your professional opinion. Begin by summarising the key points. Comment on risk level and intervention (treatment and management) needs. Reiterate the reason for the assessment, include an opening statement that reintroduces the person, the referral details and the central issues. Provide a summary and integration of the various sources of information obtained and answer to the best of your ability the referral question. Include a formulation of the person's problems. Make treatment and management recommendations (respectfully offered), but be mindful of whether these recommendations are useful within the context of options available to the board. Avoid commenting directly on whether the offender should be released or not; it is generally best to make recommendations based on risk and need and detail what may be helpful, irrespective of the outcome of the board's deliberations. A diagnosis may be offered, and is required if the referral question is for diagnosis. It is important to note that in some jurisdictions only appropriately qualified professionals may offer a diagnosis. Clarify the relationship between the data, your reasoning and the conclusions and recommendations. Despite obvious limitations in drawing conclusions, the report should nevertheless be conclusive in nature. Sometimes your conclusion will be that you do not have enough information to draw a conclusion, but the reasons for this should be spelled out.

Common difficulties/confusion

The suggestions for report writing that we have made above will hopefully help make reports useful and concise. There are, however, a few issues that need to be considered so that reports are well received. First, it is important not to make unrealistic treatment recommendations; do not recommend treatments that are unavailable or that the person is not ready to complete. Sometimes psychologists have a treatment bias in which every person is seen as suitable for treatment. Treatment outcome studies show that not every treatment is useful, not every person is ready for it and/or not every person benefits from it. Guard against over pathologising the person or overestimating his/her likely rehabilitation potential. Consider responsivity issues and be careful not to make unrealistic recommendations that create the impression a particular treatment will be effective. It is important to be mindful of prognosis and general treatment outcomes. Ensure familiarity with the types of treatments that are offered. Prior to making a recommendation for treatment at a particular service, ascertain what the referral process is, whether the person would meet referral criteria and whether, in general terms, the service is likely to accept him/her. It may be helpful to describe the treatment so the board understands the intensity and duration of the programme, so that the other conditions the board establishes do not overwhelm the person.

Do not withhold useful information that you believe will be detrimental to the person. Reports should be objective yet fair, recognising the strengths but also the issues confronting the person and his/her situation; remember the person may read your report. Be mindful of the length of the report. Although there is no correct length, the report should be 'fit for purpose'. Many statutory releasing authorities will have little time to read lengthy reports; be aware of the demands on them and tailor the report to ensure it is useful. Finally, avoid jargon, as the main purpose of your report is communication. Many psychological terms are unfamiliar to non-psychologists.

Review task

1 Identify the relevant boards in your jurisdiction and review the legislation that governs their work. In this legislation ascertain how and why psychological reports can be requested and how they are to be used. If you cannot locate this information, then ask the board.
2 Before completing a report seek an opportunity to attend a hearing. Many boards will allow students and professionals to attend a hearing as part of their training.

Checklist of steps/advice

1 Offenders are a heterogeneous group and offending behaviour is usually complex; each assessment should be individually tailored to the individual and the context in which the report is being used.
2 Use various sources of information to conduct your assessment (interviews, psychological tests, draw upon collateral information and corroborate your data).
3 Assess risk and need by drawing upon structured measures and consider measuring change using reliable and clinically significant change indices. Assess protective factors as well as risks and criminogenic needs.
4 Mullen and Ogloff (2009) have highlighted a range of ethical considerations for risk assessments that are also relevant in this context and should be considered:
   a The person consents to the assessment in the knowledge of the nature of the assessment, its purposes and the limitations on confidentiality that may apply.
   b A reasonable body of empirical evidence exists to guide the assessment and the assessment is based on a careful analysis of the relevant characteristics of the particular individual.
   c Express risks in terms of probabilities (not dangerousness) with clear admissions of the fallibility and potential variability in the prediction.
5 The body of the report should be descriptive and evaluative. Opinions should be left to the opinion section of the report.
6 Recommendations need to be fair, objective and realistic, both in terms of client factors (i.e. readiness, cognitive capacity) and services (i.e. services are available; client meets admission requirements).

Further reading

The Australian Institute of Judicial Administration has a report on a survey of problems with expert reports accessible at www.aija.org.au/online/AIJA%20PUBS%20LIST.pdf.

Dynamic Risk Assessment of Offender Re-entry (DRAOR [Serin and Mailloux, 2009]) is a measure designed to assess dynamic risk in offender's re-entering the community.

Jacobson, N.S. and Truax, P. (1991). Clinical significance: A statistical approach to defining meaningful change in psychotherapy research. *Journal of Consulting and Clinical Psychology*, *51*, 12–9. Retrieved from http://dx.doi.org/10.1037//0022-006X.59.1.12.

References

Ægisdóttir, S., White, M.J., Spengler, P.M., Maugherman, A.A., Anderson, L.A., Cook, R.S., Lampropoulos, G.K., Walker, B.S. and Cohen, G. (2006). The meta-analysis of clinical judgement project: Fifty-six years of accumulated research on clinical versus statistical prediction. *The Counseling Psychologist*, *34*, 341–82.

Bottoms, A.E. (1999). Interpersonal violence and social order in prisons. *Crime and Justice*, *26*, 205–81.

Bowen, E., Gilchrist, E.A and Beech, A.R. (2008). Change in treatment has no relationship with subsequent reoffending in UK domestic violence sample: A preliminary study. *International Journal of Offender Therapy and Comparative Criminology*, *52*, 598–614.

Daffern, M. (2010) A structured cognitive behavioural approach to the assessment and treatment of violent offenders using offence paralleling behaviour. In Daffern, M., Jones, L. and Shine, J. (eds.). *Offence paralleling behaviour: A case formulation approach to offender assessment and treatment* (pp.105–20). Chichester, UK: John Wiley and Sons.

Daffern, M., Jones, L., Howells, K., Shine, J., Mikton, C. and Turnbridge, V. (2007). Editorial: Refining the definition of offence paralleling behaviour. *Criminal Behaviour and Mental Health*, *17*, 265–73.

Douglas, K.S. and Kropp, P.R. (2002). A prevention-based paradigm for violence risk assessment: Clinical and research applications. *Criminal Justice and Behavior*, *29*, 617–58.

de Vries Robbé, M., de Vogel, V., Douglas, K.S. and Nijman, H.L.I. (2014). Changes in dynamic risk and protective factors for violence during inpatient forensic psychiatric treatment: Predicting reductions in post-discharge community recidivism. *Law and Human Behavior*, *39*, 53–61.

Douglas, K.S. and Skeem, J.L. (2005). Violence risk assessment: Getting specific about being dynamic. *Psychology, Public Policy, and Law*, *11*, 347–83.

Gobeil, R. and Serin, R.C. (2009). Preliminary evidence of adaptive decision-making techniques used by parole board members. *International Journal of Forensic Mental Health*, *8*, 97–104.

Gordon, A. and Wong, S.C.P. (2010). Offence analogue behaviours as indicators of criminogenic need and treatment progress in custodial settings, in Daffern, M., Jones, L. and Shine, J. (eds.), *Offence paralleling behaviour: A case formulation approach to offender assessment and intervention* (pp. 171–84). Chichester, UK: Wiley-Blackwell.

Hart, S., Sturmey, P., Logan, C. and McMurran, M. (2011). Forensic case formulation. *International Journal of Forensic Mental Health*, *10*, 118–26.

Hart, S.D., Eaves, D., and Ogloff, J.R.P. (eds.) (2001) HCR-20: Violence risk management companion guide. Burnaby, Canada: Mental Health, Law, and Policy Institute, Simon Fraser University.

Hood, R. and Shute, S. (2000). *The parole system at work: A study of risk based decision-making*. London: Home Office.

Huebner, B.M. and Bynum, T.S. (2006). An analysis of parole decision making using a sample of sex offenders: A focal concerns perspective. *Criminology*, *44*, 961–91.

Jacobson, N.S. and Truax, P. (1991). Clinical significance: A statistical approach to defining meaningful change in psychotherapy research. *Journal of Consulting and Clinical Psychology*, *51*, 12–9.

Jones, L. (2004). Offence Paralleling Behaviour (OPB) as a framework for assessment and interventions with offenders, in Needs, A. and Towl, G. (eds.), *Applying psychology to forensic practice* (pp. 34–63). Oxford, UK: British Psychological Society and Blackwell Publishing.

Kinnevy, S.C. and Caplan, J.M. (2008). *Findings from the APAI International Survey of Releasing Authorities* [Research Report]. Philadelphia, PA: Center for Research on Youth and Social Policy.

Klepfisz, G., O'Brien, K. and Daffern, M. (2014). Violent offenders' within-treatment change in anger, criminal attitudes, and violence risk: Associations with violent recidivism. *International Journal of Forensic Mental Health*, *13*(4), 348–62. DOI:10.1080/14999013 .2014.951107.

Lewis, K., Olver, M.E. and Wong, S.C.P. (2012). The violence risk scale: Predictive validity and linking changes in risk with violent recidivism in a sample of high-risk offenders with psychopathic traits. *Assessment*, *20*, 150–64.

Mooney, J.L. and Daffern, M. (2013). The Offence Analogue and Offence Reduction Behaviour Rating Guide as a supplement to violence risk assessment in incarcerated offenders. *International Journal of Forensic Mental Health*, *12*, 255–64.

Morgan, K.D. and Smith, B. (2005). Parole release decisions revisited: An analysis of parole release decisions for violent inmates in a southeastern state. *Journal of Criminal Justice*, *33*, 277–87.

Mullen, P.E. and Ogloff, J.R.P. (2009) Assessing and managing the risks of violence towards others. In: M.G. Gelder, N. Andreasen, J. Lopez- Ibor and J. Geddes (eds.). *New Oxford Textbook of Psychiatry*, 2nd ed., 1991–2002. Oxford, UK: Oxford University Press.

Olver, M.E., Beggs Christofferson, S.M. and Wong, S.C.P. (2015). Evaluation and applications of the clinically significant change method with the violence risk scale-sexual offender version: Implications for risk-change communication. *Behavioral Sciences and the Law*, *33*, 92–110.

Olver, M.E., Lewis, K. and Wong, S.C. (2013). Risk reduction treatment of high-risk psychopathic offenders: The relationship of psychopathy and treatment change to violent recidivism. *Personality Disorders*, *4*, 160–67.

Porporino, F.J. (1986). Managing violent individuals in correctional settings. *Journal of Interpersonal Violence*, *1*, 213–36.

Webster, C.D., Douglas, K.S., Eaves, D. and Hart, S.D. (1997). HCR-20: Assessing risk for violence (Version 2). Vancouver, Canada: Mental Health, Law, and Policy Institute, Simon Fraser University.

Wong, S.C.P. and Gordon, A. (2000). *Manual for the Violence Risk Scale*. Saskatchewan, Canada: University of Saskatchewan.

Yang, M., Wong, S.C.P. and Coid, J. (2010). The efficacy of violence prediction: A meta-analytic comparison of nine risk assessment tools. *Psychological Bulletin*, *136*, 740–67.

14

COMMUNITY TREATMENT REPORTS

Considering best practice

Lawrence Ellerby and David Kolton

Introduction

Community treatment reports are not discussed widely in the forensic literature. A literature review on community-based reports for forensic populations reveals a primary focus on risk assessment reports. Although conducting risk assessment is a central component of appropriate community risk management, treatment reports build on the information contained in risk assessments and play an equally important role in supporting clients and systems to attend to community risk management. Community treatment reports provide valuable information related to a client's ongoing functioning, management of their risk factors and response to intervention. Given risk management is not static, ongoing consideration, review and reporting of a client's participation and progress in treatment and management of identified risk factors are critical. Community treatment reports allow for communicating current information about a client and provide ongoing guidance to support risk management planning (e.g. treatment, supervision, support, monitoring). There are a myriad of reporting needs that treatment providers face. Reports may include treatment intake reports, treatment progress reports, post-suspension/ treatment closure reports and treatment completion reports. Each of these has a specific purpose and provides information important for ongoing evaluation of the client's participation and progress in treatment, therapeutic goals, assessment of the manageability of risk factors and recommendations related to ongoing or future treatment, case management and risk management needs.

Types of community reports

The following offers a synopsis of different types of community reports.

Treatment intake reports

These are typically initiated in response to a referral agency's request for a treatment proposal or as a part of a programme's intake process. The primary objective is to provide a framework for the client's treatment. Treatment plan recommendations should address the type of interventions to be provided, key treatment/ risk management targets for therapeutic intervention and strategies to working effectively with the particular client. It is important for these recommendations to be theoretically grounded to reflect the current state of knowledge related to best practice and offer a plan that will optimally support the client to address relevant issues related to risk management.

The Risk-Need-Responsivity (RNR) Model (Andrews and Bonta, 2010) can be used to guide the structure of the treatment intake report. RNR helps the clinician consider the appropriate intensity of intervention based on the client's assessed level of risk, identify relevant treatment targets and focus on responsivity issues. In regards to responsivity, intervention approaches are identified that will address treatment engagement and optimise therapeutic benefit based on client characteristics and presenting issues (e.g. age, cognitive functioning, mental disorder, cultural background, shame, trauma). Treatment goals are also identified that may not be criminogenic in nature but that should be addressed in order to enable the client to appropriately attend to the identified dynamic risk factors (e.g. practical and emotional issues related to community adjustment and integration, trauma, negative sense of self). Elements of the Relapse Prevention Model (Pithers, Marques, Gibat and Marlatt, 1983) and the Self-Regulation Model (Ward and Hudson, 2000) can also guide the identification of risk factors, pathways to offending behaviour, processes that can lead to lapses or relapse and coping strategies to support risk management. Additionally, principles from the 'New Me' and Good Lives Models (Haaven and Coleman, 2000; Ward and Stewart, 2003) can be considered to ensure treatment planning is focused on positive, approach-oriented recommendations and identify treatment goals that will support both risk management and an enhanced quality of life.

Preparing reports requires gathering and considering multiple sources of data from which to formulate the treatment plan (American Psychological Association, 2013; Heilburn, Warren and Picarello, 2003; Witt and Fogel, 2015). Sources of data for treatment intake reports should include a client interview, review of background information and an interview with a representative from the referral agency. As well, other collateral interviews with key informants may be helpful in obtaining a complete history. Many programmes administer pre-treatment psychological testing to further assess treatment needs and provide baseline data to consider when evaluating progress over the course of treatment, such as personality, emotional experience and coping skill inventories (Barnett, Wakeling, Mandeville-Norden and Rakestrow, 2012). As well, risk assessment tools structured to measure treatment change should be considered, as they allow for systematically evaluating treatment progress and goals for therapeutic intervention and risk management/ reduction over time (e.g. Violence Risk Scale – Wong and Gordon, 2006; Violence Risk Scale-Sexual Offender Version; Olver, Beggs, Christofferson, Grace and Wong, 2014).

A client interview is a central component of the treatment intake report process. These allow the clinician to begin to develop a therapeutic rapport with the client, familiarise the client with the treatment programme, assess the client's needs and begin a collaborative process with the client to develop their treatment plan (Barbaree, Peacock, Cortoni, Marshall and Seto, 1998). As part of this process, the client can be asked what treatment modalities they feel would be most helpful, what their treatment goals are and how they believe treatment could best support them to accomplish their goals and overcome obstacles they identify might challenge progress. If clients do not identify key treatment goals, these can be identified and interjected into the discussion. Oftentimes clients will acknowledge and agree with the appropriateness of suggested goals.

Treatment intake reports should offer a synopsis of the client's offending history, any past treatment and identify key information from prior risk assessments. Impressions regarding the client's presentation style, level of engagement and motivation and noted responsivity issues can be commented on. A recommended treatment plan should be offered. In terms of specific treatment recommendations, treatment intake reports can comment on:

- *Appropriate treatment modalities* (individual therapy, group therapy, arousal management/modification interventions, pharmacological intervention, couple or family/reunification therapy, adjunct interventions);
- *Treatment intensity* (recommended number of treatment modalities, frequency of treatment contact and hours in treatment, duration of treatment);
- *Treatment targets* (areas that require therapeutic intervention to facilitate risk management/reduction and an overall healthier coping repertoire);
- *Responsivity issues* (identifying additional treatment targets or recommended modifications of the treatment process based on responsivity factors);
- *Case management/supervision issues to support treatment/risk management* (recommendations related to team meetings, case communication and consultation, identification of other potential stakeholders who could contribute to the risk management team).

Treatment progress reports

These reports provide updates about the client's participation and progress in treatment at determined intervals and can offer updated recommendations for treatment, case management and/or risk management planning based on the client's current level of functioning.

The content should include providing an overview of the treatment services provided, the client's attendance, a description of their style of engagement and participation, a description of the therapeutic areas addressed and a summary of progress.

The obvious benefits of these reports are that they keep the agencies of referral appraised of the client's progress and current status in regard to risk management. Additionally, treatment progress reports are an excellent way for clinicians to regularly reflect on the case and consider progress. This can assist in evaluating if the treatment plan is on track and allow for timely and strategic modifications to the treatment as may be required to ensure interventions are focused on relevant therapeutic and risk management goals.

Sharing these reports with clients allows for an ongoing formalised feedback process to discuss and review treatment participation and progress. This includes highlighting and reinforcing positive treatment gains, discussing and processing areas of challenge and determining the next steps in the treatment planning. Clinical experience suggests clients report feeling more comfortable knowing they will have the opportunity to review these reports prior to them being completed, and this can contribute to an enhanced sense of trust and engagement (Barbaree, Peacock, Cortoni, Marshall and Seto, 1998).

Post suspension/treatment closure reports

These are completed on occasions where a client is breached or suspended for non-compliance with the conditions of their community release, when a client has incurred a new charge(s) for a criminal offence beyond non-compliance or when a client drops out or is terminated from treatment. They allow for a psychological autopsy of the non-compliance or reoffence and reflection on the client's prior participation and progress in treatment. These reports also focus on issues related to understanding the client's level of risk and risk factors, and highlight impressions related to future potential treatment, risk management and case management needs based on the factors contributing to the problematic conclusion of the client's treatment participation. They can be very important documents that have long-term usefulness as a component of the background information that accompanies the offender into the future. They provide integral information that can be used for future risk assessment, deliberations for sentencing, correctional intake and institutional or community-based case management and future treatment planning.

Treatment completion reports

These provide a final summary of a client's overall participation and progress upon the completion of treatment with a particular programme or care provider. They identify issues related to the client's attendance, level of treatment motivation and style of engagement, treatment goals addressed, progress achieved and areas of continued challenge. An opinion is provided on the client's assessed level of risk and capacity for future risk management and healthy coping. These reports are also focused on potential future risk management challenges, areas for monitoring and strategies for managing risk-related issues should they arise. Treatment completion reports can also have a life beyond the client's completion of treatment. They can be requested for the purpose of confirming a client's participation and progress in treatment for child welfare agencies, boarder service entities to seek approval for travel or in seeking a pardon. When used for these various purposes, it is typically at the client's request and requires the client to provide written consent for the report to be released to a specific person or agency.

Best practice in community reports

Best practice specifically related to writing community treatments reports does not exist per se; nevertheless, best practice pertaining to related literature can be applied to this context. A variety of best practice literature is applicable, including psychological treatment report writing, forensic psychology practice, sex offender assessment and treatment, and theoretical and practice models (e.g. RNR, Self-Regulation, Good Lives, Cognitive Behavioural Therapy, Motivational Interviewing). The following offers a clinical perspective on areas that should be considered in conducting and establishing best practice related to community reports.

Confidentiality

At the commencement of treatment, the client should be fully and clearly informed regarding how information about their participation and progress in treatment will be shared. This is particularly important in cases where treatment is mandated and when information shared could have serious ramifications for the client (Levenson and D'Amora, 2005). The client should understand whom information will be shared with, how information will be shared (e.g. personal communications, written reports), the frequency of information sharing (if there are set time frames for reports to be generated or specific milestones when reports are generated) and what type of information will be shared.

Treatment providers/programmes should have clients review and sign consent forms that outline the limits of confidentiality, practices around information sharing and mandatory reporting obligations at the onset of treatment (American Psychological Association, 2013; Association for the Treatment of Sexual Abuse, 2014). This ensures that clients are aware information will be shared prior to commencing the therapeutic process and that their awareness, understanding and agreement to this is documented. If a client mandated to treatment is not prepared to provide consent for sharing of information and refuses to sign a treatment consent form, then treatment cannot appropriately be provided and the matter should be referred back to the agency of referral (Eccles and Walker, 1998). When clients are engaged in long-term treatment it is important that policies around information sharing be re-reviewed over time so there is transparency about this issue.

Balancing information sharing and privacy

While community reports provide information about the client's participation and progress in treatment, not all treatment information needs to or should be shared. Witt and Fogel (2015) related, 'Over time a skilled evaluator develops not only a sense of what should be included in a report but also a sense of what should not be included – for some writers a more difficult task' (p. 8–16).

In providing clinical care, it is important that the client feel treatment is a safe place to share personal information and that a therapeutic relationship and environment is established that will facilitate authentic and meaningful self-disclosure, discussion and therapeutic processing. Consequently, it is critical for clients to feel they can and will have a degree of privacy when participating in treatment and that not all information disclosed will be or is required to be shared with others in treatment reports. It is important at the beginning of treatment to establish areas where the client can expect privacy and to discuss how their privacy can be protected, particularly given this is an area of practice where information sharing is common and the limits of confidentiality are stressed. In balancing this it is also important that the client know when there should be no exception of privacy and how situations will be managed therapeutically when there is a difference in opinion about what the client may want to remain private and what the therapist feels is necessary or obligatory to report.

It is possible to both provide referring agencies with relevant information to assist them in understanding their clients' participation and progress in treatment, while at the same time attending to and respecting client privacy. Providing a general synopsis of the relevant issues, as opposed to offering elaborate details, is one effective strategy for accomplishing this goal. For example, general progress concerning treatment related to a client's trauma history could be reported without providing specific details of their disclosed victimisation experiences. Similarly, reference could be made to addressing violent and/or inappropriate sexual fantasies without reporting the details of the fantasies disclosed. Clients may disclose a further history of offending behaviour in treatment (Abel, Becker, Mittelman, Cunningham-Rathner, Rouleau and Murphy, 1987). In such cases, if the disclosures do not meet the criteria for mandatory reporting, if applicable, the client could be identified as increasing their level of disclosure and accountability for past offending behaviour and as offering further information about their offending history, rather than reporting the specific details of these offence disclosures.

It is important to note that maintaining client privacy in treatment reports is not about aligning oneself with the client in an inappropriate way and certainly not about colluding with the client to keep secrets. It is about creating a therapeutic relationship and environment where the client can build trust and feel comfortable discussing issues to optimally address their risk factors and facilitate therapeutic progress and personal growth. Jeglic (2015) articulates that limited confidentiality can inhibit the development of a therapeutic alliance. Given the literature on the powerful role the therapeutic alliance plays in positive treatment outcome, it is incumbent on treatment providers to be attentive to factors that can strengthen the therapeutic alliance to enhance outcome (Norcross, 2001). It is important for forensic mental health service providers not to lose sight of the fact that professional standards dictate that appropriate and ethical client care requires attention to balancing privacy with information sharing (American Psychological Association, 2010; Canadian Psychological Association, 2000, 2001).

Case conceptualisation

When writing treatment reports it is important to not only provide information about client participation but also offer clinical conceptualisations that move beyond reporting the 'what' information to including your impressions of the 'why'. For example, if a client is resistant, rather than focus solely on identifying this and detailing the attitudinal and behavioural factors that illustrate resistance, reports should strive to offer impressions about what this behaviour could be about. Treatment interfering behaviours that are a product of factors such as trauma symptomatology, a marked experience of shame or a high level of fear and personal vulnerability, are quite different than resistant and oppositional behaviour associated with an antisocial and/or egocentric orientation. Providing clinical conceptualisations of the client's behaviour in treatment reports allows for a greater understanding of the client's functioning, styles of coping and participation in treatment (Sturmey, 2009). This information can lead to refining the case formulation and the treatment strategies used to address the factors contributing to problematic behaviours as well as inform engagement strategies for treatment providers and case managers (Yates, Prescott and Ward, 2010).

Reports should be therapeutic

Therapeutic engagement and rapport plays an important role in positive treatment outcome. While issues related to building motivation and therapeutic alliance are typically discussed in the context of treatment, these same principles and therapeutic strategies can apply during assessments to make reports part of the therapeutic process (Ellerby, 2014). Reports can be written with consideration for the client who will read it and how they may be affected by the content and style of the report. Reports can be motivating, reinforce effort and gains, and identify challenges in a manner that demonstrates understanding and support. This does not mean they are not candid or fully reflect the client's level of functioning and behaviour in treatment. It does mean being attentive to language (e.g. using non-judgmental, non-stigmatising, non-confrontational words/phrasing), reducing the use of labels, attending to how content is framed (e.g. framing issues of concern by offering a context for the problem area and recommendations for attempting to address and resolve these issues), providing a context for the information shared, and including empathic and supportive comments while focusing on approach-oriented goals. In effect, this involves applying what we know about strategies for effective client engagement (e.g. Marshall, Fernandez, Serran, Mulloy, Thorton, Mann and Anderson, 2003, Prescott, 2009) into written work.

When reports are completed in this manner, clients may still be unhappy with some of the report content; however, chances are improved that they will identify that the reports were accurate and balanced, and acknowledge areas in need of improvement and attention. This approach to report writing can also be helpful in supporting clients to continue to participate in treatment in a more engaged, open and candid manner, as well as allow for easier repair when there are threats to, or ruptures in, the therapeutic relationship.

Report collaboration

Treatment reports can and should be an integral component to the treatment process. As such, preparation of the treatment report can become a collaborative process in which the client is asked for input and there is discussion about the treatment modalities they are participating in, the quality of this participation, the treatment goals that have been attended to, and review of progress, or lack thereof. This discussion can be a therapeutic aspect of the process as well as a means of empowering the client and enhancing engagement. In addition to seeking client input when discussing the preparation of the report, clients can be offered the opportunity to review and discuss their impressions of the reports prior to them being finalised and distributed. In doing this, clients are informed that their perspectives will be considered and may be integrated into the final report; however, it is clearly established that the report will ultimately reflect the clinician's impressions, even if they are not in agreement. When disagreement occurs, it creates the opportunity for discussion and processing of the contentious issues, which are typically ongoing problematic behaviours or risk management issues that are important to address with clients.

A collaborative approach has important benefits. It can contribute to the positive development of a therapeutic alliance, enhance client trust in the treatment provider and programme, empower the client to feel a part of the process, and increase engagement and motivation. Clients are likely to be more invested in a treatment plan/process they are part of developing it (Garrett, Oliver, Wilcox and Middleton, 2003; Levenson, Macgowan, Morin and Cotter, 2009). Collaboration ensures the client's perspective is being heard and can also enhance the treatment planning, as clients are encouraged to verbalise their specific challenges and ideas about treatment goals and how they believe they can be supported during difficult times. Finally, the collaborative process around treatment reports can itself be therapeutic by providing the opportunity for developing assertiveness and communication skills.

Style matters

Much has been written about the principles of effective psychological report writing (Goldfinger and Pomerantz, 2014) and forensic report writing more specifically

(Grisso, 2010; Heilbrun, 2001; Otto, DeMier and Boccaccini, 2014). Prescriptions for report writing typically focus on data collection processes and the content to include in the report; however, the art of report writing itself is a crucial element in producing effective written communication. The style of the report and how it is organised and written has a tremendous impact on how it is received.

A central feature of effective communication is consideration of the audience (Witt and Fogel, 2015), who are rarely other mental health professionals (Heilbrun, 2001). In a community context, reports may be read and used by probation and parole officers, mental health workers, child welfare workers, law enforcement officials, lawyers, judges, correctional staff and the client. It is important that the style of language, descriptions of the client, and recommendations reflect this audience.

A number of suggestions have been put forward to enhance the effectiveness of treatment reports. These include making reports more readable, using shorter sentences, minimising the use of difficult words, reducing use of acronyms and jargon and increasing the use of subheadings (Harvey, 2006; Otto, DeMier and Boccaccini, 2014). Reports should also have a well organised structure and flow, identify the sources of the data used, be clear in differentiating case facts from clinical impressions and opinions (Otto, DeMier and Boccaccini, 2014), offer clear explanations for clinical impressions/opinions, and focus on reporting relevant information (Grisso, 2010; Witt and Fogel, 2015). Reports should be readable, understandable, helpful and have a very practical and meaningful application.

Outline of report

The report outline will vary depending on the type of community report being written; however, there are components that should be included in all reports, with the content tailored to the specific purpose of *the report*.

Identifying Information: Date, addressee, subject, index offence, sources of information, etc.

Introduction: Identify the purpose of the report; provide a synopsis of background information relevant for the report; discuss the assessed level of risk and identified risk factors; identify the current treatment plan (e.g. treatment modalities, frequency of treatment sessions and adjunct supports).

Treatment Engagement: Described treatment attendance, style of presentation, motivation and engagement.

Treatment Goals: Identify the specific treatment goals that will be or have been addressed and comment on how these target areas for therapeutic intervention are relevant to risk management/reduction (as psychologically meaningful risk factors or responsivity issues).

Treatment Progress: Speak to overall progress with a focus on areas of strength, obstacles to change, and treatment interfering behaviours; identify relevant responsivity issues and how these are being addressed; review progress in achieving recommended treatment goals.

Conclusions and Recommendations: Comment on current manageability of relevant risk factors; provide recommendations for future treatment and case/risk management (e.g. change in intervention intensity, treatment modalities, treatment goals).

Common difficulties

There are some common problems that tend to be seen in community reports related to the management of individuals who have committed violent or sexual offences. Most problematic are reports that do not have an organisational flow to them and are written without consideration of the audience. They tend to be filled with professional language, jargon and technical terms that may not be familiar to the user of the report.

It is also often evident that authors have not used a collaborative process in preparing the report. Rather, reports are accounts by the professional about the client without any client input. Further to this, it is unfortunate when authors overlook the opportunity to use the report as a therapeutic tool, preparing and writing it in a manner that has the potential to support and enhance treatment motivation and engagement.

Another common difficulty in community reports is a tendency for writers to provide information without context (Otto, DeMier and Boccaccini, 2014). The client and/or their behaviour are discussed without offering a clinical conceptualisation that can provide a better understanding and response to the identified issues.

Finally, community reports can be limited in their usefulness when the recommendations offered are generic and vague (Groth-Marnat and Davis, 2014). Often, reports do not provide recommendations that address specific issues relevant to key areas of client functioning (e.g. responsivity issues, motivation or engagement challenges, risk factor management). As well, reports often do not consider and provide recommendations to support other systems involved in case and risk management with the client (probation, parole, child welfare, mental health). Providing such recommendations can have a positive influence on case management and in turn impact the client's functioning in treatment and in life.

Review task – Key take-away points

Identify a treatment progress report that you have completed and consider the following:

Did you obtain informed consent and describe the consent process in your report? How could this report be better grounded in a theoretical model? How could the client have been included in the report writing process? If a lawyer were reading this report, how might they interpret its content? What could be included that would make the report motivating to the client? Does the report address responsivity issues? Has the report discussed the client's risk factors and how they are being addressed in treatment? Have I offered a context for behaviours and a conceptualisation of the clinical issues? Did I provide recommendations specific to the needs of the client that could be implemented by the referral source?

Checklist of steps/advice

1 Identify issues related to limits of confidentiality, information sharing and mandatory reporting. Have the client sign a treatment consent form indicating their awareness of and agreement to information sharing. Be sure that there is ongoing discussion about these issues over time.

2 Discuss the balance between information sharing and maintaining privacy and the parameters around this with the referral agency and the client.

3 Be open to having a dialogue with the client about the report and to them to reading a draft and offering feedback. This provides the client an opportunity to have input but does not mean directing the content. When there are areas of disagreement, this offers the ability to discuss these therapeutically.

4 Attend to the organisation and style of the report as the writing has an impact on the reader and how the report is viewed and used.

5 Organise reports around a theoretical model (e.g. RNR model) and focus content on addressing issues related to risk (identify level of risk and offer recommendations commensurate with assessed level of risk), need (highlight psychologically meaningful risk factors associated with offending as targets for intervention) and responsivity (identify issues that can impact the client's response to treatment and offer recommendations about accommodations to attend to responsivity issues).

Further reading

American Psychological Association. (2010). American Psychological Association *Ethical principles of psychologists and code of conduct*.

American Psychological Association. (2013). Specialty guidelines for forensic psychology. *American Psychologist*, 68(1), 7–9.

Andrews, D.A. and Bonta, J. (2010). *The psychology of criminal conduct*, 5th ed. New Providence, NJ: LexisNexis Matthew Bender.

Association for the Treatment of Sexual Abusers. (2014). *ATSA practice guidelines for the assessment, treatment and management of adult male sex offenders*. Beaverton, OR: Association for the Treatment of Sexual Abusers.

References

Abel, G.G., Becker, J.V., Mittelman, M.S., Cunningham-Rathner, J., Rouleau, J.L. and Murphy, W.D. (1987). Self-reported sex crimes of non-incarcerated paraphiliacs. *Journal of Interpersonal Violence*, 2, 3–25.

American Psychological Association. (2010). *Ethical principles of psychologists and code of conduct*.

American Psychological Association, (2013). Specialty guidelines for forensic psychology. *American Psychologist*, 68(1), 7–9.

Andrews, D.A. and Bonta, J. (2010). *The psychology of criminal conduct*, 5th ed. New Providence, NJ: LexisNexis Matthew Bender.

Association for the Treatment of Sexual Abusers. (2014). *ATSA Practice guidelines for the assessment, treatment and management of adult male sex offenders.* Beaverton, OR: Association for the Treatment of Sexual Abusers.

Barbaree, H.E., Peacock, E.J., Cortoni, F., Marshall, W.L. and Seto, M. (1998). Ontario penitentiaries' program, in W.L. Marshall, Y.M. Fernandez, S.M. Hudson and T. Ward (eds.), *Sourcebook of treatment programs for sexual offenders* (pp. 59–77). New York: Plenum Press.

Barnett, G.D., Wakeling, H.C., Mandeville-Norden, R. and Rakestrow, J. (2012). How useful are psychometric test scores in predicting recidivism for treated sex offenders? *International Journal of Offender Therapy and Comparative Criminology.*

Canadian Psychological Association. (2000). *Canadian code of ethics for psychologists,* 3rd ed.

Canadian Psychological Association. (2001). *Practice guidelines for providers of psychological services.*

Eccles, A. and Walker, W. (1998). Community-based treatment with sexual offenders, in W.L. Marshall, Y.M. Fernandez, S.M. Hudson and T. Ward (eds.), *Sourcebook of treatment programs for sexual offenders* (pp. 93–103). New York: Plenum Press, 93–103.

Ellerby, L. (2014). Clinical reflections on the assessment and treatment of a rapist. in W.T. O'Donohue (ed.), *Case studies in sexual deviance* (pp. 35–78). New York: Routledge.

Garrett, T., Oliver, C., Wilcox, D.T. and Middleton, D. (2003). Who cares? The views of sexual offenders about the group treatment they receive. *Sexual Abuse: A Journal of Research & Treatment, 15,* 323–38.

Goldfinger, K. and Pomerantz, A.M. (2014). *Psychological assessment and report writing,* 2nd ed. Los Angeles, CA: Sage.

Gordon, A. and Hover, G. (1998). The Twin Rivers sex offender treatment program, in W.L. Marshall, Y.M. Fernandez, S.M. Hudson and T. Ward (eds.), *Sourcebook of treatment programs for sexual offenders* (pp. 3–15). New York: Plenum Press.

Grisso, T. (2010). Guidance for improving forensic reports: A review of common errors. *Open Access Journal of Forensic Psychology, 2,* 102–15.

Groth-Marnat, G. and Davis, A. (2014). *Psychological report writing assistant.* Hoboken, NJ: Wiley.

Haaven, J.L. and Coleman, E.M. (2000). Treatment of the developmentally disabled sex offender, in D.R. Laws, S.M. Hudson and T. Ward (eds.), *Remaking relapse prevention with sex offenders: A sourcebook* (pp. 353–68). Thousand Oaks, CA: Sage.

Harvey, V.S. (2006). Variables affecting the clarity of reports. *Journal of Clinical Psychology, 62,* 5–18.

Heilbrun, K. (2001). *Principles of forensic mental health assessment.* New York: Kluwer.

Heilbrun, K., Warren, J. and Picarello, K. (2003) Third party information in forensic assessment, in I.B. Weiner (editor-in-chief) and A. Goldstein (vol. ed.), *Handbook of psychology: Forensic psychology,* 2nd ed. Vol. 11. Hoboken, NJ: Wiley.

Jeglic, E.L. (2015). Therapeutic alliance in working with sex offenders, in, B.K. Schwartz (ed.), *The sex offender: Insights on treatment and policy developments,* Vol. 8 (11-1-11- 20). Kingston, NJ: Civic Research Institute.

Levenson, J. and D'Amora, D. (2005). An ethical paradigm for sex offender treatment: Response to Glaser. *Western Criminology Review 6(1),* 145–53.

Levenson, J.S., Macgowan, M.J., Morin, J.W. and Cotter, L.P. (2009). Perceptions of sex offenders about treatment satisfaction and engagement. *Sexual Abuse: A Journal of Research and Treatment, 21(1),* 35–56.

Marshall, W.L., Fernandez, Y.M., Serran, G.A., Mulloy, R., Thorton, D., Mann, R.E. and Anderson, D. (2003). Process variables in the treatment of sexual offenders. *Aggression and Violent Behaviour: A Review Journal, 8,* 205–34.

Norcross, J.C. (2001). Purposes, processes and products of the task force on empirically supported therapy relationships. *Psychotherapy: Theory, Research, Practice, Training, 38,* 345–56.

Olver, M.E., Beggs Christofferson, S.M., Grace, R.C. and Wong, S.C.P. (2014). Incorporating change information into sexual offender risk assessments using the Violence Risk Scale-sexual offender version. *Sexual Abuse: A Journal of Research and Treatment, 26,* 472–99.

Otto, R.K., DeMier, R.L. and Boccaccini, M.T. (2014). *Forensic reports and testimony: A guide to effective communication for psychologists and psychiatrists.* Hoboken, NJ: Wiley.

Pithers, W.D., Marques, J.K., Gibat, C.C. and Marlatt, G.A. (1983). Relapse prevention: A self-control model of treatment and maintenance of change for sexual aggressives. In J. Greer and I. R. Stuart (eds.), *The sexual aggressor: Current perspective on treatment.* New York: Van Nostrand Reinhold.

Prescott, D.S. (2009). *Building motivation to change in sexual offenders.* Brandon, VT: Safer Society Press.

Sturmey, P. (ed.) (2009). *Clinical case formulation: Varieties of approaches.* Malden, MA: Wiley-Blackwell.

Veysey, B. (2008). Rethinking reentry. *Criminologist, 33,* 1–5.

Ward, T. and Hudson, S.M. (2000). A self-regulation model of relapse prevention, in Laws, D.R., Hudson, S.M. and Ward, T. (eds.), *Remaking relapse prevention with sex offenders* (pp. 79–101). Thousand Oaks, CA: Sage Publications.

Ward, T. and Stewart, C. (2003). The treatment of sex offenders: Risk management and good lives. *Professional Psychology: Research and Practice, 34,* 353–60.

Witt, P.H. and Fogel, M.H. (2015). Report writing fundamentals for sex offender evaluations, in B.K. Schwartz (ed.), *The sex offender: Insights on treatment and policy developments,* Vol. 8 (8-1-8-34). Kingston, NJ: Civic Research Institute.

Wong, S.C.P. and Gordon, A.E. (2006). The validity and reliability of the violence risk scale: A treatment-friendly violence risk assessment tool. *Psychology, Public Policy, and Law, 12,* 279–309.

Yates, P.M., Prescott, D. and Ward, T. (2010). *Applying the good lives and self-regulation models to sex offender treatment: A practical guide for clinicians.* Brandon, VT: Safer.

APPENDIX 1

EXAMPLE REPORT 1

This report was written in 2010 and the information (e.g. about the HCR-20) was correct at that time; please note, however, that there have been developments (e.g. the publication of version 3 of the HCR-20) that would need to be reflected in a similar contemporary report. Names and identification details have been changed or removed for reasons of maintaining confidentiality.

Our reference: XX123

DATE

Psychological Report

Client: Mr. Lee BLACK (dob: 01/08/1976)

REPORT SUMMARY

Date: 01 July 2010
Date of birth: 01 August 1976
Report writer: Full Name
Sources of information: Clinical interview (conducted on 21/06/2010 14.15–18.00); results of psychological assessment (conducted 21/06/2010); referral letter (21/06/2010); details of current DVRO (issued 11/05/10); statement on personal background; family law documents; affidavit of Karla Black (filed 12/05/2010); affidavit of Lee Black (filed 27/05/2010); affidavit of Karla Black (filed 28/05/2010); sections from affidavit of Lee Black (filed 27/05/2010); provisions of the Domestic Violence Act 1994 (SA).

1 Statement of qualifications and awareness of practice direction 46

I (NAME) am a registered psychologist (No. XXX) in South Australia who holds a degree in social psychology (University of XX), a master of science degree in applied criminological psychology (University of XX), and a doctorate in clinical psychology (University of XX). I am a member of the Australian Psychological Society and of the Forensic and Clinical Colleges of the Australian Psychological Society.

I currently hold the position of professor psychology at XX University. I have worked as a prison psychologist for the Home Office in the UK, as a clinical psychologist for forensic and mental health services in the UK and in South Australia, and as a clinical psychologist in private practice. My specific area of expertise relates to offender assessment and rehabilitation and I have published a large number of scientific articles in this area (see brief CV attached). I have a particular interest in the assessment and management of anger and violence, and have published two books in this area, including one on the management of perpetrators of domestic violence.

I am familiar with Part 15.5 of the Family Law Rules, and have also read Practice Direction 46A (Guidelines for Expert Witnesses in Proceedings in the Supreme Court of South Australia, issued 17 May 2002). I have prepared this report in a manner which is consistent with these directions.

2 Reason for referral

Mr. Black was self-referred for a psychological assessment of any difficulties with anger control and the potential risk that he presents of acting violently towards his former partner and children. This assessment is concerned with the psychological state of Mr. Black, and no comments or observations are made in this report in relation to the psychological state of others, including Mr. Black's former partner.

3 Clinical interview

Mr. Black attended the assessment alone. He was polite and cooperative through the interview and gave a detailed account of the events leading up to the referral, including the history of his relationship with his ex-partner, matters relating to the care of their children, Laura (dob 06/04/2000) and Lawrence Black (dob 26/07/2003), and the events that led to their separation. In what was quite a lengthy interview, Mr. Black displayed a good level of attention and was able to provide detailed and thoughtful answers to all of the questions posed.

History

Mr. Black is a 36-year-old man who grew up in Adelaide, South Australia. His father worked for the RAF and, in his early years, the family moved around living for periods in both Perth and Melbourne. Mr. Black has three younger brothers, although he reported that one of his brothers died 5 years ago at the age of 25. His parents were described as supportive. He sees his father as a rational man who rarely expressed anger and his mother as more emotionally expressive, occasionally getting frustrated but never aggressive. They rarely experienced conflict in their relationship and he could not recall his parents arguing often. Mr. Black described his father as 'a lot like myself' – supportive, calm, a person who did not raise his voice, emotionally controlled and never aggressive.

When asked about his education, Mr. Black described himself as 'struggling' in his first two years of school, but by Year 4 had become an 'average' student, and by Year 7 as 'in the top three of the class'. Socially he reported experiencing no difficulties, mixing with a core group of people who had similar interests. He never got into trouble at secondary school or remembers missing classes. In short, he saw himself as a conscientious student who worked hard at school and achieved well.

Mr. Black's first job was at a supermarket, before he started at Holden in 1995 – initially through vacation work, but subsequently as on contract. He has worked there ever since and currently has supervisory responsibilities. He believes that he is regarded as a hard working and reliable employee.

Mr. Black is in generally good health, but at the age of 30 experienced some problems with movement, which were later diagnosed as a form of arthritis. He has no history of mental health problems, reported that he has never tried (or used) illicit substances, and that he only drinks alcohol in moderation ('two to three beers a week, at social occasions or with a meal'). He reported that he has no previous criminal record and had not previously been in any trouble with the police.

Relationships

Mr. Black reported that he had been in a relationship with Karla Black since 1994. He was initially attracted to her 'outgoing and bubbly' personality, but from the outset of their relationship had some misgivings about their relationship. In particular, he believed that they came from different family backgrounds (seeing his own background as more stable, secure and in many ways more conservative). However, when Karla became unexpectedly pregnant, they decided to embark on family life. Karla was the first person that Mr. Black had lived with.

In the opinion of Mr. Black, problems in the relationship became apparent shortly after their daughter was born in 2000. He believes that Karla became depressed shortly after the birth, withdrawing from household responsibilities, and becoming increasingly angry towards both himself and their daughter. Mr. Black felt that their relationship improved when he was working, and soon became busy renovating properties and working long hours. They were married in 2002.

In 2003, their son, Lawrence, was born. The pregnancy was again unplanned, and Mr. Black had a vasectomy (against his wife's wishes) shortly afterwards. According to Mr. Black, a major issue in the relationship was Mr. Black's lack of time or availability for the family, as well as Karla feeling that she had few responsibilities. In an attempt to resolve these issues, Karla took over the family finances (Mr. Black would spend 30–45 minutes a day financial planning, so this arrangement gave him more time), but he felt that this did not help the family achieve its financial goals.

Shortly after their son was born, Mr. Black reported that he had an affair which lasted over 12 months. This triggered a separation and Karla moved with the children to a rental property. They remained on talking terms, but Mr. Black believed that she didn't want to return to the relationship, and subsequently he met a new person whom he became interested in. However, he reported that when Karla found out about this, she became very angry and resentful and subsequently asked if he would return to the family. Mr. Black agreed, despite some concerns about Karla's mental health (he reported that she told him she had taken an overdose on one occasion). He also acknowledged the need for him to spend more time with the family and undertook to do this.

Mr. Black recalls this period in the relationship as a 'fresh start' and remembers Karla being more caring and affectionate, and less likely to get angry, shout, or push him. This was a characteristic of their early relationship, with Mr. Black describing Karla as verbally, and at times physically aggressive towards him. They spent 18 months together, and Mr. Black reduced his work hours and spent more time with the family. A significant issue in the relationship, however, was financial independence – at the time all of the family assets were in the name of Mr. Black (by this time they had subdivided and decided to build another house). In response to this, when the family bought a car (valued at $65,000), Mr. Black put the car in Karla's name.

By October 2012 the couple had decided to undertake a major renovation of their home. He believes that Karla had become 'very depressed' again, and reported that he was attempting to get her involved in the house renovations. At this time a significant incident occurred that led to their subsequent separation. According to Mr. Black this was prompted by his attempt to leave the house with his daughter. He had asked Karla to help him unload the trailer (which contained some building equipment), so he could use the vehicle that day. When she declined, Mr. Black decided to use the lease vehicle that he had access to that day. His daughter was keen to go with him, but Karla did not consent to this and started yelling at her to 'get out of the car'. Karla then reportedly pulled the keys from the car, yelling and swearing, and then tried to lift her daughter from the car. He recalls that Karla then walked into the house, saying that she was going to transfer the money out of their account. He then walked into the house, unscrewed the internet connection to the computer to stop her accessing the account, and then attempted to take the credit cards from her purse so that she could not use them. According to Mr. Black he had done this previously, before giving the cards back 2–3 days later 'when she had calmed down'. He then tried to ring the bank to terminate the account.

Mr. Black reported that there was a struggle over the phone, during which Karla tried to punch him. They then 'wrestled' and he tried to 'restrain' her by 'pinning her arms to her sides'. They both fell to the ground and he believes that she then hit her head on the floorboards. He then continued to restrain her on the ground, before releasing her. Karla then ran out of the house, at which time Mr. Black called his father and asked him to come round to help. He then successfully changed the password to the savings account (but not the credit card). In the meantime, the police were called and Mr. Black was subsequently charged with an (domestic violence) assault. He reported that Karla experienced some injuries – bruising to her wrist and arm and a cut above her eyebrow. I note that this account of the events of 4 October is largely consistent with that of his ex-partner, Karla, as documented in her affidavit. The points of difference relate to the trigger for the incident, how emotional Mr. Black was at the time, and whether Mr. Black instigated the injury by pushing, or acted to defend himself from punches.

Since this time, Mr. Black has stayed at his parents' house, but reported that Karla had initiated and maintained contact with him. According to Mr. Black, the matter was subsequently scheduled to be dismissed in the magistrates court, but shortly before the hearing he discovered that they had decided to proceed with the charges. The magistrate then suggested that they arrive at an agreement in a pre-trial conference, and Mr. Black voluntarily entered into a restraining order for a period of 12 months, which was recently extended. I understand that Mr. Black is concerned that the order may unduly influence the outcomes of any family court proceedings, and is seeking to have it withdrawn.

4 Predicting future violence

The primary purpose of this report is to offer a professional opinion on whether Mr. Black presents a risk of violence to others, particularly his ex-partner and her husband. Methods of predicting who will be violent (and who will not) are commonly known as risk assessments. Implicit in any attempt to assess risk is the belief that some individuals are less at risk of committing violent acts than others. A considerable amount of research over the last decade has sought to identify those factors that are associated with violent offending (e.g. Douglas, Yeomans and Boer, 2005), although the focus of much of this work is on predicting violent offending in those already known to have committed violent offences.

Risk factors are those variables that impact systematically on violence, either by increasing or decreasing its likelihood. Predicting whether someone will commit further offences typically involves establishing which risk factors are relevant to the individual case. Professional approaches to assessing risk are typically based on two main approaches, commonly known as the ***clinical*** and the ***actuarial***. There has been considerable, and at times heated, debate between practitioners and researchers about the value of each approach (e.g. Lievore, 2003). Clinical predictions of risk primarily involve professional judgements about an individual's likelihood of reoffending based upon a practitioner's knowledge of that individual. The actuarial approach involves assessing risk solely on the basis of the statistical probability that offenders with a particular set of characteristics will reoffend. Predictions are based on empirically established correlations between a risk measure (typically based on known characteristics of both the offender and the offence) and recidivism. The use of an actuarial instrument with a particular offender results in a statement to the effect that 'Mr. X scored a ??% on this risk assessment instrument. Individuals with these characteristics, on average, reoffend at ??% over 5 years'. A third method, the clinically adjusted actuarial approach (also known as the structured professional judgement model) involves the use of one (or more) actuarial instruments followed by adjustments based on clinically derived case considerations.

There is a consensus within the scientific community that purely clinical approaches to risk assessment possess inadequate inter-rater reliability and predictive validity (Grove and Meehl, 1996). This means that clinical assessments of risk are not only likely to be less accurate than actuarial assessments but also that different assessors are more likely to reach different conclusions. As such, most experts in this area recommend the use of structured risk assessment methods which use actuarial data. The Australian Psychological Society (2005), for example, in their 'Guidelines for Working with People Who Pose a High Risk of Harm to Others' suggest that members 'working in contexts of increased risk will need to be informed about the structured and systematic assessment of risk' (p.1). This is the approach adopted in this assessment.

Incorporating professional judgement in any final classification of risk is important when applying any estimate of risk to an individual case given that while purely actuarial approaches provide estimates of how likely it is that offenders with similar profiles will reoffend, they do not offer information about the risk presented by a particular individual in a particular context. In this report, the results of a clinical interview are used to supplement the result of a structured assessment of risk. Further, formal assessments were conducted relating to Mr. Black's experience and expression of anger, attitudes towards domestic violence, personality and propensity to respond to questionnaires in a valid and forthright manner. Each of these is described below.

The Historical-Clinical-Risk Management-20 (HCR-20)

The *HCR-20* (Douglas, Webster, Hart, Eaves and Ogloff, 2001) is a structured guide for the assessment of risk of violence among civil psychiatric, forensic and criminal justice populations. It contains 20 items (10 historical variables, 5 clinical variables and 5 risk management factors) as well as an item based on the Hare psychopathy checklist (PCL-R). Variables include relevant past, present and future considerations.

The 10 items of the Historical (H) scale are primarily static and unlikely to fluctuate over time; they include: (a) previous violence, (b) young age at first violent incident, (c) relationship instability, (d) employment problems, (e) substance use, (f) major mental illness, (g) psychopathy, (h) early maladjustment, (i) personality disorder and (j) prior supervision failure. The Clinical (C) scale has five items referring to current mental, emotional and psychiatric status, including dynamic risk markers that are changeable in nature: (a) lack of insight, (b) negative attitudes, (c) active symptoms of major mental illness, (d) impulsivity and (e) unresponsive to treatment. The Risk Management (R) scale also has five items that are concerned with predicting the future social, living and treatment circumstances of an individual and anticipating the reactions of the individual to those conditions: (a) plans lack feasibility, (b) exposure to destabilisers, (c) lack of personal support, (d) non-compliance with remediation attempts and (e) stress. The HCR-20 is derived conceptually through consideration of the relevant literature; the constructs represented by its items have support across many studies and, therefore, it may generalise across a variety of settings and populations. Mr. Black's HCR-20 assessment resulted in a final risk judgement of '*low risk of violence*', the lowest category available. The only risk factors endorsed were those relating to a history of relationship instability and stress.

The *Hare PC:SV* is a 12-item scale based on a subset of PCL-R items that can be used in civic and forensic settings in psychiatric evaluations, personnel selection and community studies. It assesses the Interpersonal/Affective, Social Deviance, Impulsive Lifestyle and Antisocial Behaviour components of psychopathy. Mr. Black scored 3 on this measure, suggesting that psychopathy was unlikely to be present and that further assessment of psychopathy was not required.

5 Psychometric assessment

The questionnaires selected for use in this assessment included two measures of anger experience and expression (to determine the extent of any problems with anger); an assessment of his attitudes and behavior relevant to domestic violence; and a measure of mental health symptomatology, interpersonal style and valid responding. This latter measure is important to establish the extent to which Mr. Black provided responses which might be regarded as those the assessor (and the court) might have wanted to hear. It thus provides some safeguard against deliberate deception in the assessment process. Each of these measures allows for responses to be compared directly with the broader population (matched for age), offering some reference points from which to understand Mr. Black's current presentation.

The *State-Trait Anger Expression Inventory* (STAXI-2 [Spielberger, 1999]) is a 57-item self-report measure which assesses state anger, trait anger and styles of anger expression and control. It is the most widely used and best validated measure of anger currently available. The Trait Anger subscale of the STAXI-2 (T-Ang; 10 items) measures an individual's general propensity to experience anger and its concomitant components over time. This scale is the most important in determining whether an individual has an anger problem or not. Respondents are asked to indicate their general anger experience with a number of items, with 1 (almost never) and 4 (almost always) the end points. Higher scores are indicative of high levels of trait anger. Sample items include 'I am quick tempered', 'I am a hotheaded person' and 'I get angry when I am slowed down by other's mistakes'. Alpha coefficients of 0.84 (female) and 0.86 (male) have been reported (Spielberger, 1999). Mr. Black's score of 12 on this subscale places him within the normal range. People in this score range report that they are *sometimes* quick tempered. They do not block the experience of anger and report that they feel angry about as often as most people. Anger is generally seen as a signal that they need to take action to deal with the problem causing the anger. People with these scores would not be expected to get into trouble as a result of any angry feelings.

The *Anger Disorders Scale: Short Form* (DiGuiseppe and Tafrate, 2004) is a scale which has been designed to assess aspects of anger that may lead to impairments in functioning. It is based upon a model of anger which identifies a number of different domains in which anger may be experienced and expressed (e.g. cognitive, behavioural) and has been well validated with clinical populations. The short form provides a total score, along with three subscale scores: reactivity/expression, anger-in and vengeance. Mr. Black's profile was below the 35th percentile for all domains of this measure, suggesting that he is below average in his reactivity, expressiveness of anger and vengeance. His profile suggests that he has *'no significant anger pathology'*, according to the test manual (p. 28). Rather, these results suggest that Mr. Black is likely to experience angry feelings less often than most other men, less likely to express anger and to have a higher than average level of emotional control.

The *Personality Assessment Inventory* (Morey, 1991) is a 344-item self-report measure of psychopathology which has been designed to assess specific aspects of personality and mental health functioning. The measure contains four validity scales, 11 clinical scales, five treatment scales and two interpersonal scales. It is a particularly useful assessment instrument for these purposes as it provides a broad screening of a wide range of mental health problems in a manner where the responses can be compared to those of the broader population, as well as providing assessing for invalid responding (the tendency to present an overly positive impression of oneself in a self-report measure), and some scales that are useful in determining the likely level of engagement with psychological treatment. The results of this assessment show that none of the scores on the clinical scales are elevated. This suggests that Mr. Black currently does not experience any significant mental health symptoms to a degree where they are likely to have an influence on his ability to function effectively.

Mr. Black scored above average (T=60) on the interpersonal scales of dominance and warmth, suggesting that he is likely to be assertive, although not distant, in his relationships. These scores should, however, all be interpreted in the light of a slightly elevated score (T=66) on the Positive Impression subscale. This subscale purports to measure an overly positive self-presentation, although high scores may also reflect careless responding. As such, these results should all be interpreted with some caution, given that they potentially provide a slightly over-positive picture of his current mental health.

The *Inventory of Beliefs about Wife Beating*, an 11-item version of the instrument originally developed by Saunders, Lynch, Grayson and Linz (1987), purports to measure attitudes toward physical abuse by husbands towards wives. It consists of two subscales: the 'Wife Beating Is Justified' subscale (eight items) measures attitudes regarding the acceptability of the use of such violence (e.g. 'A husband has no right to beat his wife even if she breaks agreements she has made with him'); and the 'Help Should Be Given' subscale (three items) which measures beliefs that government/social agencies should provide help to victims of abuse (e.g. 'Wife-beating should be given a high priority as a social problem by government agencies'). Higher scores on both subscales indicate stronger levels of agreement with such notions. Mr. Black's score on this measure (total score 12) indicated that he does not hold attitudes that are supportive of violence towards women. The lowest possible score on this measure is 11.

Abusive behaviour, rated for the 6-month period prior to separation, was assessed using the *Revised Conflict Tactics Scales* (Straus, Hamby, Boney-McCoy and Sugarman, 1991), a self-report measure of abusive behaviour in intimate relationships. Questions ask about four types of abusive behaviour, including psychologically aggressive tactics. Mr. Black indicated that in this period he had *occasionally* 'called her names or criticised her', 'ended a discussion with her and made the decision yourself', and 'put down her family and friends'. He did not endorse any items that related to physical or sexual aggression.

6 Opinion

The opinion presented in this report is based on the results of the clinical interview, psychometric assessment and documentation received in the course of referral, and my clinical and academic experience in working with individuals who have acted in violent and antisocial ways. I have structured this section of the report in order of the three primary referral questions, as follows:

1   Alleged problems with anger management
    The results of this assessment suggest that Mr. Black does not have any major difficulties with anger. His scores on the scale measuring the disposition to feel angry place him in a category that is below the normal range for the male adult community population. This suggests that Mr. Black is less likely to experience feeling anger than other men of a similar age. I do not see any need for him to attend an anger management program.

    It is important to consider the possibility that Mr. Black is pathologically overcontrolled in his emotional style, as in some instances this in itself can be a risk factor for serious violence. In addition, some domestically violent men can be characterised as callous, unemotional and superficial in their interpersonal style. Mr. Black certainly presented as a very logical and rational person. In describing the incident of 4 October 2008, for example, he described his attempt to disconnect the internet as 'mitigating the risk', and generally saw himself as someone who didn't argue, but 'had discussions'. Such comments reflect an interpersonal style that is somewhat detached but provide no indication of significant problems related to over-regulated anger, and as such are not suggestive of any area of concern relevant to this assessment.

2   Risk of committing acts of domestic violence in the future.
    Mr. Black's clinical profile suggests that he currently experiences no significant psychiatric symptomatology. He is not anxious or depressed, does not experience psychotic symptoms, and has no problems in relation to substance use or

abuse, including alcohol. The structured assessments employed in this report show that he should currently be classified as at low risk of committing acts of violence.

3   Need to be subject to a domestic violence restraint order.
The risk assessment did not identify any factors in Mr. Black's history or current presentation that suggest there is cause for concern about the risk of future violence. In fact, this assessment suggests that the risk of Mr. Black acting violently would appear to be very low. I also note here that Mr. Black has no previous convictions for violence and, to my knowledge, there have been no previous reports to the police of domestic violence.

4   My experience in the area of domestic violence, however, suggests that many incidents do not come to the attention of authorities, and that perpetrators often do not acknowledge many aspects of their abusive behaviour. Caution is always warranted in drawing conclusions based primarily on the self-report of one party and, as such, the possibility of Mr. Black misrepresenting his history and details of the case is an issue that requires further consideration. In this assessment, such tendencies were assessed in a number of ways as follows: (a) careful monitoring of his emotional state when answering questions directly related to abusive behaviour; (b) psychometric assessment of invalid responding styles; (c) the presence of psychopathic personality traits associated with deceptiveness and manipulative behaviour; (d) an ability to acknowledge some aspects of behaviour in relationships that are problematic. The results of this assessment provided no evidence that Mr. Black had attempted to mislead the assessor or to misrepresent his history. Indeed, his ability to acknowledge aspects of his behaviour that might be perceived as abusive (such as controlling the family finances, ending discussions and making decisions himself) offers some reassurance that Mr. Black had been forthright in the assessment.

My conclusion from this assessment is that there is little psychological evidence to suggest that those around Mr. Black are at significant risk of harm. Rather, it suggests that Mr. Black is capable of exercising considerable restraint over his behaviour. There is little, if anything, from this assessment to suggest that anger management problems or violent and aggressive behaviour should be considered as relevant factors in such matters. However, I am unwilling to comment on the need for a domestic violence restraint order to be imposed, given that this is ultimately a matter for the court to determine.

I, [NAME], have made all inquiries which I believe are desirable and appropriate and no matters of significance as I regard as relevant have, to my knowledge, been withheld. I hope that this report is useful. Please contact me if you require any further information.

Yours faithfully,
Signature and name and contact details

Enc. Curriculum vitae

Selected References

Australian Psychological Society. (2005). *Guidelines for working with people who pose a high risk of harm to others*. Melbourne, Australia: Australian Psychological Society.

DiGiuseppe, R. and Tafrate, R.C. (2004). *Anger Disorders Scale (ADS): Technical manual*. North Tonawanda, NY: Multi-Health Systems Inc.

Douglas, K.S., Webster, C.D., Hart, S.D., Eaves, D., and Ogloff, J.R.P. (eds.) (2001). *HCR-20: Violence risk management companion guide*. Burnaby, Canada: Mental Health, Law, and Policy Institute, Simon Fraser University.

Douglas, K.S., Yeomans, M. and Boer, D.P. (2005). Comparative validity analysis of multiple measures of violence risk in a sample of criminal offenders. *Criminal Justice and Behavior, 32*, 479–510.

Grove, W.M. and Meehl, P.E. (1996). Comparative efficacy of informal (subjective, impressionistic) and formal (mechanical, algorithmic) prediction procedures: The clinical-statistical controversy. *Psychology, Public Policy, and Law, 2*, 293–323.

Harris, G. (2003). Men in his category have a 50% likelihood, but which half is he in? Comments on Berlin, Galbreath, Geary and McGlone. *Sexual Abuse: A Journal of Research and Treatment, 15*, 389–92.

Saunders, D.G., Lynch, A.B., Grayson, M. and Linz, D. (1987). The inventory of beliefs about wife beating: the construction and initial validation of a measure of beliefs and attitudes. *Violence Against Victims, 2*, 39–57.

Spielberger, C. D. (1999). *STAXI-2 professional manual*. Odessa, FL: Psychological Assessment Resources.

Straus, M.A., Hamby, S.L., Boney-McCoy, S., and Sugarman, D.B. (1991). The revised Conflict Tactics Scale (CTS2): Development and preliminary psychometric data. *Journal of Family Issues, 17*, 283–316. doi: 10.1177/019251396017003001.

APPENDIX 2

EXAMPLE REPORT 2

This report was written in 2014 and the information was correct at that time. Names and identification details have been changed or removed for reasons of maintaining confidentiality.

Psychological assessment

Name:	Mr. X
Address:	HMP Prison
Date of Instructing:	1 month 2014
Solicitor:	A Solicitor, Firm & Co. Solicitors
Author:	Ms. Smith, BSc (Hons), MSc, CPsychol (foren), AFBPsS, BPS Chartered/HCPC Registered Forensic Psychologist
Date of Report:	1 month 2014

Contents list *[Not included here for space reasons]*

1   Author's credentials

1.1   I am a forensic psychologist, chartered with the British Psychological Society and registered with the Health Professions Council. I have a BSc (Hons) in psychology and an MSc in forensic psychology. I have 20 years of experience working with offenders and people who may pose a risk to others. I am currently employed as a psychologist in practice and at a university. I have vast experience of working in prison custodial and secure and community mental health services. I have experience of preparing reports and giving evidence for criminal and family court, immigration and asylum tribunals, parole boards and mental health tribunals. I prepare 18–24 reports per year for legal proceedings. Full details of my career and experience are found in my CV in Appendix 2.

2   Summary of conclusions

2.1   Mr. X poses a high risk of further offending and a high risk that serious harm would arise from such offending. This opinion is based upon Mr. X demonstrating a versatile pattern of offending, including violence, sexual violence and drug-related offending. Whilst his offending occurred as a juvenile, Mr. X has continued to offend within prison and has accrued further convictions in prison from the commission of serious violence. Mr. X has not engaged in treatment within prison that is of sufficient duration or intensity to address the risk posed by him to others. Mr. X presents with a high number of risk factors that are as yet unaddressed. He does not present as someone who has matured significantly in prison and unfortunately is not able to present evidence that the support available to him in the community is sufficiently positive and robust to manage the risk.

3   Instructions

3.1   Instructions were received from A Solicitor of Firm & Co. to conduct a risk assessment commenting on the risk of further offending and risk of harm caused by such offending. This assessment will comment on the risk assessment only and not on matters relating to immigration law or the political/cultural position in Somalia.

4   Assessment process

4.1   Mr. X was assessed in a private room within the legal visits department of HMP Prison on Date 2014. The duration of the assessment was over 4 hours, with the assessment conducted over morning and afternoon sessions with a break in the middle due to the prison regime.

4.2   Mr. X completed the Paulhus Deception Scale (PDS)[i], which is a 40-item self-report questionnaire that measures one's tendency to give socially desirable responses. The PDS contains two subscales: Self-Deceptive Enhancement, the tendency to give honest but inflated self-descriptions; and Impression Management, the tendency to give inflated self-descriptions to an audience. The PDS assesses socially desirable responding as a temporary tendency caused by situational demands and as a trait-like tendency apparent whenever the individual gives self-reports. Mr. X's responses on the impression management scale suggested that his response style was probably invalid due to giving unduly positive responses 'faking good'. Mr. X's scores across the PDS on the whole indicated an above average response suggesting not only that he is influenced by the situation but also that he has a trait-like characteristic towards self-enhancement, lacking insight into problems. There are a number of possible explanations for this. It is possible, given the demands of the situation, that Mr. X was 'faking good'. It is also possible that Mr. X's response pattern occurred as a result of extreme maladjustment, confusion, carelessness or acquiescence. The results suggest that caution is exercised with regards to Mr. X's self-report and triangulation with collateral information is required. It is notable that during the interview Mr. X had a tendency to deny the offence of rape and to minimise his behaviour in other offences and in relation to fights in prison, which is consistent with the socially desirable responding. However, Mr. X openly disclosed some fights that would not otherwise be known and thus is not solely deceptive or in denial. Mr. X's self-report is nonetheless reviewed cautiously with reference to supporting documentation where it is available to corroborate his assertions.

4.3 A large bundle of documents was reviewed as part of the preparation of this report. The index is included in Appendix 1.

5 Context of the assessment

5.1 Mr. X arrived in the UK on Date 2003 aged 11, from Ethiopia where he had been resident in a refugee camp with his older brother, younger brother, sister-in-law and nephew. It is understood that Mr. X was issued with entry clearance under family reunion and granted Indefinite Leave to Enter to join his half-brother who was residing in the UK, having been recognised as a refugee. Refugee status had been inferred from his older brother's grant of asylum status, arising from reported persecution by Hawiye and Darood tribes due to belonging to the Ashraf clan, and the subsequent issue of reunion visas and ILE.

5.2 It is understood that the Home Office are intending to cease Mr. X's refugee status as a result of his conviction on Date 2009 for four counts of rape of a female aged 16 or over and a further conviction on Date 2011 for wounding, inflicting grievous bodily harm, this offence having occurred in prison. Mr. X was released from custody on Date 2013 and re-detained on Date 2013 under Immigration Powers. He has been at HMP Prison since this time.

5.3 On Date 2010 Mr. X was notified of his liability to deportation under the 1971 Immigration Act. On Date 2013 Mr. X was notified of his liability for automatic deportation under the UK Borders Act 2007. Subsequently a notice of the Home Office's intention to cease his refugee status was issued on Date 2014.

5.4 Mr. X has completed the custodial part of his sentence and could be released into the community where he would be on licence until Date 2017.

6 Personal history

6.1 Mr. X reported that he was born in Mogadishu, Somalia. Mr. X reported that he has three brothers: A (age 35–6), B (age 26–7), C (age 19). Mr. X suggested that he could not recall anything about life in Somalia due to the young age he was when he left there. Mr. X stated that he left Somalia when he was approximately 7 with his brother's wife, her child, his brother B and his brother C to travel to Ethiopia. He stated that his brother A was already in the UK. Mr. X reported that his brother A informed him that his parents had been killed in the war in Somalia but that he personally had no actual recall of this. Mr. X stated that he was shocked that in one of the Home Office reports his brother A is referred to as his 'half brother'. Mr. X stated that he believed they were all full siblings and has not had the opportunity to discuss this with his brother.

6.2   Mr. X suggested that life in Ethiopia was 'ok'. He stated that although he did not speak the language at first, he was able to learn it in the time he was there. Mr. X stated that he attended school and that there were no difficulties. Mr. X suggested that his brother B was his predominant carer, as his brother's wife and child traveled to the UK soon after arrival in Ethiopia, with money being sent over from A. Mr. X suggested that he and his brothers traveled to the embassy a few times until they were able to obtain visas to travel to the UK. Mr. X reported that he traveled to the UK with his brothers, where they were given refugee status as a result of his brother's application. Mr. X suggested that he was excited at the prospect of coming to the UK to be reconciled with his brother. He further reported that he had never seen a white person before arrival at Heathrow airport. Mr. X described that he felt 'different' but was unable to describe in more detail how he felt.

6.3   Mr. X suggested that on arrival in the UK they all lived in Tooting with his brother and family. Mr. X suggested that A worked a lot although he did not know what he did. Mr. X reported that he started school at the end of Year 6 but that he did not learn a lot due to not being able to speak English. Mr. X reported that as a family they moved quite a lot, resulting from A's changes in employment or to obtain larger properties. Mr, X reported that they moved to Town where he attended Town High School. The family moved again after one year to Cricklewood as a result of his brother finding alternative employment. Mr. X suggested that after 6 months his brother B moved back to South London and that he and his brother C ran away to live with him. Mr. X suggested that he and C did not get on with A, suggesting A could be violent.

6.4   Mr. X reported that the Local Authority became involved after he moved in with B due to his non-attendance at school and being apprehended on a train without a ticket. Mr. X stated that he was able to remain with B but that they moved hostels, initially living in Streatham and then moving to Mitcham. Mr. X suggested that they achieved some stability in Mitcham but that they then had to move again within Mitcham, although he did not know why. Mr. X acknowledged that his education was disrupted due to the frequent moves and his non-attendance at school. Mr. X suggested that each time they moved it would take 8 or 9 months to get into a new school. Mr. X admitted that he got into a few fights at school, sometimes protecting his younger brother and sometimes arising from his own problems. Mr. X also admitted that he started to smoke cannabis at a young age and was caught with this in school. Mr. X admitted that he was suspended and expelled as a result of his poor behaviour at school. He attended approved schools, but continued to be disruptive and stopped attending following being arrested for criminal damage.

6.5   Whilst Mr. X acknowledged that his education was disrupted, he argued that his ability to form relationships was not, suggesting that he made friends wherever he went, largely through playing football. Mr. X suggested that most of his friends were Somali. Mr. X suggested that he had difficulty at first learning English and that he learned most of it from television. However, Mr. X suggests that now his ability to speak English far exceeds his ability to speak Somali.

6.6   Mr. X reported that he had one relationship, after he was charged with rape, with a girl named Y. He suggested that they met at a rave for under 18s, through friends. Mr. X suggested that the relationship lasted for about 8 months, before her mother took her back to Somalia for education. Mr. X suggested that Y was the only girl he had ever liked, and that prior to his conviction he was too young to have relationships. Mr. X admitted that he had engaged in one sexual experience prior to being charged with rape and prior to his relationship with Y. He stated that friends older than him encouraged him to use a brothel. Mr. X suggested that he did so but thought very little of this experience. Mr. X suggested that he had engaged in two one-night stands after he was charged with rape.

7   Offending history

7.1   On Date 2009 Mr. X was convicted at XX Juvenile Court of destroying or damaging property. He received a conditional discharge for 6 months. Mr. X suggested that this offence involved him putting his foot up against the door of a bookmakers and the owner/manager alleging he had damaged the door. Mr. X denied that he had forcefully kicked or damaged the door and suggested that there was a small crack in the door that could have already been there.

7.2   On Date 2009 Mr. X was convicted at XX Juvenile Court of possessing a controlled drug – class B (cannabis) with intent to supply. Mr. X was sentenced to a 12-month referral order and a 6-month parenting order. Mr. X reported that the context of this offence was that he was a regular, although he suggested infrequent, smoker of cannabis. He stated that he had a £10 bag of cannabis that he was offered £20 for. He stated he agreed to sell the cannabis and the transaction was observed by the police. Mr. X insisted that this was the first occasion that he had sold drugs. Mr. X stated that although the conviction is dated prior to that for rape, the offence occurred after the offence of rape, whilst he was on bail, and he attributed his use of cannabis to the stress of the proceedings.

7.3   On Date 2009 at XX Crown Court Mr. X was convicted of four counts of rape. The offence was committed when he was aged 15. He was sentenced to 7 years' detention in a Young Offenders' Institution and required to sign the sex offender register for life. The victim of the rape was a young woman Mr. X and his friends met on a tram. The trial judge commented that it was apparent that this young lady engaged in sexual activity with a friend of Mr. X. This friend was charged with rape but was acquitted. The judge commented that the sexual act had, however, upset the young lady and that she sought support from Mr. X and another friend of his. It is suggested by the trial judge that the victim had placed her trust in Mr. X but that Mr. X and his friend raped her simultaneously. The judge commented that he was satisfied that the victim's distress was evident through uncontrollable crying. The victim was reported to have escaped and been incoherent and thoroughly distressed, in a state of undress on her lower body, when she presented herself at a nearby house for assistance. The judge commented that he considered that Mr. X had planned the attack shortly before it occurred and not when they met the young girl. Further, the judge commented that although no actual violence was used on the victim and no actual threats were made, that the victim knew what was coming and was absolutely terrified. She opened up her belt to get the ordeal over with. The judge described her as 'frozen'. The trial judge reported the victim to have had mental health problems prior to the rape, evidenced by a previous suicide attempt, and that these were exacerbated by the rapes, evident in two subsequent suicide attempts.

7.4   When interviewed for this assessment, Mr. X was unable to recall the name of the girl who became the victim. He stated he and four friends got on the tram and met the girl. He suggested that they all got off the tram at XX. Mr. X stated that two of the friends left, and that one 'Tom' was with the girl alone somewhere else in the park. Mr. X suggested that Tom and the girl returned to him and his friend Peter, with Tom, subsequently leaving and the girl sitting smoking with him. Mr. X suggested that she was happy and had even asked if she could stay the night with him. Mr. X admitted that he had sexual intercourse with the girl but claims she consented. Mr. X stated that the girl then stated she had lost her key, that he found it for her and then left the park, leaving her with Mr. Y. Mr. X stated that Mr. Y told him the next day that he had also had sex with the girl. He said he did not know how she had gotten home but suggested that together, he, Mr. Y and Tom telephoned her to check if she was all right. Mr. X denied the offences of rape. Mr. X suggested that he considered appealing against his conviction but that his co-defendant implicated him during the trial so he could not. It would appear within the trial that the two defendants blamed each other. Mr. X disputed the victim's account of the offence. He suggested that she had provided different accounts of her background and argued that she did not report that she had been raped when she arrived at a nearby house. Mr. X stated that he believed that his conviction occurred only because his 'so-called friend' panicked and implicated him. Mr. X was aggrieved that his co-defendant was apparently released over one year ago. Mr. X has not engaged in any intervention work to address the offence of rape due to his denial. Mr. X stated that he does not give any thought to the victim, stating that he 'can't'. He was not able to identify what effect the offence may have had upon her. In an attempt to support his position, Mr. X suggested that he does not believe in sex outside of marriage. He reported that engaging in casual sex is part of a 'western lifestyle'. Whilst Mr. X did not directly seek to blame the victim, this comment suggested that he might hold underlying attitudes about British females that contributed to his decision making in relation to the offence. This comment was also contradictory to his earlier sexual experiences, suggesting further that it served as a means of distancing himself from the offence.

7.5 On Date 2010, whilst on remand for the offence of rape, Mr. X was convicted at XX Juvenile Court of assault of a constable (prison officer). He was given a conditional discharge of 9 months. Mr. X suggested that he was using the telephone when a prison officer tried to turn off the phone. Mr. X stated that he pushed the officer back and the officer reported him for assault. Mr. X said that he did not consider that the offence was assault, but was unable to prove this due to the CCTV footage 'disappearing'.

7.6 On Date 2011 at XX Crown Court Mr. X was convicted for wounding/ inflicting grievous bodily harm on another young offender whilst he was serving his sentence at HM YOI. Mr. X was sentenced to 15 months' detention in a young offenders' institution to be served consecutive to his sentence for rape. The judge's comments indicated that this was an 'extremely violent' reaction to the most 'innocent provocation'. Mr. X is reported by the trial judge to have committed a 'frenzied attack' with some decorative scissors, resisting commands to stop and when finally restrained, commenting that he wished he had 'stabbed him in the head'. Mr. X's account of this offence was that he had a disagreement with another prisoner in the workshop. He argued that he had seen what happens in prison and is aware of the need to act first to protect oneself. Mr. X did acknowledge that he 'lost control' and 'blacked out'. Mr. X suggested that the argument was 'just prison life' but that the other prisoner swore at him. Mr. X said, 'I had scissors, the next thing I know I've attacked him'. Mr. X believed that he had no alternative than to use violence. He suggested that it is not possible to walk away in prison. Further, he suggested that to seek help from an officer after an argument is 10 times worse than attacking someone due to the stigma attached to being seen as a 'snitch'. Mr. X denied saying that he wished he had stabbed him in the head. He suggested that there were no officers present only prisoners who tried to stop him. Mr. X suggested that officers arrived as a result of the victim's screaming. Mr. X suggested that when officers arrived he put the scissors down and was taken peacefully to the segregation unit. Mr. X suggested that he pleaded guilty to the offence, as he knew he had 'done something wrong'.

7.7 It is notable that Mr. X moved around the prison estate frequently. *[Details]* Mr. X also admitted to having weapons in prison, which consisted of homemade knives that he had fashioned to protect himself from perceived problems with other inmates. Mr. X suggested that there was a prisoner from East London who 'thought he was running the wing'. Mr. X suggested that he does not get involved in gangs. Mr. X stated that he had disclosed his offence and challenged the prisoner that if he had a problem with that he knew where to find him. Mr. X said he did this believing people would find out about his offence anyway. He suggested that he was subsequently subject to attempts to attack him and thus fashioned weapons to protect himself. Mr. X had previously refused to relocate to the vulnerable prisoners' unit.

8   Risk assessment

8.1   This approach is not a predictive assessment using an actuarial tool, which would provide a defined level or category of risk. Tools that do this are actuarial assessments that are optimised to predict a specific outcome (likelihood of reoffending) within a specific population over a specific period of time creating a statistical profile of an individual compared with specific groups. However, such tools are limited in their application to the specific populations upon whom they were developed and may not be generalisable to individuals who fall outside of the population of the original group. Furthermore, actuarial tools do not take into account situational factors, the impact of treatment or intervention or circumstances that may increase or decrease risk. There are problems with predictive tools in Mr. X's case due to the age he was at the time of the offence and the age he is now. Also the actuarial tools available are not normed on individuals from Somalia or who are refugees; as such their utility would be questionable.

8.2   This assessment constitutes a discretionary approach to risk assessment, a holistic approach considering developmental/historical factors as well as the current situation to make an assessment of the potential for future risk of violence and reoffending. Risk assessment is the process of evaluating people to characterise the risks that they will commit offences in the future, as well as the steps that could be taken to minimise the risks. Two risk assessment tools are utilised here due to the risk of both sexual offending and violent offending.

8.3   For the purpose of assessing risk of sexual offending, the Risk Of Sexual Violence Protocol (RSVP)[ii] is used. The RSVP considers the risk of sexual violence occurring in five separate domains. These are sexual violence history, psychological adjustment, mental disorder, social adjustment and manageability. Factors are considered as to whether they were present and relevant at the time of the offending and thus are related to risk. If they are risk-related factors, then presence at the current time is also considered. Sexual violence is defined as the actual, attempted or threatened contact or communication of a sexually violent nature with another person that is deliberate and non-consensual. This risk assessment considers the totality of circumstances in the case at hand.

8.4   To assess the risk of violence, the HCR-20 version 3[iii] is also used. This tool considers risk factors across three temporal domains: historical, current and future. Violence is defined as the actual, attempted or threated infliction of bodily harm of another person.

8.5   These tools are forms of risk assessment known as structured professional judgement guides and are the currently professionally preferred and empirically informed approaches to risk assessment. These tools have been demonstrated through research to be valid and reliable assessments of sexual violence and violence and are currently acknowledged as best practice in the assessment and management of risk of sexual violence and violence.

8.6   The risk factors evident from each protocol will be outlined first. This will be followed by a formulation that seeks to explain the risk of both violence and sexual violence arising from the factors. Risk scenarios are then considered resulting in the development of a risk management plan.

9   Risk of sexual violence protocol

9.1   *Sexual violence history*

9.1i   Mr. X has been convicted of a sexual offence on one occasion. Although four counts of rape are recorded, these are all against the same victim on the same occasion, arising from Mr. X's actions of raping the victim both orally and vaginally and swapping places with his friend. The following risk factors are **not** present based on this pattern of sexual offending.

1   Chronicity of sexual violence
2   Diversity of sexual violence
3   Escalation in sexual violence
4   Physical coercion in sexual violence

9.1ii   The trial judge's remarks relating to the offences of rape suggest that the victim was terrified and knew what was going to occur. This fear meant that the use of physical violence or coercion did not occur. However, it is noted that Mr. X and his co-defendant apparently lulled the victim into a false sense of security before raping her. Therefore, the following factor is **present and relevant** to the risk of sexual violence.

5   Psychological coercion in sexual violence

9.2   *Psychological adjustment*

9.2i   **All** of the factors within this domain are considered to be **present and relevant**. These are:

6   Extreme minimisation or denial of sexual violence
7   Attitudes that support or condone sexual violence
8   Problems with self-awareness
9   Problems with stress or coping
10   Problems resulting from child abuse

9.2ii   As is evident in section 7.4, Mr. X denies the offence of rape, suggesting that the sexual activity was consenting. He denied that he and his co-defendant acted together. Mr. X suggested that the victim willingly engaged in sexual activity and disputed both her account of the rape and the level of distress she reported. Consequently, Mr. X's denial of the rape is relevant to the risk of further sexual offences, due to this impacting on engagement in treatment approaches aimed at reducing risk, and may also impact on willingness to engage in monitoring and supervision strategies.

9.2iii Mr. X expressed some attitudes that may support or condone sexual violence which related to casual sex being part of a 'western lifestyle'. This comment seemed aimed at supporting his assertion that the victim was consenting, which was in part assumed due to her being a western/English girl. This is related to Mr. X's denial of the offences and also his lack of ability to empathise with the victim at all.

9.2iv Mr. X demonstrated little insight into his motivation to commit sexual offences. He did not accept the conviction for rape and was unable to provide an explanation for his behaviour. He maintained his position that the victim consented. He did not report any sexual arousal or attraction to the victim. He was unable to discuss his offence in relation to his experiences with peers and maintenance of relationships or status with them. Mr. X was not able to discuss the offence within the context of his lifestyle; as such, he is considered to have problems with self-awareness.

9.2v Mr. X demonstrates a vulnerability to stress and a propensity to cope with situations he finds stressful using antisocial means including use of violence and use of cannabis. Mr. X's difficulty in responding to stress in more adaptive means is predisposed by his experiences in childhood, the lack of parental guidance when living in Ethiopia and the difficulties in developing a secure relationship with his oldest brother when in the UK. Mr. X also reported that his brother was absent a lot of the time and also that he would use violence as a means of chastising him. Mr. X admitted that his use of cannabis increased when he was feeling under stress when on bail for the offence of rape and that this contributed to his offence of supplying cannabis. Within prison, Mr. X continued to respond to stress using violence and cannabis. There have been some periods of greater stability; however, it is not clear how Mr. X has achieved this and how he would cope in the community.

9.2vi Mr. X described that he and his brothers were left alone in Ethiopia when his sister-in-law traveled to the UK. Whilst he stated his oldest brother sent money for them, there is some evidence that Mr. X was neglected with regards to ensuring his overall well-being. Once in the UK, Mr. X reported that his oldest brother hit him and that he ran away from home. Mr. X also described that he was frequently not able to attend school due to house moves and that there was local authority involvement. This factor is only partially present due to acknowledgement that the experiences of Mr. X were not wholly abusive and in recognition of cultural differences. Nonetheless, Mr. X's childhood experiences did not equip him to effectively build relationships, to integrate into the UK lifestyle or to refrain from offending and, therefore, there is partial presence and relevance assessed in relation to this factor.

9.3 *Mental disorder*

9.3i Mr. X does not present with a stable pattern of deviant arousal to violence. Whilst the offence was rape, the victim was a similar age and therefore there is not an indication that he has a sexual preference for people younger than himself. It is accepted that the rating of this factor is limited by his incarceration since conviction; however, there is not sufficient evidence to indicate a positive rating. Further, Mr. X has not been diagnosed with a major mental illness. The following items are therefore assessed as not **present or relevant**

11 Sexual deviance

12 Major mental illness

Mr. X has not been assessed for

13 Psychopathic personality disorder

This item is therefore omitted.

9.3ii Mr. X has in the past had difficulties arising from use of cannabis. Mr. X reported that he began to use cannabis at the age of 14 as a result of friends using. He suggested that at the beginning this was occasional use only, but that subsequent to being charged with rape that he began to use heavily on a daily basis due to struggling to cope with the situation he was in. Mr. X was convicted of supplying cannabis. Mr. X stated that he had bought the cannabis from a friend for £10 for personal use. He was later offered £20 for it but was observed and arrested. Mr. X stated that he used to use khat regularly also. Mr. X denied that he offended to obtain funds for his cannabis use, not withstanding the conviction. He suggested that he funded his use out of money his brother gave him. Mr. X reported that he has never drunk alcohol. He suggested that he has seen what it does to people; specifically, that they get to a point where they do not know what they are doing. Mr. X suggested that use of cannabis does not have the same effect on people as alcohol. Mr. X suggested that he has abstained from use of cannabis in prison except for one occasion following surgery on his eye, when he used it to help with pain. Mr. X suggested that he is able to distract himself and occupy his mind to manage the risk of further cannabis use. This factor is therefore present and relevant with regards to ongoing risk of sexual offending.

14 Problems with substance use

9.3iii Mr. X has historically expressed thoughts of harming others and has acted on impulse. This was evident, for example, in the offence of wounding perpetrated against another prisoner, where Mr. X is reported to have said that he wished he had stabbed the victim in the head. No such reports are available indicating this is an ongoing concern and, therefore, the following factor was present historically, although does not appear to be present currently. This factor is not currently relevant to risk of further sexual violence:

15 Violent or suicidal ideation

9.4 *Social Adjustment*

9.4.i All of the factors in this domain are assessed as present and relevant to ongoing risk of future risk of sexual violence. These factors are:

16 Problems with intimate relationships

17 Problems with non-intimate relationships

18 Problems with employment

19 Non-sexual criminality

9.4ii   Mr. X has had difficulty in establishing intimate relationships in the community. It is accepted that there are limitations to this risk factor arising from Mr. X's age at the time of his imprisonment. However, this item is assessed as present and relevant due to Mr. X's attitudes towards relationships and willingness previously to engage in casual impersonal sexual encounters through paid sex or one-night stands. Mr. X did report one relationship with a girl he referred to positively and as such this item is only partially present. Mr. X also had difficulties with non-intimate relationships in that his peer group was also antisocial young men with whom he offended. Mr. X also had difficulties with his oldest brother and, although he reports close relationships now with his family, he actually reported very limited contact with them and was not able to provide names of his nieces and nephews which could suggest the relationships are not as well established as they could be in order to provide positive support to him that is likely to be protective. Mr. X suggested that he does not need support from anyone and that he does not ask for anything. Mr. X stated that he gets stressed when he talks to friends and family outside due to them being able to continue with their life whilst he is imprisoned. It is notable that Mr. X remains in contact with Tom, who was acquitted of sexual offending. Contact with Mr. Y is prohibited and thus has not occurred.

9.4iii Problems with employment refers in this case to Mr. X's engagement in education due to his age, which was fraught with difficulties arising from his truancy and aggression. It is accepted that Mr. X had some difficulties in education arising from language differences; however, it was his attitude and behaviour that resulted in the problems above and beyond language barriers.

9.4iv   Further, it is clear from Mr. X's conviction record that he has experienced problems in relation to non-sexual offending, including violent offending and drug-related offending.

9.5   *Manageability*

9.5i   All three risk factors in this domain are present and relevant for Mr. X:

    20   Problems with planning
    21   Problems with treatment
    22   Problems with supervision

9.5ii   Mr. X does not describe clear plans for the future. He is unclear where he will live, how he will secure employment or how he will constructively spend his time. It is accepted that Mr. X's ability to formulate plans is impacted upon by his incarceration and uncertainty regarding his immigration status. Nonetheless, this has affected his ability to meaningfully plan for the future.

9.5iii Mr. X stated that he has completed anger management and victim awareness courses. No information regarding his progress was available. Mr. X argued that he does not believe he has an anger management problem anymore, as he believes he has learned to control himself. Mr. X has not undertaken any intervention work in relation to his sexual offence, although he stated that he would be prepared to do this whilst on licence. In this regard Mr. X is considered to be an untreated sexual offender.

9.5iv There have been a number of problems arising whilst Mr. X has been under supervision that do not bode well for his manageability on licence. Mr. X has engaged in a number of fights in prison resulting in various institutional adjudication penalties, including having days added to the date of his release. Mr. X suggested that the fights were simply 'prison fights' arising from other prisoners suggesting that he was not respectful. Mr. X suggested that he had never had a fight that was his problem, suggesting that all of the fights arose due to 'other people trying to start on me'. Mr. X did, however, suggest that he did what he felt he had to do to protect himself. Mr. X stated that some problems he had in prison were related to the friends he had; he emphasised that he was not referring to gangs, but that he would also defend his friends. Institutional records contain entries suggesting that on Date 2012 he was making threats to assault staff, stab staff and go on to the netting. Mr. X was taken to the care and separation unit in handcuffs. Further, on Date 2011 Mr. X was reported to have swung a knotted sock with a heavy article in it at another prisoner. Additionally, on Date 2013 Mr. X had to be restrained when he became aggressive. Mr. X suggested that he was transferred to HM YOI in 2012. Mr. X suggested that things were better there as no one was bothering him. Mr. X reported that he was attacked by two other prisoners with a plank of wood resulting in him suffering a detached retina for which he continues to need treatment. Mr. X stated that he did not inform officers that he had been involved in a fight/was attacked. He said instead that he had been play fighting and had been elbowed in the face. Mr. X did suggest, however, that he is currently getting on well in HMP Prison. He suggested that there have been no problems with either staff or prisoners.

10 HCR-20 version 3

There are a number of items within this risk assessment that overlap with the items in the RSVP. Where this is the case, rather than repeating evidence, the relevant risk factor and paragraph will be referred to.

10.1 *Historical items*

10.1i These 10 items reflect features of the person's history of psychosocial adjustment. It indexes a set of core important risk factors for violence that may have arisen during a person's past and can provide crucial evidence for understanding a person's violence. The following risk factors are both present and relevant for Mr. X.

H1. History of serious problems with violence

H2. History of problems with other antisocial behaviour (see 9.4iv)

H3. History of problems with relationships (see 9.4ii)

H4. History of problems with employment (see 9.4iii)

H5. History of problems with substance misuse (see 9.3ii)

H8. History of problems with traumatic experiences (9.4vi)

H9. History of problems with violent attitudes (9.3iii)

H10. History of problems with treatment or supervision response

10.1ii   The evidence for these factors has been covered in the previous sections as indicated in parentheses. It is significant to note, however, that Mr. X has engaged in a clear pattern of serious violence as an adolescent including rape, wounding and other fights not resulting in a conviction. He has reported less serious violence as an adult over the age of 18 within institutions.

10.1iii The following items are not present and are omitted respectively.

H6. History of problems with major mental illness

H7. History of problems with personality disorder

10.2   *Clinical factors*

10.2i   These five factors reflect an individual's current psychological adjustment and are rated on information over the last 12 months. The following factors are assessed as present and relevant:

C1. Recent problems with insight

C3. Recent problems with instablity

C5. Recent problems with treatment or supervision response

As is indicated in paragraph 9.2vi, Mr. X demonstrated very little insight into his risk factors and expressed very little understanding of the reasons he committed the offences. Mr. X had a tendency to externalise blame, and with regards to violence, he appeared to consider this the only realistic response available to him given what he considered to be provocation. Mr. X failed to give consideration to the role his lifestyle, associates, mood, drug use and lack of positive support in his life played in his offending. This has impacted upon his ability to engage effectively in treatment programmes and to change his behaviour. This lack of insight is highly likely to continue to impact on his engagement with supervision and treatment in the community also. Mr. X reported a continued fluctuation in his moods and occasionally behaviour, although there are no reports available suggesting violence has continued in prison. Mr. X did report anger towards the prison system and immigration processes for denying him medical treatment for his eye and this impacts on his mood state.

10.2ii The following factors are not present or relevant to the risk of further violence

C2. Recent problems with violent ideation or intent

C3. Recent problems with symptoms of major mental disorder

10.3   *Risk items*

10.3i   These five items refer to future problems in factors which research demonstrates are related to risk. All factors are assessed as present and relevant to the risk of future violence:

R1. Future problems with professional services and plans

R2. Future problems with living situation

R3. Future problems with personal support

R4. Future problems with treatment or supervision response

R5. Future problems with stress or coping

10.3ii Mr. X has no explicit plans regarding the role of professional services. At the current time, due to Mr. X's immigration status, the role of professional services is not clearly defined. Due to his young age at time of offending and ongoing denial, it is unlikely that professional services will be able to intervene at a level that manages the risk. When this is combined with uncertainty about living situation and likely housing in a hostile environment with will be unstable by virtue of the residents and the short-term accommodation this offers, concerns about professional service input are exacerbated.

10.3iii Whilst Mr. X suggests that he has good positive support from friends and family, this is not borne out in his description of their relationships, the lack of consistent contact and the lack of protection offered from these relationships historically. It is unclear how such relationships would now be protective rather than a risk factor.

10.3iv Whilst Mr. X states that he would comply with his supervising probation officer, his conduct in custody does not suggest that this is likely to be the case. Mr. X does not express positive attitudes towards supervision that reflect that he is likely to engage in a positive manner recognising the role supervision plays in managing his risk. Rather he refers to supervision as a process that should meet his needs in finding him accommodation and employment. Whilst stable accommodation and employment both have the potential to be risk reducing, Mr. X described this process in entitled egocentric terms, rather than acknowledging the risk-reducing component.

10.3v Mr. X is also going to continue to face very stressful living circumstances as a result of the immigration proceedings. His coping ability has not been evidenced over a significant period of time to have developed his resilience to this life stress, nor does it indicate that Mr. X will turn to positive coping methods. It is likely that Mr. X will seek to use cannabis as a means of coping, which is a risk-increasing factor.

11 Opinion

11.1 As a result of the application of the HCR-20 version 3 and the RSVP, the conclusions are based upon a formulation approach. Formulation is the process by which clinicians seek to conceptualise the roots of a person's problems with a view towards increasing understanding and identifying intervention. This formulation is based upon Weerasekera's (1996)[iv] 'Four P' model that encourages consideration of *predisposing*, distal vulnerabilities, *precipitating* trigger factors, *perpetuating* or maintaining factors and *protective* factors, that reduce the influence of the risk factors.

11.2 In my opinion based on the information available during this assessment the most significant *predisposing* factor relating to Mr. X is the lack of secure attachments in childhood arising from his fragmented upbringing, the loss of his parents, the lack of a consistent adult role model and the frequent moves, including moving from his native Somalia to Ethiopia and the UK, and then frequent moves within the UK. These experiences resulted in Mr. X having a lack of boundaries, and his offending is an expression of that. It appears that there was an expectation that Mr. X would be resilient both emotionally and practically evident in the expectation that he and his siblings could fend for themselves. This is likely to have resulted in an emotionally disconnected experience and the development of beliefs that mean Mr. X is intrinsically motivated to protect himself at all costs. **Precipitating** factors are the development of an antisocial peer group, which Mr. X was drawn to due to their acceptance of him, and this is likely to have fed into his sense of being safe within a group. Offending is further **perpetuated** by Mr. X having antisocial attitudes that support offending, which includes attitudes towards western lifestyles and western girls and also the use of violence as a means of defending oneself. Further, the use of cannabis is likely to have dishinbited Mr. X. In the future, Mr. X's lack of insight into his offending is likely to be a perpetuating factor as this is likely to present a barrier to treatment and engagement in supervision. In my opinion, Mr. X's offending demonstrates a range of delinquent behaviours, and sexual violence is one such manifestation. There is not evidence that Mr. X is predisposed to act in a sexually violent manner due to deviant sexual interests.

11.3 If Mr. X offended again, the most likely scenario is a violent offence. This is most likely triggered by a perceived threat to himself and the belief he needs to defend himself. Violence could escalate to serious harm if Mr. X chooses to use a weapon, which he does have the potential for given his prior use of weapons. Warning signs may be limited due to Mr. X's impulsivity unless those managing him are aware of the perceived threat. Violence is more likely if Mr. X has been using cannabis. Further sexual violence is not likely to be a planned offence or to be motivated by sexual deviance. If a sexual offence occurred, this is again likely to be in the context of an opportunity arising as part of an antisocial lifestyle.

11.4 It is difficult to conclude that risk in this case has significantly reduced due to the lack of significant intervention work occurring with Mr. X. Unfortunately, within HMP Prison where he is detained under immigration powers, Mr. X is unlikely to be offered such intervention. Mr. X could be offered intervention in the community whilst on licence in the form of the thinking skills programme; however, this is unlikely to be of sufficient intensity to manage the risk posed by Mr. X. Given that the close supervision of prison has not managed the risk, it is not possible to be confident that supervision in the community would be sufficient. Mr. X would need to be subject to significant monitoring and supervision, including the use of curfew and electronic tagging as well as intervention. It is unfortunate that Mr. X is not able to provide evidence that his family and peer group would act as protective factors, and therefore, the risk in this case of further offending and of serious harm remains high.

12   Declarations

12.1 Statement of compliance

I understand my duty to the court and have complied and will continue to comply with that duty. This report includes all matters relevant to the issues on which my expert evidence is given. I have given details in this report of any matters which might affect the validation of this report. I have addressed this report to the court.

12.2 Statement on conflicts of interest. I confirm that I

a   have no conflict of interest of any kind, other than any conflict disclosed in my report;

b   do not consider that any interest disclosed affects my suitability as an expert;

c   will advise the instructing party if, between the date of my report and the final hearing, there is any change in circumstances which affects my answers to (a) or (b) above.

12.3 Statement of truth

I confirm that insofar as the facts stated in my report are within my own knowledge I have made clear which they are and I believe them to be true, and that the opinions I have expressed represent my true and complete professional opinion. Should further information be revealed regarding Mr. X's life history or relating to offending then this assessment may be invalidated. Signature and name and date.

Appendix 1 – Index of documents reviewed

55 items listed *[Not included here for space reasons]*

Appendix 2 – CV *[Not included for space and confidentiality reasons]*

Notes

i   Paulhus D.L. (1998). *Paulhus Deception Scale - Formerly known as the Balanced Inventory of Desirable Responding.* North Tonawanda, NY: Multi-Health Systems Inc.

ii Hart S.D., Kropp R., Laws R.D., Klaver J., Logan C. and Watt K. (2003). *Risk of sexual violence protocol.* Burnaby, BC, Canada: Mental Health Law and Policy Institute, Simon Fraser University.

iii Douglas, K.S., Hart, S.D., Webster, C.D. and Belfrage, H. (2011). *HCR-V3 Historical Clinical Risk Management (Version 3): Professional guidelines for evaluating risk of violence.* Burnaby, BC, Canada: Mental Health, Law, and Policy Institute, Simon Fraser University.

iv Weerasekera, P. (1996). *Multiperspective case formulation: A step towards treatment integration.* Malabar, FL: Krieger

APPENDIX 3

EXAMPLE REPORT 3

This report was written in 2011 and is based on a real case. Names have been changed to protect the identities of those involved, and the report has been shortened due to space constraints. Where shortening has occurred, this has been through the deletion of complete paragraphs rather than the editing of the text; paragraph numbers have been kept as per the original report so that the deletions can be identified.

Case No:	XXX132
For:	XX Court
Final Report of:	Jane Smith BSc; MSc; CPsychol (foren)
Specialist Field:	Forensic Psychology
Instructions:	Led by XX Solicitors
Subject:	Rachel White (d.o.b. 01.01.2007) and Louise White (d.o.b. 01.01.2010)
Subject Matter:	An Independent Risk Assessment of Sarah White
Date:	28 November 2011

Contents Page (*not included here due to space constraints*)

1   Introduction

1.1   I am a forensic psychologist, chartered with the British Psychological Society and registered with the Health Professions Council. I have over 15 years' experience working with offenders and people who may pose a risk to others. I have experience working in custodial and mental health services. I have experience preparing reports for criminal and family court, immigration tribunals, parole boards and mental health tribunals. I am a parole board member and lecturer at Anywhere University. Full details of my career and experience are found in my CV in Appendix 2.

2 Summary of conclusions

2.1   Miss White's full scale IQ is in the borderline range. This, however, may not be the most reliable indicator of cognitive ability as there is a significant difference between her scores on the verbal comprehension index and the perceptual reasoning index. Miss White's performance on the verbal comprehension index is within the extremely low range, suggesting that she has the most difficulty with verbally presented information and information reliant upon word use and understanding. This likely results in Miss White having difficulty in fully understanding information she is given and also difficulties in expressing herself.

2.2   There is an irrefutable relationship between Miss White's childhood experiences of domestic violence and her inability to protect her own children. Miss White's mother failed to protect Miss White and her siblings from a number of violent men and resisted the interventions of social workers. Miss White is repeating the same patterns. Miss White did not have an alternative role model to mediate against such experiences or to more adequately develop her parenting skills.

2.3   Miss White accepts the concerns raised by the local authority but does not have the capacity to address them. Miss White has not changed the pattern of her relationships even after her children were removed and is unlikely to be able to without significant intervention and support.

2.4   Miss White vehemently denies injuring Louise but accepts she did not protect her children from violent men. Miss White suggested that she would protect her children by not allowing men into her house until she knew them better. This is not an adequate strategy and she did not follow this when she met Mr. Brown.

2.5   Risks would remain to Miss White's children if they were returned to Miss White's care as a result of relationships likely to involve domestic violence and a failure to fully accept the risks. Miss White is accepting of the concerns but does not consider social workers to be a welcome assistance to her. Rather she sees them as an interference, based on her experiences in childhood and her mother's experiences.

2.6   It is noted that Miss White is reported to have a good bond with her children as demonstrated from the supervised contact. Whilst some concerns have been expressed by supervisors about the language Miss White uses, this relates more to Miss White's limited verbal fluency rather than reflecting Miss White's attitudes towards her children. The distress expressed by Miss White during the assessment seemed genuinely related to the loss of her children and her desire to be with them. Miss White presented as someone who had a sincere intention to protect her children, although her actual ability to do this may be limited.

3   Background Information

3.1   Proceedings were issued by the Local Authority on 23 February 2011. Both Rachael and Louise were placed together with Local Authority Foster Carers under Section 20 of the Children Act 1989. The children remain there at the current time.

3.2   An anonymous referral was received by the Local Authority on 10 January 2011 advising that Louise had bruising to her face and body. During a social worker visit and Child Protection Medical, a number of bruises were noted which were believed to be 'non-accidental'.

3.3   The children's birth father, John Black, has no contact with the children. He was convicted in 1996 of willful neglect and cruelty (shaking her, causing permanent brain damage) to one of his older daughters. The author has prepared an assessment relating to risks he poses.

3.4   Miss White's partner at the time of the injuries to Louise, Joe Blogs, was granted intervenor status for the purpose of the finding of fact hearing.

3.5   Miss White's mother, Mrs. Jones, was also granted intervenor status for the purpose of the finding of fact hearing.

3.6   At the finding of fact hearing on 5 and 6 September 2011, it was accepted that the injuries to Louise were non-accidental. There was a possibility that Miss White and Mr. Blogs caused the injuries. The injuries were not premeditated but caused by a momentary loss of control. It was not possible to say whether the injuries were caused on one occasion. Miss White was not ruled out as a potential carer.

3.7   Miss White has supervised contact with the children three times per week at Surestart Centres.

4   Instructions

4.1   Instructions requested a psychological assessment of Sarah White, in particular reference to the following issues:

1   An analysis of Miss White's cognitive functioning.

2   Whether or not her life experiences have affected her psychological functioning and her ability to offer her children good enough and safe parenting.

3   Her ability to care for two young and dependent children on her own and the potential risk, if any, of a momentary loss of self control, in light of the findings made by the district judge, and how that risk can be reduced or eliminated in the future.

4   Her understanding of the Local Authority's concerns in this case over and above matters referred to above and to what extent Miss White is able to cooperate with professionals to improve her parenting and protecting her children.

5   Her ability to take on board and implement/action advice given to her, in particular relation to advice about caring for her children.

6   Her ability to meet all her children's needs, including their developmental needs.

7   The potential risk, if any, to her children if either or both were placed in her care, and if so, the nature of that risk.

8   Any other matters that you consider appropriate to consider.

9   In the event that any issues or problems are identified in relation to the above questions, please advise as to what work can be done with Miss White in order for improvements to be made. Who would carry out such work and over what timescale? What is the prognosis of achieving a successful outcome and a rehabilitation of either/both children into her care?

5   Assessment process

5.1   Miss White was assessed at the offices of XX Solicitors in Town. The duration of the assessment was over 6 hours. The assessment consisted of a clinical interview, administration of the Wechsler Adult Intelligence Scale – Fourth Edition (WAIS-IV) and the Personality Assessment Inventory (PAI).

6   Assessment
Presentation during interview

6.1   Miss White was motivated to engage in the assessment. She arrived early for the appointment and was waiting outside of the solicitor's office when I arrived. She immediately expressed her anxiety regarding the assessment, stating that it was so important for her to get her children back. Miss White stated that she had been informed by her solicitor that the outcome of my assessment would dictate whether her children were returned to her care; therefore she saw this assessment as incredibly important. Whilst the importance of the assessment was acknowledged and discussed, it was reiterated that the decision would be made by the court. It was acknowledged that this assessment was to assist the court in making their decision but that the assessment itself was not the final factor. The nature of the instructions was shared with Miss White. Miss White suggested that she understood this. The process of disclosure was also discussed and understood by Miss White.

6.2   Miss White frequently became distressed during the interview, breaking down in tears. This occurred when she spoke of her children being removed from her, her recognition that she had failed to protect her children, the length of time she has been away from them and when discussing her fears that her children may not be returned to her care.

7   Current situation

7.1   At the current time, Miss White has contact three times per week with her daughters, Rachael and Louise. She expressed her frustration that the contact was supposed to be for 2 hours each time but recently the social workers have reduced the contact to just over an hour on Monday, and then on Fridays, she has only been seeing the children for one hour and 15 minutes. Miss White suggested this has been due to administration problems and difficulties in finding supervisors or due to Rachael now attending school. Miss White expressed her frustration that this was not addressed earlier as it has been known for a long time that Rachael would start school in September. Miss White stated that as of this week, contact would be on Tuesday instead of Monday, which she hoped would mean that she would get her full time.

7.4   Miss White also expressed her frustration that at times events have occurred without her being informed of them in advance. She stated that there had been times when she was informed by Rachael that the foster carer had been on holiday and she had been placed with other carers. Miss White believed that she should have been informed of this in advance of this occurring and by a social worker, not by her 4-year-old daughter. In addition, Miss White stated that she was angry with the content of the social worker's report, suggesting that most of the things she said have been misinterpreted.

8   Account of events resulting in proceedings

8.1   Miss White was adamant that she had not inflicted the injuries to Louise. Miss White stated that she did not know at what point Mr. Blogs inflicted the injuries upon Louise. She accepted fully that Louise had been injured as a result of her failure to protect her and believes that she needs to live life very differently in the future to make sure that her children are her priority and are always protected. Miss White stated that she had only recently discovered, when the judge gave her feedback, that Louise had been hurt on more than one occasion. She stated that until recently she believed that Louise had only been hurt once.

8.2   Miss White gave an account of events that was consistent with some of the documentation. It is acknowledged that the recent social work report regarding Miss White highlighted some inconsistencies in the specific details of Miss White's disclosure. However, largely Miss White's statements during this interview were consistent with what she had said to more recent interviewers.

8.3   Miss White indicated that she had slept downstairs on the night of 10 January 2011 as she had a bad cough and did not want to wake either Mr. Blogs or her children. She also stated that because she was not sleeping very well, she was concerned that if she went back to bed she might fall asleep and not wake in time for the court hearing relating to Mr. Black seeking contact with the children. Miss White suggested when Louise woke, she gave her a bottle, but as Louise went back to sleep, she did not change her and therefore did not notice any bruising on her body. She stated that she did not notice the bruising on Louise's cheek as her cheeks were already red due to her teething. Miss White left the children in the care of her mother whilst she went to court.

8.4 Miss White stated that she was shocked when her mum contacted her to say that Louise had bruises. She stated that she wanted to return home to see the extent of them. Miss White stated that when she saw them, she was concerned that if she told social workers, the children would be removed from her care and therefore made a decision not to. Miss White realises now that her actions now have made the situation much worse and demonstrated her failure to protect her children adequately.

8.6 With regards to Mr. Blogs' contact with the children, Miss White suggested that her children liked Mr. Blogs and her children had formed good relationships with him. It is noted that Mr. Blogs had only been released from prison some 12 days before the injuries were discovered. It is not clear what contact the children had with Mr. Blogs whilst he was in prison and how they had formed what were perceived or described by Miss White as good relationships. She stated that she has become aware since Mr. Blogs left and the children were removed that Rachael has told her grandmother that she didn't like Mr. Blogs, though she said that no one had made this clear to her.

8.7 Despite having suggested that her children had a good relationship with Mr. Blogs, Miss White suggested that Mr. Blogs could not cope with Louise's crying and would say to her frequently 'can you shut her up!' and on one occasion was overheard to say he could 'volley' Louise. Miss White suggested that she had tried to communicate with Mr. Blogs that Louise was crying as it was her way of communicating. She stated that she understood that babies cry for many reasons – because they are teething, hungry or if they need changing and that she tried to make Mr. Blogs understand this. We spent a long time discussing the types of language that people use and whether she, at the time he said this, believed that there was no intention to harm. Miss White seemed quite vague about this and at times quite contradictory, saying that she didn't believe that Mr. Blogs was saying this with any kind of seriousness, but would also say at the same time that this should have been a sign that she should have 'got rid of him'. Miss White also acknowledged that Mr. Blogs had taken Louise outside in the cold. She stated that she had told him to bring her in and that she believes that she did try to protect her child on that occasion.

8.8 Miss White stated that she could not think how most of the bruises were caused, although maintained it was Mr. Blogs who was responsible.

8.9 Miss White emphasised that she knows how to cope with crying babies as she was given advice by her GP after she had suffered with postnatal depression with Rachael (GP records confirm this as October 2007-March 2008). She stated that she had been advised to 'take 5 minutes to go outside and have a breather'. She stated that the doctor had told her that as long as the children were fed and changed and she had given them teething powder that the children would calm down. She stated that she had only ever needed to do this once and the rest of the time she felt that she coped well enough with the children.

8.11   Miss White stated that she stayed in a relationship with Mr. Blogs for a week after her children were removed whilst she thought things through and needed his support. She felt that Mr. Blogs was there for her at that time and did not feel that her mother was. She stated that she then told him to leave as she realised that it must have been him who had harmed Louise and therefore the relationship needed to end. Miss White had suggested to other report writers that her solicitor advised her to end her relationship; she stated that this was not true, and that she did not know how to tell Mr. Blogs to leave and was afraid of the consequences and so used her solicitor as an excuse. She also claimed that this is one of the reasons why she had not confronted him about the possibility that he had harmed Louise. She stated this was because she knew 'what he was capable of'. Miss White stated that she had tried to end the relationship with Mr. Blogs before and he had kicked her door. She stated that she was scared about what he might do. However, notwithstanding these events, Miss White had failed to consider the possibility that Mr. Blogs posed a risk to her or her children, or make more efforts to end the relationship.

8.13   Miss White suggested that the only reason that social workers have stayed involved in her life is because the children have the father that they do and that her social workers only became involved when they found out about Mr. Black. Miss White was reminded that social workers remain involved and that the children were removed because the children were injured whilst they were in her care, and that irrespective of who the father is, had social workers not been involved, the outcome would have been the same following the anonymous referral about the injuries.

8.14   Miss White suggested that she did not want social workers involved in her and her children's lives. She said that she didn't want them knocking on the door all the time and wanted a good life for her and her children. Miss White was encouraged to think about herself and social workers ultimately having the same goals, with each wanting the best for her children, and that social work involvement was not necessarily a bad thing, if it meant that her children were safe. However, Miss White's experiences of having a social worker in her own life and in the lives of her children are seen by her as a negative interference.

9   Personal history

9.1   There is a great deal of documentation relating to Miss White's childhood experiences due to the long-term involvement of Children and Young People's Services with her mother relating to the care of Miss White and her siblings. It is clearly recorded that Miss White's mother engaged in a number of relationships with men who were violent to both her and her children. One of her partners is alleged to have sexually abused Miss White. Miss White's mother is also reported to have resisted the involvement of social workers, at times continuing relationships when she said she was not, therefore putting both herself and her children at risk.

9.3 Miss White was prompted with regards to the documentation suggesting that there were a number of adverse events in her childhood relating to her mother's relationships. Initially Miss White suggested that the only partner of her mother's that she had difficulty with was Martin Jones. She stated that he was violent when he drank alcohol and that she felt that she had to keep checking on the safety of her mum and the other children.

9.4 Miss White was further prompted about the extent of background history recorded on files. She admitted that she had lived with her nan when she was 15 years old, as her mother's ex-partner, Nigel Wood, father of Jason and Clare, would hit her a lot. She stated that if her mother stuck up for her, then he would hit her mother, and that Miss White therefore decided to move in with her nan to protect her mum.

9.5 Miss White was prompted for further information about her relationship with Nigel Wood and the allegations that he had sexually abused her. Miss White acknowledged that she had disclosed to people at school that he had kept touching her sexually. She stated, however, that when social workers got involved, nothing was done about it, and that this was another reason why she had moved in with her nan. Miss White stated that Mr. Wood would regularly try to kiss her, touch her breasts and her genital area. She stated that he had tried to have intercourse with her on one occasion, but that this was interrupted. She said that she did not say anything straight-away as she did not know how people would react. Miss White dismissed this experience as not having a great deal of significance. It seemed that essentially Miss White has split off from this experience. However, when asked to recall how she felt at the time as a 15-16-year-old girl in this situation, Miss White acknowledged that she felt very scared and hoped her mum would protect her, but she did not. Miss White suggested that this was one of the reasons that she wanted her children to know what was happening to them, as she wants her children to be able to talk to her and know that they are going to be kept safe. Miss White was not able to explain or think about the impact her own experience of sexual abuse might have had upon her. When asked to think about it, she said simply that she did not know.

10 Reflections on childhood

10.1 Miss White was encouraged to think of the parallels about her own situation with her children now and that which she experienced in her own childhood. Miss White acknowledged that she appeared to be repeating the pattern of her mother. She argued that her mother was trying to protect her but that her mother was also scared. Miss White stated that her mother was trying to protect her now as she does not want her to go through what she has been through, and Miss White argued that she wants her children to grow up differently and have good lives and good relationships and not get themselves pregnant at 16.

10.2   Miss White was not able to articulate, however, how she might break the cycle that she has found herself in going from one bad relationship to another. Her answer seemed to be that she would not let men into her house and that she would spend longer trying to get to know them. Whilst this might go some way to protecting herself and her children, it seemed to be quite a naive response to the situation, and whether Miss White has the capacity to make the different decisions about the men she has relationships with remains a concern.

11   Relationship history

11.1   Miss White stated that her first sexual relationship was at 16 with Simon Wilson. She stated that they met at a friend's party and he was 4 or 5 years older than her. She stated that this relationship lasted approximately 2.5 years. Miss White suggested that the relationship was good at first and that he looked after her and claimed her benefits for her. She stated, however, that as the relationship developed, they would argue about everything. She stated that Simon started to be violent towards her and eventually her auntie persuaded her to leave. She stated that she was also aware that he almost had sex with her sister. Miss White had a miscarriage whilst she was in this relationship (confirmed by GP records).

11.3   Miss White stated that her next relationship was with Mr. Black, who she met whilst on a training course. Again, she described that this was a good relationship at first. She stated that, however, when she had Rachael, Mr. Black did not take his responsibilities seriously and that he lived his life like a teenager. Miss White suggested that there was only one occasion when Mr. Black hit her and this was during a drunken argument. Miss White suggested that the relationship was not a violent one and that it ended because she did not like his lifestyle and lack of responsibility. She stated, however, that when they had met up on a night out, they had a drunken sexual encounter resulting in her pregnancy and subsequent birth of Louise. Miss White denied that she had been violent to Mr. Black. Miss White acknowledged that social workers had expressed their concern about Mr. Black due to the harm he had caused his older daughter. Miss White stated she thought Mr. Black had broken his daughter's arm. Miss White expressed her concerns that she had not been fully informed by social workers of exactly what Mr. Black had done and stated that it was only when she read my assessment report and the addendum report regarding Mr. Black that she was aware of the full extent of his actions. She suggested she may have taken different actions if social workers had told her the truth. However, that is not supported by her more recent decisions. Miss White stated that she believes the children should have contact with Mr. Black, but acknowledged that at first she was not sure if she wanted them to see him because of what he had done to his older daughter. Miss White stated that when she realised contact could be supervised, she decided that she would not mind if Mr. Black had contact with his children as she thought that it would be safe. She stated, however, that the children do not really know their father. She stated that Louise has never really met him and Rachael has only met him a few times.

11.5 Miss White then developed a relationship with Chris Blogs. She stated that she was in contact with him through Facebook on a chat site and then she had met up with him outside her backyard. She stated that she let him into the house and a sexual relationship started immediately. Miss White was 5 months pregnant with Louise when they met. She stated that initially their relationship was very good and he would help her around the house and with Rachael when she was unwell during her pregnancy. She stated that people told her that he had been violent, but she did not believe this as he was so different with her. Mr. Blogs went to prison not long after they met in June 2010 and was released on New Year's Eve 2010. Mr. Blogs lived with her upon release. She reported that he used a lot of cannabis and made lots of verbal threats. Miss White suggested that she asked him to leave on one occasion but let him back in as she was afraid of what he was going to do as he was kicking the door. Reports from a friend indicated that Mr. Blogs had said things like he could 'volley' Louise. Miss White acknowledged that she should have taken more action but was afraid of him.

11.8 I discussed with Miss White her choice of partners and how she has been informed on a number of occasions about the risks posed by her partners having a history of violence which she has chose to ignore. Miss White acknowledged this and began to cry, displaying her distress. She acknowledged that she had not listened to the risks when they were pointed out to her and believes that people must think she is 'stupid'. Miss White suggested that she felt bad, because if she had listened to advice that she had been given in the first place, her daughter would never have been hurt. Miss White was asked why she had not taken note of risks when they were pointed out to her. Miss White suggested that she had fallen into a trap which she could not get out of.

11.9 She stated that all of her partners seemed to be different at first in the way that they treated her and she believed that their exes were trying to cause trouble. She stated, 'With Mr. Blogs, for example, I had never seen him be violent, but I should have known because he had stolen loads of times from me and my mum'. She stated that she had been told by her friends that he had stolen Louise's milk tokens whilst she was in hospital. She stated that she always made excuses for him and always thought that each partner might be different, or that she might be able to change them. Miss White expressed the belief that all men are nice in the beginning, but then they change. She therefore expressed that if she waited a few months before she let them into her house, that she would know whether they were risky or not. Miss White admitted that when she is a relationship, she is blind and cannot see what everybody else sees.

11.11 Miss White stated that she had been to Women's Aid to see if they could help her address the problems she has in her relationships with men. She stated that Women's Aid have told her they can assist her in developing her confidence and self-esteem. She has not commenced any courses with them yet as she said she needs to read through some paperwork first before she can go back to them. Miss White also stated that she is willing to do a parenting course and believes she will need to contact 'Sure Start' about this.

12 Offending

12.1 Miss White does not have a concerning offending history. Miss White has only one offence as a teenager for theft.

13 Psychiatric history

13.1 There is no known psychiatric history.

14 Alcohol and drug use

14.1 Miss White stated that she does not, and never has, used drugs. She stated that nowadays she does not often drink alcohol, only occasionally on weekends or in privacy when the kids are in bed. Miss White asserted that her children were her priority, even when she was drinking. She suggested that even if she was paralytic –i.e. heavily intoxicated – if the children were to wake and they needed her, this would make her immediately sober, and therefore minimise the impact that alcohol might have on her impact to care for her children adequately.

15 Employment history

15.1 Miss White participated in a training course when she left school. She had worked infrequently and short-term work before she had her children. Miss White has not worked since Rachael was born.

16 Social support

16.1 Miss White reported difficult relationships with family members and stated that she did not know whether she can trust her mother or her cousins. She described a belief that her mother and auntie have reported her to social services in the past, as have a number of her friends. She stated that she would rather not live where she does and would rather move away and start a new life.

16.2 Despite comments reported above, Miss White went on to report a very supportive relationship with her mother. She described that they were more like friends and that it was not a particularly maternal relationship. It seemed from the account that Miss White had given of her history that she provided as much support to her mother as her mother provides to her. Miss White was questioned about her mother stating that she did not feel able to speak to Miss White about her concerns about Mr. Blogs. Miss White could not understand why her mother had said this. Miss White also denied that she had made her mother lie in court as is suggested in her mother's statement. Miss White suggested that there had been problems with her siblings (particularly her half siblings) who are not allowed contact with children, although Miss White stated that she did not know why or who had caused trouble for her in the past. Miss White stated that her half siblings have had behavioural problems as a result of their experiences. She stated that her brother Jason has been referred to a CAMHS worker, which has helped him.

16.3 Miss White stated that there were very few people that she would call friends. She suggested that all of the people who she had previously thought were friends had been 'backstabbers'. She stated that they all thought they were better than her because they have got a boyfriend and children. She stated that she is not able to trust any of her friends. She stated that a number of her friends have had children removed from their care but have now had them back, which she did not think was fair in relation to how long she has had to wait. Miss White expressed her frustration that she might see things that are inappropriate but she does not report people to social services and thought it was unfair that people reported her. Miss White was asked why she would not report something that she saw if it was putting children at risk, and why she did not think it was appropriate that people reported her if her children were at risk. Miss White then retracted her statement and said that if children were clearly at risk and being beaten, then she would report it, but for other things she would not.

17 Future plans, perceptions of what is needed to change

17.1 Miss White was desperate to have her children returned to her care and believes that this is the place they should be. She stated that she will do anything that she is asked to do by social workers. She stated that she is willing to complete a parenting course run by 'Sure Start' and will do any of the courses or work that she is able to with Women's Aid. She stated that she has not done it to date as she has been concentrating on the paperwork and the contact.

17.3 Miss White stated that the way that she would protect her children in the future is to not allow men in her house. She suggested that when it has been just her and her girls living on their own then everything has been fine. Miss White suggested that her daughters don't need to see men coming in and out of their life. However, the periods when Miss White has not been in a relationship have been rare. Miss White suggested that her children only needed contact with their own father.

17.4 Miss White suggested that things would be different in the future as she would listen to people if they told her that her partner had been violent. Miss White suggested that if people told her that her partner had been violent in the past then she would not get involved with them. Miss White was adamant that she would not get involved with another man who would jeopardise her contact with her children. She stated that she is fully aware of her priority being the safety and protection of her children. Miss White suggested that she would not allow men into her house until she knew them better and that she would ask social workers to do a background check. However, when Miss White was asked to be specific about what she would look for and how she would know if a person was a safe person to let into her and her children's lives, she found it difficult to articulate this. Miss White stated that she would have relationships where she would meet men in town and not allow them into her house. Miss White stated that she thought she would realise after a few months whether the men were okay or not. She based this on the fact that she had been through so much with men, she thinks that she would know now. She argued that she just needs a second chance. She repeated over and over again that she would just not let them into her house and that she would listen to what other people told her.

17.5 It is concerning that Miss White did not take this action in relation to Mr. Blogs and raises questions about her capability/willingness to follow through with this. Further, it is concerning that Miss White was not able to think of other strategies with regards to the safeguarding of her children – for example, avoiding relationships or thinking of her own issues and how she should manage her relationships. Engaging in a relationship remains very important to Miss White. This is perhaps understandable given her history, personality and vulnerability. However, it raises concerns regarding her ability to identify risks to herself and her children and implement adequate measures to safeguard them.

18   Tests administered
Wechsler Adult Intelligence Scale - 4th edition (WAIS-IV)[1]

18.1 Miss White completed the Wechsler Adult Intelligence Scale-fourth edition (WAIS-IV) as part of the assessment process. This is an individually administered clinical assessment designed to assess cognitive and intellectual functioning. It examines non-verbal reasoning skills, spatial processing skills, visual motor integration, attention to detail, and acquired knowledge such as verbal reasoning and comprehension. The WAIS-IV comprises up to 15 subtests measuring both verbal and non-verbal abilities from which index scores and composite scores are derived. The indexes considered are verbal comprehension, perceptual reasoning, working memory and processing speed.

18.2 Miss White was keen to participate in the assessment; at the beginning she said that she preferred this type of test to the clinical interview as it was not so emotional. Miss White did show signs of tiring during the assessment and was offered a break which she declined. Miss White was self-conscious during the testing process; she was anxious about getting questions wrong and needed encouragement throughout that she was doing okay. Miss White was also observed to talk to herself throughout the assessment, effectively coaching herself through. Miss White had particular difficulty during the verbal subtests and expressed that she often finds it difficult to explain things.

Full scale IQ

18.3 The full scale IQ is interpreted as an estimate of an individual's over-all level of functioning. **Miss White's full scale IQ score fell within the 'borderline'[2] range of functioning. She performed better than 8 percent of similar age peers (confidence level 95 percent)[3].** The full scale IQ gives an indication of Miss White's intellectual functioning; how-ever, consideration of Miss White's cognitive functioning across the different indexes gives a more detailed indication of Miss White's learning strengths.

Verbal comprehension index

18.4 The verbal comprehension index (VCI) is designed primarily to assess the use of specific cognitive capacities applied with orally presented verbal information. This involves elements of understanding and defining words, making concrete and abstract links between pairs of words and general knowledge. The index reflects the individual's verbal conceptualisation, ver-bal reasoning and verbal expression, acquired knowledge, learning ability and degree of abstract thinking. **Miss White's VCI score fell within the extremely low range, performing better than 2 percent of the gen-eral population (95 per cent confidence level that the scores are in the extremely low-borderline range).** An exploration of the subtests which make up the VCI highlights that Miss White's performance was gen-erally consistent. The subtests do not highlight any particular strengths or weaknesses in this index. This suggests that Miss White's performance across the three subtests is likely to be as a result of global difficulties with verbal ability and knowledge. Miss White's responses on the subtests indicated that she had a very limited word pool to draw upon for defining words and explaining concepts. She had difficulty with verbal fluency. It is likely that Miss White's limited educational achievement will have impacted on her abilities in this area.

Perceptual reasoning index

18.5 The perceptual reasoning index (PRI) is designed to primarily assess the application of reasoning with non-verbal, visual stimuli, including the ability to analyse and synthesise abstract visual stimuli. The index reflects the indi-vidual's ability to organise and think with visual symbols and patterns, process non-verbal material, spatial visualisation, simultaneous processing and rea-soning. **Miss White's PRI scores fell within the borderline range, per-forming better than 8 percent of her age-related peers (95 percent confidence level that Miss White's level of functioning is within the borderline - low average range).** Analysis of subtests did not highlight any significant strengths or weaknesses with performance being generally consistent.

Working memory index

18.6   The working memory index (WMI) is designed to assess the capacities involved in the initial registration and holding of information, referred to as short-term memory, and the mental manipulation of information that is being held in mind, referred to as working memory. **Miss White's scores on the WMI fell within the average range, performing better than 37 percent of her peers (95 percent confidence level that her score is within the average range).** There were no significant strengths or weaknesses identified and generally her performance across subtests was consistent. This suggests that generally the problems with Miss White's cognitive abilities relate to her ability to process and apply the information, not to her ability to retain and recall it.

Processing speed index

18.7   The processing speed index (PSI) was designed to assess processing speed with non-verbal, visual stimuli. The index requires the individual to copy or search for abstract symbols at speed. It reflects ability in short-term visual memory, thinking speed, reaction time and speed of visual-motor coordination. **Miss White's scores on the PSI fell within the average range, performing better than 50 percent of her age-related peers (95 percent confidence level that her performance was in this range).** There were no significant strengths or weaknesses. This suggests, as with working memory, that the problems Miss White experiences relate to overall functioning rather than speed of processing, particularly with regards to non-verbal information.

18.8   There was a significant difference between Miss White's verbal comprehension index score and perceptual reasoning score. This suggests that the full scale IQ may not be the best indicator of functioning as this is brought down by the extremely low performance on the verbal subtests. Given that most information is presented verbally and proceedings involve complex assessments and information giving, care needs to be taken to ensure that Miss White understands adequately what she is required to do.

Implications of the cognitive assessment

18.9   Professionals working with Miss White need to give her information in simple chunks. Information needs to be repeated and presented in a number of formats, written and pictorial, where appropriate, to aid understanding. Miss White needs to be allowed time to express herself, and professionals need to be aware that she does not have the verbal facility to explain herself easily. Professionals should clarify with Miss White that she understands what is required of her and the implications of assessments by asking her to express her understanding to ensure there is not a misunderstanding. Similarly, professionals should clarify with Miss White what they think she has said as her ability to express herself may result in misunderstandings. This may have occurred in the social worker's assessment with regards to the discussions about ending the relationship with Mr. Blogs where each party thinks they have understood the meaning of the other, but in fact, have not.

Personality assessment interview (PAI)

18.10 Miss White completed the personality assessment inventory[4]. The personality assessment inventory is a self-report, objective inventory of adult personality. Her responses on this scale suggested that she responded to the item content consistently. Miss White did not try to portray herself in either a positive light nor did she exaggerate problems.

18.11 On the clinical scales of the PAI there were moderate elevations on the anxiety and anxiety related disorders scales which suggested that Miss White was experiencing stress, not unexpected given the circumstances of the testing, and that she was feeling worried about specific events, sensitive, emotional and lacking in self-confidence. Miss White's responses also indicated high levels of dysphoria (depression scale). This suggests that Miss White feels despondent predominantly and has withdrawn from social activities. Individuals with scores at this level are often guilt-ridden, moody and dissatisfied with life. This is certainly consistent with Miss White's reports during the clinical interview that she feels a tremendous amount of guilt for her failure to protect her children and that she is generally very unhappy with the way her life is currently. If Miss White continues to report such feelings, it is likely that she will feel worthless, hopeless and a personal failure. She may exhibit difficulties in concentrating and in decision making. Miss White may experience problems with her sleep pattern, changes in activity levels and loss of appetite. If Miss White becomes aware of such signs she may benefit from discussing interventions with her GP, which could include short-term medication or referral to talking therapies.

18.12 Miss White's responses also resulted in elevations relating to paranoia. Miss White's response pattern indicated that she is overly suspicious and hostile at times. This is consistent, it seems, with her response to social workers particularly. Individuals with response patterns like this tend to be distrustful of close friendships and probably have few close friends. This is consistent with Miss White's description of her friends and family (see also Section 16, social support). During the clinical interview Miss White presented as someone who felt persecuted by other people. She stated that she believes people frequently informed on her to social services and that social workers are always ringing and checking up on her, even when she has done nothing wrong. Miss White openly admitted that she has no real friends and does not trust either friends or family. The most significant feature of Miss White's pattern of responding was her tendency to blame others for her predicament. It is noticeable, however, that despite this elevation, on the scale relating to 'non-support' Miss White's responses indicated that she has generally close, supportive relationships with family and friends. This inconsistency is also recorded in Section 16, social support, and reflects the changing views

Miss White has of friends and family. It is likely that day to day Miss White can engage in positive relationships with friends and family and that the suspicious, mistrustful characteristics relate specifically to problems relating to the loss of her children and the role she considers family and friends to have had in this.

18.13 On the treatment consideration scales, Miss White's responses do indicate that she is able to recognise that there are major problems in her functioning that need intervention and that she is willing to engage in this. This too is consistent with Miss White's statements during the clinical interview. The scale does not, however, assist in assessing likely patterns of engagement or prognosis, which is more of a concern in Miss White's case.

18.14 On the interpersonal scales, Miss White's responses indicated that she feels self-conscious in social interactions and is not skilled in asserting herself. This obviously contributes to her failure to stand up to partners easily, particularly when coupled with her childhood experiences and prior relationships. She is likely to be uncomfortable if she is the centre of attention. In addition, Miss White's pattern of responding indicates that she does not value close lasting relationships.

19   Opinion

19.1 Instructions requested a psychological assessment of Sarah White, in particular reference to the following issues:

1   An analysis of Miss White's cognitive functioning.

1.a Miss White's overall level of cognitive functioning (full scale IQ) is in the borderline range. However, this may not be the most accurate measure of IQ for Miss White due to there being a significant difference between her performance on the verbal comprehension index (VCI) subtests and the perceptual reasoning index (PRI) subtests. Miss White's performance on the VCI subtests was in the extremely low range, indicating significant difficulties communicating verbally. Her performance on the PRI was in the borderline range, indicating some difficulties, although not extreme. There is a need to be cautious about assuming understanding of complex processes, or that Miss White has expressed herself in the way she intended. This will need constant clarification on both sides. There is also an implication for learning from future programmes. Group work may not be the most effective medium for therapeutic interventions to occur as there is more danger that Miss White will not understand material and this could be overlooked.

2   Whether or not her life experiences have affected her psychological functioning and her ability to offer her children good enough and safe enough parenting.

2.a There is an irrefutable relationship between Miss White's experiences in her childhood and her experiences of parenting her own children. Miss White observed her mother engaging in repeated relationships which were characterised by domestic violence. She is undoubtedly the victim of domestic violence both vicariously and experientially. Miss White was physically and sexually abused by her mother's partners. Miss White also observed her mother remain in and return to destructive relationships, despite concerns for her own and her children's safety, and also deceiving social workers who were involved. Miss White described a pattern of trying to protect her mother as well as trying to protect herself in her childhood.

2.c   Miss White struggled to link her own childhood experiences of her mother's failure to protect her from domestic violence situations and physical and sexual abuse with her life now and what her children have and continue to experience, thus demonstrating little insight of the problems or what she needs to change. Although Miss White can recognise that patterns are being repeated, she presented as someone who feels powerless to make changes to her situation without significant intervention.

3   Her ability to care for two young and dependent children on her own and the potential risk, if any, of a momentary loss of self-control, in light of the findings made by the district judge and how that risk can be reduced or eliminated in the future.

3.a   Miss White continued to emphasise that she did not injure the children and that she believes the injuries were caused by Mr. Blogs. It is therefore difficult to accurately assess the potential risk of a momentary loss of self-control as Miss White categorically denied injuring Louise, or losing control, ever, with her children. Miss White asserted that she had learned techniques from her GP to cope with a crying baby, which she needed to employ rarely.

3.b   It is significant that there are few substantiated reports of violence in other areas of Miss White's life. Although it is suggested that Miss White has in the past assaulted partners, this is not substantiated and indeed she denied this during the current assessment. Generally, it is not suggested that Miss White is an individual who has problems with self control. This is not apparent from the documentation, from the clinical interview or the psychometric testing. It is therefore unlikely that Miss White poses a direct risk of harm to her children in the future due to a loss of control. It is more likely that Miss White is not able to protect her children from harm by men with whom she has a relationship, as she is not able to prioritise the needs of her children over her own. Miss White has not demonstrated the ability to engage in relationships with men who are not violent and shows limited insight and ability in changing this pattern. Miss White is likely to minimise and even ignore risks posed by future partners, particularly if she feels loved and supported by them.

3.c   It appears from information contained in the assessment reports of other professionals, e.g. social work assessment 3.10.11, that Miss White has struggled to attend to basic needs in the past relating to offering a healthy diet, access to dental care, the previous referral to children's services and, of course, the recent injuries to Louise and the ongoing concerns relating to Miss White's pattern of relationships. It is positive that Miss White ended the relationship with Mr. Blogs when the social worker discussed this. However, it remains a concern that she embarked upon the relationship in the first place, following a similar pattern to previous relationships, meeting on Facebook and entering into a sexual relationship immediately on meeting. Miss White places herself and, when in her care, her children, in vulnerable situations. Miss White does not seem to have taken on board the key concerns and does not have the ability to change her behaviour without significant support and intervention. In short, Miss White's ability to care for her daughters adequately is limited.

4   **Her understanding of the Local Authority's concerns in this case over and above matters referred to above and to what extent Miss White is able to cooperate with professionals to improve her parenting and protecting her children.**

4.a   Miss White presented as someone who did not have a great deal of insight into what it would take for her children to be rehabilitated into her care. She focused on whether her children would be naughty rather than how she would deal with the emotional stress and the issues related to them being removed. She did not seem to have insight into the fact that Louise had not lived with her since she was 7 months old and there might be some difficulties in her being returned to her care.

4.b   Miss White is aware on a superficial level that she needs to make changes relating to her relationships and that she needs to protect her children. Quite how she will achieve this is unclear to Miss White. Miss White suggested that she would not allow men into her house; however, this was not the case with Mr. Blogs.

4.c   Miss White has indicated that she is willing to engage in anything asked of her by social workers and the court to enable her to keep her children. Whilst she is willing, her ability is another matter and may hinder her capacity to benefit from intervention. It is also concerning that Miss White has identified some appropriate interventions, e.g. Sure Start parenting courses and work with Women's Aid, but has not engaged with this at present.

5   **Her ability to take on board and implement/action advice given to her, in particular relation to advice about caring for her children.**
       Miss White's only strategy to protect her children was to not let men into the house, but this seems to be a naive strategy. It sounded as though she was still continuing to look for a relationship and that she was falling into the same traps as before in believing that the men were different, that they would be nice this time. Such thinking limits Miss White's ability to assess the potential risks. Because of the areas and social circles where Miss White resides, it is likely that her partner choice will be limited to men of a similar background and that she will continually place herself at risk if she gets involved in these relationships. As indicated above Miss White has indicated a willingness to engage in work but has a limited capacity to benefit from this.

6 **Her ability to meet all her children's needs including their developmental needs.**

6.a This has been covered in the answers to questions 3, 4 and 5 above. There is no more to add to this point.

7 **The potential risk, if any, to her children if either or both were placed in her care, and if so, the nature of that risk.**

7.a The fact that she got into a relationship with another violent person so soon after her children were injured is concerning. This is with Miss White saying that she is aware of the risks, but then not doing anything about them and still questioning when she is given feedback about the violence, the risk of violent relationships and concomitant risks to the children remain.

7.b It is positive that Miss White has identified possible interventions, e.g. through Women's Aid. She has not, however, embarked upon such work as yet. Miss White would need to demonstrate that she had learned from such work and had made changes to her pattern of relationships. Examples of such changes would be abstaining from relationships for a period of time as she suggested she would or demonstrating more openness regarding relationships and the capacity to make more informed and safe judgements about men she comes into contact with and not engaging in relationships with men who have violent temperaments.

8 **Any other matters that you consider appropriate to consider.**

8.a There are no other matters.

9 **In the event that any issues or problems are identified in relation to the above questions, please advise as to what work can be done with Miss White in order for improvements to be made. Who would carry out such work and over what timescale? What is the prognosis of achieving a successful outcome and a rehabilitation of either/ both children into her care?**

It is likely to take a significant amount of work with Miss White to help her see the patterns from the past and to be able to break them. Such help would be available with Women's Aid, but is likely to take a significant amount of time. The court would need to decide whether this is within acceptable timescales for the children. Supervised contact could continue whilst this work was occurring, with a view to increasing the level of contact. However, until such intervention is completed successfully, the children could not necessarily be protected in Miss White's care.

20 **Declarations**

20.1 Statement of compliance

I understand my duty to the court and have complied and will continue to comply with that duty. This report includes all matters relevant to the issues on which my expert evidence is given. I have given details in this report of any matters which might affect the validation of this report. I have addressed this report to the court.

I am aware of the requirements of Family Procedure Rules Part 25 and Practice Direction 25.

20.2 Statement on conflicts of interest

I confirm that I:

a   have no conflict of interest of any kind, other than any conflict disclosed in my report;

b   do not consider that any interest disclosed affects my suitability as an expert witness on any issue on which I have given evidence;

c   will advise the instructing party if, between the date of my report and the final hearing, there is any change in circumstances which affects my answers to (a) or (b) above.

20.3 Statement of truth

I confirm that I have made clear which facts and matters referred to in this report are within my own knowledge and which are not. Those that are within my own knowledge I confirm to be true. The opinions I have expressed represent my true and complete professional opinions on the matters to which they refer.

Signed:_____ Date:_____

Appendix 1 - Documentation reviewed:

Due to the large volume of documentation, the index to the bundle is copied and included. Documents read are ticked for clarity.

Additional documents reviewed are as follows: [*Six documents listed – not included here for space reasons.*]

Appendix 2 – CV [*Not included here for space and confidentiality reasons*]

Notes

i   Wechsler, D. (2008). *Wechsler Adult Intelligence Scale*, 4th edition. San Antonio, TX: The Psychological Corporation.

ii Qualitative description of the IQ and index scores; <69 = extremely low, 70–79 = borderline, 80–89= low average, 90–109 = average.

iii Confidence interval is the range within which we can be 95 per cent confident that an individual's true score falls.

iv Morey, L.C. (1991). *Personality Assessment Interview (PAR)*. Lutz, FL: Psychological Assessment Resources Inc.

INDEX